SHAKESPEAREAN
FANTASY AND POLITICS

THOMAS BETTERIDGE

UNIVERSITY OF HERTFORDSHIRE PRESS

First published in Great Britain in 2005 by
University of Hertfordshire Press
Learning and Information Services
University of Hertfordshire
College Lane
Hatfield
Hertfordshire AL10 9AB

British Library Cataloguing in Publication Data
A catalogue record for this book is available from the British Library

ISBN 1-902806-39-5 hardback
ISBN 1-902806-40-9 paperback

Design by Geoff Green, Cambridge, CB4 5RA
Cover design by John Robertshaw, Harpenden, AL5 2JB
Printed in Great Britain by Alden Group Ltd, OX2 OEF

Contents

Acknowledgements

I HAVE DISCUSSED MY WORK with numerous colleagues and students. The following is by no means an exclusive list: Deborah Allabush, Hannah Bedson, Madeline Casey, Rebecca Colling, Sue Cotton, April Croman, Brian Cummings, Jodie Daly, Michael Dobson, Louise Duffield, Kelly Edwards, Joshua Facey, Bethan Fletcher, Tim Greany, Henrietta Griffiths, Siobhan Halliday, Margaret Healy, Astrid Hunt, David Scott Kastan, Adam Kennedy, Erica Longfellow, Paul McGarry, Rhiannon Morgan, Joanne Murray, Claire Partridge, Ruth Skelton, Althea Stewart, Harriet Taper and Joanna Tuff.

All quotes from the works of William Shakespeare in this study come from the Arden Shakespeare series. All emphases in secondary quotes in this study are emphasised in the original.

This book is dedicated to the wonderful students of Kingston University.

Introduction: History, criticism and Shakespeare

Every artwork is an instant; every successful work is a cessation, a suspended moment of the process, as which it reveals itself to the unwavering eye. If artworks are answers to their own questions, they themselves thereby truly become questions.

Theodor Adorno, Aesthetic Theory[1]

W HAT QUESTIONS DOES the work of William Shakespeare pose for us at the beginning of the twenty-first century? Are plays like *King Lear* or *Othello* still capable of creating a space for thought five hundred years after they were written? Why read Shakespeare today? These questions are, however, at one level clearly redundant since it is an indisputable fact that Shakespeare is still being read. Why is this?[2] One reason is that Shakespeare's drama is centrally concerned with questions of truth, language and ethics. Its complexity and open-endedness mean that it operates as a space for thought – a linguistic arena for the production of truths. This study is concerned with truths produced in and through an engagement with the writing of Shakespeare. In other words it is a piece of literary criticism. It draws extensively on the critical work of Slavoj Žižek and other contemporary thinkers in order to discover the truths of Shakespeare's drama and relate them to contemporary issues within the discipline of English literature but also in the wider field of cultural studies – again this is no more than to say that this study is a piece of literary criticism.

This Introduction is in three unequal parts. The first section is a polemical discussion of the until recently dominant New Historicist approach to the study of Shakespeare. This focus is developed and extended in the second part of the Introduction through a detailed analysis of *King Lear*. The final part of this Introduction consists of a relatively brief introduction to some of the key concepts in Žižek's thought applied to *Romeo and Juliet*. What unites the disparate parts of this Introduction is a shared concern with the aesthetics and ethics of literary criticism – what it means to produce ethical criticism.

Shakespeare and the historicists

New Historicism has been the dominant force in Shakespeare studies over the last twenty years.[3] Its historicist approach to the study of Shakespeare has largely set the agenda for the study of his work. There are, however, a number of serious theoretical and historical problems with New Historicism's general methodological treatment of Shakespeare's work. David Scott Kastan has recently commented that: "For all of its 'density of specification', New Historicism is finally insufficiently historical, both in subject and methodology, and arguably insufficiently 'new' in its refusal or inability to theorize its work."[4] Kastan's criticism of New Historicism is that it lacks the rigour of history and fails to fully theorise its basic methodological assumptions and procedures. I shall discuss the historiographical failings of New Historicism in the next part of this Introduction with reference to its use of feudalism as a historical concept. In this first short section I want to briefly engage with Kastan's perspicacious second point concerning New Historicism's theoretical refusal. A key element in New Historicist criticism is the turn to history as an appropriate object of study for the literary critic. This turn is, however, theoretically fraught. In particular, it is based on a slippage between the truths of history and those produced by the study of works of literature. History as a discipline pursues the truths of the past. This is its ethical justification. Mark Poster, commenting on the historiographical work of Michel de Certeau, suggests that:

> The discipline of history ... bears a burden ... Historians must insist that the stories they tell are not stories but truths, representations of past realities. But they must also spurn the prescription of truth to acknowledge openly its own assumptions, to lay bare its procedures to critical

inquiry, to question its conditions of possibility. The trick for historians is to normalise a condition of writing that is anything but normal.[5]

New Historicism is history without burden. It consistently exposes the unnaturalness of history, its tricks, while failing to subject itself to similar scrutiny. In particular, New Historicism's truth claims are based on the burden free appropriation of the conditions of history writing. As a form of literary criticism New Historicism's turn to history means that it locates the truths of its objects of study, works of literature, outside its own discursive norms so that, for example, the truth of *King Lear* becomes the extent to which it reflects a truth of history – the death of feudal England. In particular, the basic structure of New Historicist criticism, exemplified with great wit and skill in the work of Stephen Greenblatt, is that of a fascinating anecdote, a brief schematic reference to some grand historical narrative, for example the death of feudalism, and then a detailed analysis of a literary text. What this model does is produce literary criticism that obscures the grounds, the basis, of its own articulation. New Historicism avoids explicitly justifying itself as a form of literary criticism by making a number of claims about its validity that refer beyond its objects of study. It validates itself by referring to history and in the process becomes a kind of history-lite – history without the burden of producing a truth of the past since in the end the truths it produces are based on the close textual analysis of works of canonical literature.

New Historicism has largely turned its back on the aesthetic and has tended to dismiss the idea that works of literature produce truths that can be critiqued on the basis of their truthfulness. The price New Historicism pays for this rejection is, however, its inability to account for its dependence upon a relatively conservative canon of literary works. The denial of the aesthetic as a real or meaningful category means that New Historicist critics cannot interrogate the canonical status of the works they study. Shakespeare's privileged status within New Historicism is the classic example of this failure since it is based upon a valorisation of his work as literature that cannot emerge within the scope of New Historicism – in other words given the questions that New Historicism constructs as valid and answerable on the basis of its methodology the aesthetic value of Shakespeare's work cannot be addressed. In these terms New Historicism exemplifies a loss of confidence within literary criticism in itself as an ethical discourse, one capable of producing truths. New Historicism is exemplary of much recent literary criticism in its use of history to finesse this failure, its deployment of history as an ersatz aesthetic. One can see this in the kind of arguments advanced in Hew Historicist studies of Shakespeare in which, for example, the study of *King Lear* is validated on the basis of its reflection of the death of feudalism – and not because of its status as a piece of literature. Peter Uwe Hohendahl comments that New Historicism:

> … de-emphasises aesthetic difference through thick description of cultural details. Since the art-work is no longer guaranteed a special status (aesthetic theory has been discarded as ideology), it can be rescued from indifference only through linking and weaving.[6]

The process of 'linking and weaving' is, however, asymmetrical in New Historicist work. The point of New Historicism is to engage in the textual analysis of literary works and to justify this by referring to history. The typical polemical strategy of New Historicist criticism, however, effectively reverses this process since it is the analysis of intricacies and complexities of the literary text as a privileged object of study that sustains the truth claims of New Historicism. Joan Copjec comments that "some notion of transcendence is plainly needed if one is to avoid the reduction of social space to the relations that fill it".[7] In the field of history Copjec's 'notion of transcendence' is provided by the claim to produce a truth of the past. Whatever one may think of this claim it is a necessary requirement for history as a discourse to have meaning. New Historicism seeks to make history its transcendental principle, but without accepting, with history, the ethical cost: the burden of producing truths of the past.

The problem of aesthetics lies at the heart of the failure of New Historicism as a form of literary criticism since without an engagement with the aesthetic it is not possible to properly address the questions posed by Shakespeare's work. Indeed it is impossible to seriously justify the study of his work. It is laughable to suggest that if one wants to understand early modern English society one should privilege as a source the writings that one man produced within a very specific theatrical context over a relatively short period of time – *c.* 1580 to 1615. Equally without some notion of aesthetics, or at least some sense that it is the role of the literary critic to engage with the truths of works of literature, the idea that there are contemporary reasons for studying Shakespeare is bizarre. New Historicism's rejection of the aesthetic, however, reflects a deeper malaise within the field of cultural theory, which is the reduction of analysis to a form of weak nominalism in which concepts and ideas are made meaningful within a contextual frame whose boundaries are far from clear.[8] In other words New Historicism's methodology will allow one to analyse the misogynist imagery in *King Lear* but will block any justification for this critique that goes beyond an undertheorised assumption that misogyny is bad.[9] Slavoj Žižek comments that:

> When a typical cultural theorist deals with a philosophical or psychoanalytical edifice, the analysis focuses exclusively on unearthing a hidden patriarchal, Eurocentrist, identitarian 'bias'. The theorist does not even ask the naïve but nonetheless necessary question, OK, but what *is* the structure of the universe? How *is* the human psyche 'really' working? Such questions are not even taken seriously in cultural studies, since its proponents simply tend to reduce them to the historicist reflection on conditions in which certain notions emerged as the result of historically specific power relations.[10]

New Historicism shares in this failure since it does not ask – what is the truth of Shakespeare's mediation of history in *Richard III*? How valid is his discussion of the costs of desire in *Twelfth Night*? Instead it reduces the truths of these plays to their historical context. In the process it effectively silences the most important questions that Shakespeare posed in his plays which are concerned with ahistorical questions relating to the self, history, language and desire.

King Lear, *history and the birth of feudalism*

David Kastan's critique of New Historicism is that it is undertheorised and often lacks historical rigour. I would argue that Kastan's critique of New Historicism's history is particularly pertinent in relation to the tendency of New Historicist critics to deploy historical motifs and concepts that historians have long since stripped of any real explanatory potential.[11] A classic example of this is the idea of the death of feudalism.[12]

It is now twenty years since Paul Delaney published his seminal article, '*King Lear* and the Decline of Feudalism'.[13] Delaney's argument in this piece, that Shakespeare's play reflects or even describes the death of feudalism, has become a critical commonplace within New Historicism, and indeed in the larger field of literary criticism. Certainly much of the recent published work on *King Lear* takes as a given, something which requires no interrogation, that the period during which Shakespeare wrote *King Lear* witnessed the traumatic destruction of a feudal society and its violent replacement by modern capitalist understandings of subjectivity, signification and society.[14] There are, however, a number of problems with this representation of Shakespeare's age. At a basic level it is important to note that despite the fears of contemporaries the succession of James I was peaceful and relatively unproblematic.[15] If feudalism was dying in this period and its death causing traumatic upheavals this was not witnessed at the level of political struggle. John Morrill points out that England during the period 1569 to 1642 was, in a European context, uniquely peaceful and the English amazingly law-abiding.[16] At another level while critics working on *King Lear* are largely in agreement about the effects of the change from a feudal to a capitalist society, they fail to agree on, and often do not even address, the question of how or why feudalism declined; they know what feudalism was, what capitalism is, but are vague about how the one declined into or grew out of the other.

This lack of understanding in terms of the process that led to the decline of feudalism and its replacement by capitalism has recently taken on a new salience as a result of a number of historians raising serious questions over whether feudalism has ever been more than an early modern historical myth. In her seminal work, *Fiefs and Vassals: The Medieval Evidence Reinterpreted*, Susan Reynolds points out that:

> It is not just that all the phenomena and notions of feudo-vassalic institutions never existed together anywhere, but that they are too incoherent, too loosely related, and too imperfectly reflected in medieval evidence to be envisaged as anything like an ideal type.[17]

Reynolds goes on to argue that:

> What the concept of feudalism seems to have done since the sixteenth century is not to help us recognise the creatures we meet but to tell us that all medieval creatures are the same so that we need not bother to look at them. Put another way, feudalism has provided a kind of protective lens through which it has seemed prudent to view the otherwise dazzling oddities and varieties of medieval creatures.[18]

I would argue, however, that, far from being a protective lens, feudalism as imagined in the work of Shakespeare's contemporaries, and in that of modern literary critics, has acted as a distorting prism or magnifying glass. Feudalism has operated as an excuse to gaze, an incitement and justification for viewing the past as other, a monstrous object fit for inspection, analysis and interrogation.

The status of feudalism within both modern criticism and Stuart historiography is particularly pressing in terms of *King Lear* since one of the main concerns of Shakespeare's play is the status of history: the production of historical myths, stories, lies and truths. One of the key intellectual developments of the Jacobean period was the emergence of feudal England as an object of historical study. It was during the early Stuart period that the historians John Selden and Henry Spelman developed the idea of feudalism, and its decline, as an explanatory historiographical tool that could account for the tensions and conflicts within Jacobean society. As a work of history *King Lear* addresses the same issues as those reflected in Selden's and Spelman's work. It is, however, surely more than simply coincidence that Shakespeare wrote a play which modern commentators have claimed depicts the death of feudalism at the same time as fellow Jacobean writers were giving birth to the idea of feudal England.[19] In *King Lear* what Shakespeare shows us is a collapse and then partial restoration of an imaginary feudal order. It is Lear's rejection of feudalism in the opening scene that creates the play's narrative, the matter of its history. As in the work of Selden and Spelman, in *King Lear* it is the birth and death of feudalism that provides the historical text with its motivation; the feudal is the fantasy that enables the Jacobean text to produce a narrative explanation for social antagonism and conflict.[20] In these terms *King Lear* reflects not on the death of feudalism but the historiographical needs that led to its birth, in particular the desire to create a magisterial historical myth that could account for the fractured and antagonistic nature of Jacobean society in a way that obscured the real reasons for social conflict in seventeenth-century England – the oppressive and arbitrary division of wealth, power and authority.[21]

In his early historical work, *Jani Anglorum Facies Altera*, John Selden discussed the history of southern England. In this text, although he specifically distances himself from those who argue that the origin of English laws was the Norman Conquest, Selden argues that:

[William the Conqueror] liberally bestowed the Lords and Estates of the *English* upon his fellow-soldiers … Upon which account, some while since the coming of the *Normans*, there was not in *England* except the King himself, any one, who held Land by right of *Free-hold* (as they term it) since in the sooth one may well call all others to a man only Lords in trust of what they had; as those who by swearing fealty, and doing homage, did perpetually own and acknowledge a *Superior Lord*, of whom they held, and by whom they were invested into their Estates.[22]

Clearly what is being described here is the creation of a feudal system of landholding in England. Selden, however, specifically rejects the idea that English law originated in the Norman Conquest and argues that the reason William did not embark on a wholescale re-writing of English law was entirely politic. Selden writes that:

It is a remark amongst Statesmen, That new acquired Empires do sowe some hazard by attempting to make new laws: and the Norman did warily provide against this danger, by bestowing upon the yielding conquered Nation the requital of their ancient Law: a requital, I say, but more, as it should seem, for show than use; and rather to curry favour with the people at the present, than in good deed for the advantage of the English Name.[23]

In Selden's narrative the Norman Conquest becomes the point at which the laws of England became corrupted by a fall into a kind of performative politics, when show became separated from act. Selden argues that during the Saxon period there was not a distinction between the appearance of the law and its use – this division was introduced by William the Conqueror as a political response to his status as a foreign invader.

In *Jani Anglorum Facies Altera* the advent of the Normans is equated with a fall into politics as performance and the division of the country into feudal estates. Selden also, however, equates the Conquest with another form of corruption – the establishment of primogeniture in England. He writes that, "anciently, if I be not mistaken, most inheritances were parted among the Children …".[24] Later he claims that, during the Saxon period,

Everyone's Children [were] their Heirs and Successors, and there was no Will to be. Nor was it lawfull with us down to our Grandfathers time, to dispose of Country Farms or Estates by *Will*, unless it were in some *Burroughs*, that had a peculiar Right and Priviledge of their own.[25]

Selden's historical narrative effectively equates the writing of wills, and specifically the practice of primogeniture, with William's corrupt separation of the law's use from its appearance. For Selden, during the Saxon period there was no distinction in the law between saying and doing.[26] Indeed he argues that under the Saxons the law's guardians were also its makers.[27] Within this schema, political division and conflict, indeed social antagonism itself, are products of the Norman Conquest. Selden's historiography is driven by a fantasy of a time – for him the Saxon period – when the law escaped the play of signification and society was not corrupted by the particular wills of individual landholders.

Selden's contemporary, Sir Henry Spelman, has been credited by a number of scholars with the invention or discovery of feudalism.[28] In his work *The Original, Growth, Propagation and Condition of Feuds and Tenures of Knight-Service in England* Spelman spelt out in detail the nature of English feudalism. He opens this work by drawing a clear distinction between hereditary and temporary feuds.

> As for temporary Feuds, which (like wild fig-trees) could yield none of the feudal fruits of *Wardship, Marriage, Relief* etc unto their Lords, they belong nothing to our argument, nor shall I make other use in setting them forth, than to assure the Reader they are not those that our Laws take notice of.[29]

Spelman goes on to tell his reader that he is only interested in hereditary feuds since they alone "can bear the feudal fruits we speak of, Wardship, Marriage etc".[30] Having set up the proper limits of his study Spelman goes on to discuss in detail the relationship of vassals to lords and how this related to feuds. In the process his text constructs a model of a functioning feudal society which it locates in post-Conquest medieval England.

This functionality is, however, bought at the price of the corruption of pure feudalism by the hereditary principle. Spelman explicitly argues that true or proper feuds cannot be inherited, since "in true feudal speech the Tennant or Vassal hath nothing in the propriety of the soil it self, but it remaineth intirely unto the Lord ...".[31] In *The Original, Growth* the advent of hereditary feuds is related directly to usurpation. Spelman writes:

> ... let us now go on in examination, when and how *Feuds* became *hereditary* ... the truth is, that when *Hugh Capet* usurped the Kingdom of *France* against the *Carolinges* he, to fortifie himself and to draw all the Nobility of *France* to support his Faction about the year 987 granted to them in the year 988 that whereas till then they enjoyed their *Feuds* and Honours but for life or at the pleasure of their Princes; they should from thenceforth for

ever hold them to them, and their heirs, in Feudal manner ...[32]

In this passage Spelman associates the moment when feuds became hereditary with faction and usurpation. Hugh Capet is depicted here as a politic corrupter of the feudal ideal, a man who used his status as monarch to distort the system of landholding within his lands purely in order to 'fortifie' his position and that of his followers.

Spelman goes on to relate Capet's behaviour with that of William the Conqueror, writing that his actions were "a fair direction for *William* of *Normandy* (whom we call Conqueror) how to secure himself of his new acquired Kingdom of *England* ...".[33] Hereditary feuds in England are therefore represented in *The Original, Growth* as being the product of the importation of a foreign and clearly potentially corrupt practice designed to enable usurpers and conquerors to keep the lands they have won. Spelman writes that William the Conqueror:

> ... presently transfer'd his Country-customs into England ... and amongst them ... this new French custom of making *Feuds* hereditary, not regarding the former use of our Saxon Ancestors; who, like all other Nations, save the French, continued till that time their *Feuds* and *Tenures*, either arbitrary or in some definite limitation ...[34]

There is therefore a strange tension running through Spelman's work between his opening remarks about the proper object of study in terms of feudalism, which is hereditary feuds, and his history of their advent. Real feudalism in *The Original, Growth* existed before feuds were made subject to inheritance but this kind of feudalism is wild, natural and arbitrary, making it an illegitimate object for judicial study or historical analysis.

There is, however, a final twist in Spelman's work. It concludes by giving the entire preceding text a very specific spin.[35]

> It was neither my Words nor my Meaning to say, that he [William the Conqueror] first brought in either *Feuds* or *Military Service* in a general sense, but that he brought in the Servitudes and Grievances of Feuds viz *Wardships*, *Marriage*, and such like, which to this day were never known to other Nations that are govern'd by the *Feudal Law*.[36]

Ultimately the argument of *The Original, Growth* is that 'fruitful' feudalism is untruthful, newfangled and foreign – perhaps even bastard. It is directly associated with the corruption of the law by a usurping ruler only concerned with protecting his own position and that of his supporters. In the work of Selden and Spelman the Norman Conquest is constructed as a fall into a world of political conflict and faction: a world in which the law's meaning is undermined and the feud is transformed from a reward for service and valour to a hereditary possession, a tool for building factions and maintaining power.

In Selden's and Spelman's work pre-Conquest feudalism functions as a fantastical image of a non-antagonistic but class based society in which the magistrates or ruling class have access to a disproportionate and oppressive amount of wealth and power. It embodies the fantasy that one could have a society based on non-equitable distribution of wealth and power but which was free from conflict, one in which the law is transparent, where there is no need for politics and people achieve positions of eminence on the basis of worth and not their family name. In these terms the fantasy of 'true' feudalism is explicitly humanist and implicitly magisterial since it embodies in such texts as *The Original, Growth* a contradictory commitment to the non-equitable distribution of wealth as normative with an insistence that wealth ought to distributed on the basis of worth and not family.[37]

The decline of feudalism is written into its initial conceptualisations; it was always dying, always being bastardised. This is undoubtedly why it has proved so difficult for historians since Spelman's time to explain how or when pure feudalism started to decline, what was the agent for this change and when this process was completed. Arthur B. Ferguson points out that: "[Spelman] addressed himself ... to the problems which present-day historians still have not entirely solved, namely the rise and decline of feudalism."[38] The point to notice here, however, is not that feudalism's decline was written into its emergence as a concept, although this is undoubtedly the case; it is rather that the difficulty of accounting for feudalism's demise is the invisible, the non-explainable, of the ideology embodied in the work of Selden and Spelman: *its* visible point of invisibility.[39] The real not-seen of these texts is the inherent and non-historical status of social conflict and antagonism within early Stuart society.[40] The decline of feudalism, and the impossibility of explaining this event or process, is the blind-spot of early Stuart historiography, the invisible it produced as a condition of its own possibility. Trying to explain how feuds changed from being pure and natural into being artificial and hereditary – and inevitably failing at this – creates the need for historical narratives, interpretations and explanations *and* guaranteed that they would never be final or complete, that the lens would never need to be removed.

In *King Lear* Shakespeare reflects upon history as a discourse by placing the matter of history at the centre of the play's narrative motivation. Early modern history writing was based on a number of privileged sources of information and knowledge. Tudor historians relied upon the work of earlier historians, written records from the past, in particular letters and official publications, and a set of fairly basic assumptions about character motivation in order to produce the truth of the past.[41] Thomas Blundeville, in his work *The True order and Methode of wryting and reading Hystories*, claimed that:

> Every deed that man doth, springeth eyther of some outwarde cause, as of force, or fortune, (which properlye ought not to be referred to man:) or else of some inward cause belonging to man: of which causes there be two, that is, reason and appetite.[42]

For Blundeville proper history writing produces a text that combines an explanation of public events and private motivations within the context of a deterministic understanding of time as chronological. He writes that: "And bycause tyme doth accompany all maner of actions, and every action hath his proper and peculier tyme, the writer must giue to every action his dewe time accordingly."[43] For Blundeville historical actions do not so much exist in time as 'accompany' it. The implication of this understanding of the relationship between time and historical events is that the latter are external to time but are in a strange way time's matter, the web that materialises the abstraction of time. *King Lear* as a piece of history provocatively fails to live up to Blundeville's strictures. In particular, the status of letters in this text subverts their importance as part of the validating matter of Tudor history writing. Letters in *King Lear* are constantly misread, forged or misdirected. Even more subversively it is impossible to place the letters in *King Lear*, and in particular those from Cordelia to her supporters in England, within a clear chronological framework. It is equally difficult, as Richard Knowles has recently pointed out, to provide a convincing narrative of Cordelia's movements between her banishment and her appearance in Dover accompanied by a French army.[44] And yet these are precisely the things, letters out of time and events that cannot be explained, that Blundeville regarded as signs of historiographical failure. *King Lear* is a historical play that consistently flaunts its failure as history.

This subversion of the historical extends beyond such particularities as letters and events to encompass the status of history itself as a discourse. *King Lear* is a play about the death of feudalism which reflects directly on the cost of feudalism's birth, in order to die, in seventeenth-century historical writing. Lear, acting like a parodic modern [i.e. seventeenth-century] monarch treats his realm as something he owns and not as part of a coherent feudal society in which possession of land brings with it dues and obligations. It is Goneril and Regan in their attempts to restore the relationship of land to responsibility who act like typical 'Jacobean' feudal lords. The moment in Act 2 Scene 4 when the two sisters torment Lear over the number of followers he can keep can be seen as an enactment of a return to feudalism since what is happening at this point in the play is that the people who actually possess the land are claiming the right to be the ones who provide the monarch with his knights. Within a pure feudal system a king with his own knights would be an anomaly, a potential source of conflict that would need to be addressed. Similar feudal themes are addressed in the Gloucester/Edmund plot. Here the issue is not one of the relationship between land and duty but of that of inheritance. Primogeniture, the concept that robs Edmund of his birthright, is not an inherently feudal concept. Indeed strict primogeniture, as both Selden and Spelman pointed out, is antithetical to feudalism since, like Lear's view of his kingdom, it is based on an understanding of land as a possession. When Edmund wins his noble title and his land through loyalty to his chief over-lord, Cromwell, he is behaving in an entirely feudal fashion. While Lear and Gloucester obsessively treat their land as subject to their wills, and as will-able, it is Edmund who behaves in a 'natural' feudal manner, as defined by Spelman, when he insists that the possession of feuds should depend on one's worth and not one's name or place in the family tree.

Act 1 Scene 1 of *King Lear* stages the extent to which Lear's abstract language of property ownership requires a fantastical other to provide it with motivation. It enacts the truth that Lear's attitude towards his land requires the fantasy of the feudal in order to obscure its true nature. Lear as monarch treats his land as private property, but, because this is clearly problematic in terms of the dominant ideology of seventeenth-century English political discourse, it has to be made to look like an aberration or a fall. The historical narrative of feudalism's growth and decline, and that of Lear's torment, seeks to account for a crisis, the social as constitutively antagonistic, on the basis of a fantasy of a time before or after hegemonic struggle, a place that escapes the play of signification, a pre-political world of fixed meanings and social stability. In Spelman's, and to a lesser extent Selden's, work true or natural feudalism seems only to have ever existed as a moment or a point of origin. It is feudalism's decay, its retreat from its natural state, that provides the matter of their narratives. But of course this decay is written into the way in which Spelman places the true feudalism outside the scope of his study.

Shakespeare's play has a similar structure, since Lear's fall, like feudalism's in *The Original, Growth*, has already happened before a single word is spoken. *King Lear* opens with a brief exchange between Gloucester and Kent:

> Kent: I thought the King had more affected the Duke of Albany than Cornwall.
> Gloucester: It did always seem so to us; but now, in the division of the kingdom, it appears not which of the Dukes he values most; for equalities are so weigh'd that curiosity in neither can make choice of either's moiety.

Act 1, Sc 1, L 1–6[45]

The politics embodied in this exchange are inherently monarchical but this passage also reflects the extent to which Lear's kingship fails in terms of contemporary understandings of the proper ordering of the polity. For example, in his seminal work of Tudor political writing, *The Governour*, Sir Thomas Elyot argued that true or proper kingship was distinguished by its transparency and publicness.[46] Clearly the political world that Kent and Gloucester inhabit is neither transparent nor public – it is a world in which curiosity (implying lack of publicness) and affection (suggesting private desires) occupy a central place.[47]

The fantasy at the heart of *King Lear* is that the play's tragedy is caused by Lear's madness, his staging in Act 1 Scene 1 of a love competition. By making the violent and traumatic events of *King Lear* explicable as the story of Lear's fall into madness, that play reproduces the structure of the historical work of Selden and Spelman; the tragedy of Lear, like the decline of feudalism, is a historical myth that works to obscure the antagonistic and conflict riven truth of the past and present. However, this is only the case if one fails to note the extent to which Shakespeare's play is different from Lear's. While almost all the characters in *King Lear* do seek to make sense of the play's events by reference to Lear and his madness, what Shakespeare remorselessly shows us is the failure of these attempts; what happens in Act 1 Scene 1 may be mad, and is certainly bad kingship, but it does not explain the play's ultimate moment of violence and horror – Cordelia's murder.

Shakespeare's appropriation of Samuel Harsnett's *Declaration of Egregious Popish Impostures* also reflects his awareness of the ways historical myths work.[48] This text needs to be understood as part of a tradition of anti-popish tracts going back to the 1530s that use popery's tendency to produce a false, protean, sophistic language to provide their narrative motivation and authorial justification. Harsnett deploys his ability to penetrate the foggy reasons and obscure words of his popish enemies to claim an authoritative voice within Elizabethan culture. In the process he constructs his opponents as his antithesis: popish inquisitors (and as a sub-text Harsnett's Puritan enemies) who corruptly encourage their victims to produce a false disordered language that they can then penetrate and explain in order to claim authority.[49] Popery, and the demonic speech that it generates, like the idea of feudalism in the work of Selden and Spelman, works as a fantastical other within the *Declaration* to justify Harsnett's status as examiner and his (it is an inherently masculine role) right of inspection, examination and interrogation.[50]

It is this interrogative examining role that Lear desires to play in relation to his own daughters. When he stages the competition over the division of his land what he wants is not only to hear his daughters tell him that they love him (although the *hearing* is clearly important) but also that they do so in a way that allows, indeed incites, him to adopt the role of interpreter of their words. It is for this reason that Goneril's speech so satisfies Lear:

> Gon: Sir, I love you more than word can wield the matter;
> Dearer than eyesight, space and liberty;
> Beyond what can be valued, rich or rare;
> No less than life, with grace, health, beauty, honour;
> As much as child e'er lov'd, or father found;
> A love that makes breath poor and speech unable,
> Beyond all manner of so much I love you.

Act 1, Sc 1, L 55–61

Goneril's speech is complex and self-consciously literary. It repeats the familiar poetic trope, for example used in the first sonnet of Philip Sidney's Petrarchan sonnet sequence Astrophil and Stella, in which the inability to write becomes itself the occasion for the production of poetry. Goneril claims she cannot find the words to say how much she loves and takes seven complex lines to confirm this linguistic failure. The poetic nature of the conceit underlying Goneril's words is important because it reflects the extent to which this speech is a performance designed to construct its audience as the privileged producer and consumer of its meaning. Lear's desire to hear the truth of his daughter's love is satisfied by the production of a speech that demands interpretation; like the words of the demonics in Harsnett's text Goneril's figurative and poetic words need to be interpreted by a privileged reader.[51]

Cordelia's 'Nothing' demands no such interpretation. Indeed as far as Lear is concerned it positively resists being read. When he tells Cordelia that 'Nothing will come of nothing' he is of course wrong on a number of levels. Most notoriously he is wrong in terms of the early modern misogynistic pun on 'nothing' = female genitalia. He is also, however, being dishonest since ultimately it is not Cordelia's nothing he is concerned with here but his own.[52] Lear in this scene is demanding not only that his daughters tell him how much they love him but also that they do so in a way that allows, indeed requires, him to add something to their words.[53] At one level this is of course his land; however, at another it is his interpretative validation of their love. Lear desires to make Cordelia's truth his own by being its privileged interpreter: to make her love, her 'nothing', some-thing by filling it with matter, with his words.

The desire to occupy the position of privileged interpreter, one at the heart of Harsnett's text, requires the production of a veil or body, a hidden or fantastical object/text, against which to define itself. In the work of Selden and Spelman this screen is the idea of feudalism, in the Declaration it is the language of the demonics and in King Lear it is, at one level, the bodies of Lear's daughters. Lear has a desperate need to know, to penetrate, almost literally, to the heart of their beings in order to find, or more accurately to confirm, the truth of his interpretation of their words. It is for this reason that Lear's madness is so misogynistic; he desires to see what his pun in Act 1 Scene 1 shows is nothing more than his own fantasy. Lear's desire to "anatomize Regan" (Act 3, Sc 6, L 73) indicates the extent to which his madness embodies his earlier desire to know the truth of her love *and* turn it into speech. However, at another level, Lear does not need to anatomise Regan since he already *knows* the truth. The depth model underlying Lear's attack on Regan is in practice tautological since in his world depth only exists in order to be turned into surface, to be turned inside out. One cannot, however, anatomise 'nothing' without making it 'something' while, on the other hand, one cannot but anatomise the kind of Petrarchan language that Goneril speaks.

Lear's desire to anatomise Regan also relates to the play's status as history. When sixteenth-century historians used concepts like feudalism or popery were not these fantasies precisely what allowed them to anatomise the past? To claim the right of inspection? And to therefore construct themselves, and their texts, as authoritative and magisterial while simultaneously allowing them to avoid or obscure a basic failure of interpretation – the impossibility of explaining within a magisterial framework the fact of oppression and class conflict.[54]

The truths that Lear and Gloucester desire to see and know through examination and interrogation lead them only to see their own desires and fantasies.[55] When Lear tells Cordelia that 'Nothing will come of nothing', it is his fear of his nothingness, the fact that Cordelia gives him nothing to interpret and anatomise, that provokes his anger. A similar structure can be seen in the scene when Edmund presents Gloucester with the forged letter purporting to come from Edgar:

> Glou: You know the character to be your brother's?
> Edm: If the matter were good, my lord, I durst swear it were his; but, in respect of that, I would fain think it were not.
> Glou: It is his?
> Edm: It is his hand, my lord: but I hope his heart is not in the contents.
> Glou: Has he never before sounded you in this business?
> Edm: Never, my lord. But I have heard him oft maintain it to be fit that, sons at perfect age and fathers declined, the father should be as ward to the son and the son manage his revenue.
> Glou: O villain, villain!
>
> Act 1, Sc 2, L 62–75

Gloucester reads the forged letter wearing glasses tinted with his own fantasies and fears. As a consequence he sees only that which he has put there himself. Like an early modern critic writing about the death of feudalism,

Gloucester sees in the written record a fantasy that he has himself produced.

Lear's and Gloucester's acts of false interpretation do not, however, produce nothing – the nothing they produce is the play *King Lear*; they therefore in effect make history. There is, however, another history present in Shakespeare's play, one that is antithetical to the kind of historical narratives produced by such fantasies as feudalism and popery. When the Fool speaks his prophecy in Act 3 Scene 2 he is drawing on a history that is not magisterial or even explanatory in a conventional sense. The Fool's prophecy is that:

> When priests are more in word than matter;
> When brewers mar their malt with water;
> When nobles are their tailors' tutors;
>
> …
>
> Then shall the realm of Albion
> Come to great confusion:
> Then comes the time, who lives to see't,
> That going shall be us'd with feet.
> This prophecy Merlin shall make; for I live before his time.

Act 3, Sc 2, L 81–95

The Fool's prophecy is of a time when oppression exists – in other words it is a prophecy that has already come to pass and is always coming to pass.[56] It is for this reason that although it is a prophecy it exists in the Fool's words before it is made by Merlin. This prophecy has a direct relationship to the kind of writings that emerged from the Peasant's Revolt and which Shakespeare draws on in a number of plays.[57] As a historical play *King Lear* embodies a conflict between history as an endless record of moments of oppression and history as narrative, explanation and inquisition – history as a story and history as a constantly repeated catastrophe whose end is not yet in sight but will come.[58]

This tension over the status of history as a discourse is brought to its conclusion at the end of the play around the horror of Cordelia's death. This event is not reducible to simple words or narrative explanation. Ultimately its truth exists beyond history.[59] At the end of the play, when Lear enters carrying the body of his youngest daughter, there are three attempts to make sense of Cordelia's death – Kent's, Edgar's and Albany's:

Kent: Is this the promised end?
Edg: Or image of that horror?
Alb: Fall, and cease.

Act 5, Sc 3, L 261–3

Kent asks if Cordelia's death is part of an apocalyptic narrative, Edgar emphasises its visual horror, while for Albany it is the end of history. There is, however, another response which is Lear's desperate attempt to deny the reality of Cordelia's death and therefore to escape the pressure, the need, to make it meaningful, to historise it. The play concludes with Edgar's injunction to "Speak what we feel, not what we ought to say" (Act 5, Sc 3, L 323). There is a real irony in these words since if it were possible to speak what we feel, if Cordelia's love could have been spoken, the tragedy of *King Lear* would not have happened. Certainly Lear does speak what he feels at the moment of Cordelia's death but all he says is one word, 'Howl'.

In Shakespeare's play Lear's fall, as an explanation for the tragedy that is history, functions in the same way as feudalism's decay does in the work of Selden and Spelman. It allows, indeed incites, the production of historical explanation. If feudalism had not decayed, if Lear has not been mad, all would have been well – Jacobean society would not be conflict ridden and Cordelia would not have died. Shakespeare, however, undermines this fantasy in a moment of radical authorial denial.[60] Confronted with the truth of the past in Cordelia's meaningless, pointless death, Lear's response is simply to 'howl': one word repeated over and over again which does not allow, indeed positively resists, interpretation. Lear's howl represents a rejection and denial of a model of interpretation based on the desire to know, to produce explanations, to write history.[61]

Cordelia's death is the truth of the past. It cannot be simply reduced to words, made into a story or used as the justification for someone to have the right of inspection; it cannot be anatomised, as Petrarchan poetry is designed to be, as part of a process that enables the emergence of a masculine desire premised on the need to penetrate in order to know; and it cannot, like the fantasy of feudalism, be used to create a narrative of the past that writes over the Fool's history of oppression and the oppressed. Kent, Edgar and Albany, when confronted with the fact of Cordelia's death, instantly try to make it meaningful. The differing strategies that these characters adopt are moreover part of this process since what is important in their reaction is not the truth of their various attempts to explain Cordelia's death but the way in which Kent's, Edgar's and Albany's words construct it as explainable. The promise, and temptation, that Shakespeare holds out to his audience at this moment is that they can make sense of Cordelia's murder – they can create a narrative, deploy a historical myth, tell a sad tale, anything, just to fill in the expanse of nothing that opens at the end of the play.[62]

The conclusion of *King Lear* can be read as a direct challenge to the historicist study of Shakespeare. Claire Colebrook has suggested that: "The textualisation of history, as well as an attempt to think beyond history as text, is perhaps the clearest identifying feature of new historicism."[63] The desire to fill history with text, with explanation, is one that ultimately fails at the end of *King Lear*; whatever Kent, Edgar or Albany say their attempts to 'textualise' Cordelia's death fail. Even a powerful myth like feudalism ultimately cannot recuperate the trauma. Lear's howl cannot be linked and woven into a historical narrative or turned into one detail among many as part of a "thick description of cultural details".[64] It simply is – repeated night after night, outside history and narrative – the howl of injustice that only a Fool can answer.

Romeo, Juliet, Shakespeare and Žižek

Slavoj Žižek's work represents in its totality an attempt to restore truth as a category to critical thought. In pursuit of this agenda Žižek consistently returns to the founders of modern Western materialist thought, primarily Marx and Lacan. This return is what makes his work so important for the study of literature, and in particular Shakespeare. In plays like *Richard III* and *Othello* Shakespeare's agenda is profoundly materialist and strangely Lacanian in its concern with the implications of language's status as inherently flawed or incomplete – as always saying too much and/or too little. It is important to note moreover that Žižek's work represents a radical break with existing postmodern and post-structuralist thought. In particular, Žižek is committed to a specific materialist understanding of Lacan's and Marx's work as the truth – or at least as capable of producing truthful cultural analysis. The implications of this in terms of literary criticism can best be illustrated by briefly discussing a small number of key elements in Žižek's thought in relation to Shakespeare's work, and particularly *Romeo and Juliet*.

Three key inter-related terms for Žižek are the Real, fantasy and reality. Their structural relationship functions within Žižek's work to sustain its truth claims. The fundamental point to understand about this triad is that it reverses the common-sense assumption of the relationship between reality and fantasy. Žižek writes:

> ... for Lacan, fantasy is on the side of reality – that is, it sustains the subject's 'sense of reality': when the phantasmic frame disintegrates, the subject undergoes a 'loss of reality' and starts to perceive reality as an 'unreal' nightmarish universe with no firm ontological foundation; this nightmarish universe is not 'pure fantasy' but, on the contrary, *that which remains of reality after reality is deprived of its support in fantasy.*[65]

The implication of this reversal of the common-sense relationship between fantasy and reality is that 'reality' is a product of 'fantasy' – it is the fantastical that allows the emergence of reality. Brian Nical comments that: "It is natural to think of fantasy as an escape into a realm of wish-fulfilment, divorced from reality, but Žižek emphasizes that reality actually *depends* upon subscribing to the fantasy."[66] This subscription to fantasy is a product of the symbolic order's arbitrary violent imposition of meaning on to the mass of matter that is the pre-symbolic Real.

The Real, for Žižek, can strictly speaking never emerge or indeed be. He writes:

> The Real is ... simultaneously both the hard, impenetrable kernel resisting symbolization *and* a pure chimerical entity which has in itself no ontological consistency. ... the Real is the rock upon which every attempt at symbolization stumbles, the hard core which remains the same in all possible worlds (symbolic universes); but at the same time its status is thoroughly precarious; it is something that persists only as failed, missed, in a shadow, and dissolves itself as soon as we try to grasp it in its positive nature.[67]

The Real only exists as a series of traumatic effects within the symbolic order. It is, in Žižek's words, "a certain limit, a pure negativity, a traumatic limit which prevents the final totalization of the social-ideological field".[68] Fantasy protects reality from the effects of the Real but at the same time draws its energy from its proximity to the Real. It sustains the narrative that produces reality but its motivation is to narrate away, through and over the Real. In other words the Real remains at the centre of the fantasy but only as an effect – as that which motivates the fantastical narrative that tells reality.

Romeo and Juliet opens with the Chorus creating a narrative explanation for the tragedy that is about to unfold:

> Chorus: Two households both alike in dignity
> (In fair Verona, where we lay our scene)
> From ancient grudge break to new mutiny,
> Where civil blood makes civil hands unclean.
>
> …
>
> The fearful passage of their death-mark'd love
> And the continuance of their parents' rage,
> Which, but their children's end, nought could remove,
> Is now the two hours' traffic of our stage;
> The which, if you with patient ears attend,
> What here shall miss, our toil shall strive to mend.

Prologue, 1–14

This speech suggests a link between the death-marked love of Romeo and Juliet and the feud between their families. But it does no more than suggest this. The Chorus's words leave open the possibility that their love is death-marked for other, perhaps more fundamental, reasons. What these might be is unclear but the lack of names in this Prologue is indicative of Shakespeare's concern in *Romeo and Juliet* with language and its costs.

The fantasy that sustains the reality of fair Verona is that without the feud it would be a settled, ordered city. In particular, the feud operates to order and frame the fundamentally violent nature of masculinity in Verona. *Romeo and Juliet*, the world's most famous love story, opens with two servants, Sampson and Gregory, indulging in violent sexual banter:

> Greg: The quarrel is between our masters and us their men.
> Samp: 'Tis all one. I will show myself a tyrant: when I have fought with the men I will be civil with the maids, I will cut off their heads.
> Greg: The heads of the maids?
> Samp: Ay, the heads of the maids, or their maidenheads; take it in what sense thou wilt.
> Greg: They must take it in the sense that feel it.

Act 1, Sc 1, L 18–26

Gregory and Sampson are participating in the feud as a way of sustaining their sense of what it means to be a man. Or to put it more accurately the feud works to allow them to articulate a particularly violent misogynist version of masculinity as the norm. The fantasy at work in this exchange, and indeed throughout the play, is that it is the feud that normalises Gregory's and Sampson's sense of identity when in fact it operates as its apology. The feud protects the dominant model of masculinity within Verona from acknowledging its fear of the feminine by creating a narrative frame, the feud itself, within which men can define themselves against a reductive misogynist version of femininity. Shakespeare gives Gregory's and Sampson's banal reduction of women to sex objects, things to be taken and had, a particular linguistic form. Gregory and Sampson talk in puns – words whose 'humour' is dependent on a reductive analogy with sex and the female body. Their language strives to fix and contain the feminine, to pun it into place, as a way of asserting their masculinity.

Romeo and Juliet ends with a moment of apparent reconciliation with Montague and Capulet agreeing to raise a golden statue to their dead children. The final lines are spoken by the Prince who clearly intends them to produce closure:

> Prince: A glooming peace this morning with it brings:
> The sun for sorrow will not show his head.
> Go hence to have more talk of these sad things.
> Some shall be pardon'd , and some punished,
> For never was a story of more woe
> Than this of Juliet and her Romeo.

Act 5, Sc 3, L 304–9

There is, however, something a bit strained about this final speech. It seems designed to remind the audience that they have been watching a story, a fiction. Ending with the names of the two lovers uncannily reminds one that it was the names that were lacking from the Chorus's Prologue. This creates a strange sense of repetition and therefore of the emptying out of meaning since the implication is that the play's sad story is simply about to start again. Finally the Prince's concluding couplet with its expansive rhyme of 'woe' with 'Romeo' suggests that the truths of the play are being dispersed into language.[69] This dispersal, however, sits uneasily with Montague's and Capulet's decision to create a statue of Romeo and Juliet, which in turn pre-figures the attempted textualisation of Cordelia's death by Kent and his colleagues at the end of *King Lear*.

What form will this statue take? If it is simple realistic figures of Romeo and Juliet will this be a proper representation of their love? Indeed what would a statue of Juliet's love look like? What would it be? Shakespeare concludes *Romeo and Juliet* with images of linguistic expansion and material fixity, a golden statue and endless woe. What this suggests is that the tragedy of *Romeo and Juliet* is only tangentially related to the feud. Their deaths cannot 'solve' the violence and fear expressed by Gregory and Sampson at the start of the play. *Romeo and Juliet* ends with an attempt by the Prince, Montague and Capulet to shore up the reality of Verona: to produce a new fantasy, the fiction of *Romeo and Juliet.*

One of the key moments in *Romeo and Juliet* is Mercutio's famous Queen Mab speech. This appears at first sight strange since what Mercutio is describing in this speech has little or no relevance to the play's plot, but in practice it is this lack of utility that marks the importance of Queen Mab. Mercutio's speech opens with an evocation of Mab as a fairy-tale creature:

> Mer: [Queen Mab] is the fairies' midwife, and she comes
> In shape no bigger than an agate stone
> On the forefinger of an alderman,
> Drawn with a team of little atomi
> Over men's noses as they lie asleep.

Act 1, Sc 4, L 54–8

In the opening lines of his speech Mercutio constructs Mab as the principle of fantasy and imagination. As the speech progresses, however, she becomes a nightmarish figure associated with ambitious dreams and violent desires. By the end of the speech Mab has been completely transformed from a fairy-tale creature into a horrific hag:

> Mer: This is that very Mab
> That plaits the manes of horses in the night
> And bakes the elf-locks in foul sluttish hairs,
> Which, once untangled, much misfortune bodes.
> This is the hag, when maids lie on their backs,
> That presses them and learns them first to bear,
> Making them women of good carriage.
> This is she —

Rome: Peace, peace, Mercutio, peace.
Thou talk'st of nothing.

Act 1, Sc 4, L 88–96

What is it about Mab that causes Mercutio to lose control to the extent that he has to be stopped by Romeo? Why does Mercutio's own fantasy seduce him into linguistic excess? To answer these questions it is useful to briefly discuss the subject as it appears in Žižek's work. Žižek argues that subjectivity should be understood as split between the subject as a particular individual and the Subject emptied of a subject's particularity – the difference between *a* subject and the idea of *the* Subject, that which is the Subject before it is filled with the particular details that constitute subjecthood. The Subject, for Žižek, is strictly speaking a void or lack that exists only as the potential space for a subject to emerge. The relationship between Subject and subject is fundamental in Žižek's work in terms of the production of meaning. He argues that:

> … in order for the series of signifiers to mean *something* (to have a determinate meaning), *there must be a signifier (a 'something') which stands for 'nothing'*, a signifying element whose very presence stands for the absence of meaning (or rather, for absence *tout court*). This 'nothing', of course, is *the subject itself* …[70]

Mercutio's Queen Mab speech is a series of signifiers that spins out of control. Mercutio finally cannot stop his rant since it is precisely its productivity, its protean qualities, that are what he fears and desires. Mercutio's sense of self is built upon a model of masculinity based on the violent denial of lack displaced on to a fear of the feminine. In the Queen Mab speech what really threatens Mercutio is his own image of Mab as a chimera, a protean, fantastical figure that escapes all definition since at one level this is himself – what he is and what he desires to be. Mercutio, like Mab, is ultimately a nothing, a fantasy, a lack, constantly filled with words that produce a subject/something/Mercutio from the Subject as nothing.[71] The Queen Mab speech is, therefore, the other side of Gregory's and Sampson's banal reduction of the feminine. Mab represents the protean qualities of language, the endlessly expanding woe, while the sexist puns of the opening exchange articulate a desperate desire for linguistic fixity, the concretisation of meaning.

Romeo's intervention works because it reminds Mercutio of another nothing – one that Gregory and Sampson would recognise. This is the nothing of the female sex – the nothing, the lack, that in misogynistic thought signifies the dangers and fears lurking in the female body. Romeo's nothing can, therefore, be related to a Lacanian *object a*. Žižek writes that:

> *Object a* is simultaneously the pure lack, the void around which the desire turns and which, as such, causes desire, *and* the imaginary element which conceals this void, renders it invisible by filling it out. The point … is that there is no lack without the element filling it out: *the filler sustains what it dissimulates.*[72]

Nothing in Verona is an object and cause of desire. It signifies and reduces femininity to a banal bawdy pun – the nothing of the female sex. At the same time, however, nothing in its expansiveness provokes desire. It is a fixed banal 'thing' and an expanse of woe in which the male subject fears (and desires) losing himself.

Language for Žižek is profoundly violent. He writes:

> Word is murder of a thing, not only in the elementary sense of implying its absence – by naming a thing, we treat is as absent, as dead, although it is still present – but above all in the sense of its radical *dissection*: the word 'quarters' the thing, it tears it out of the embedment in its concrete context, it treats its component parts as entities with an autonomous existence: we speak about colour, form, shape, etc as if they possessed self-sufficient being. The power of understanding consists in this capacity to reduce the organic whole of experience to an appendix to the 'dead' symbolic classification.[73]

Žižek's violent and gloomy language in this passage, words as the death of matter, is problematic. Certainly it is true that language can be used to cut up the world but this can also be a productive communal process – weaving together new live meanings out of the chaos of the Real. This is the possibility that Shakespeare produces around the figure of Autolycus in *The Winter's Tale*. The central point of Žižek's argument is, however, less contentious, which is that there is a tension between word and matter – that turning the latter into the former is at one level a violent process of naming and ordering. Juliet's rejection of Romeo's name reflects this violence:

> Juliet: Tis but thy name that is my enemy:
> Thou art thyself, though not a Montague.
> What's Montague? It is nor hand nor foot
> Nor arm nor face nor any other part
> Belonging to a man. O be some other name.
> What's in a name? That which we call a rose
> By any other name would smell as sweet;
> So Romeo would, were he not Romeo call'd,
> Retain that dear perfection which he owes
> Without that title. Romeo, doff thy name,
> And for thy name, which is no part of thee
> Take all myself.
>
> Act 2, Sc 2, L 38–49

For Juliet the naming of Romeo is a violent imposition of an alien meaning on to his person. His name forces him into a place within the symbolic order that has no relationship to who he really is. Juliet's love offers him the possibility of escape from this 'false place', this 'forced choice' – freedom from the burden of subjectivity in an ever expanding oceanic feminine expanse of desire:

> Juliet: My bounty is as boundless as the sea,
> My love as deep: the more I give to thee
> The more I have, for both are infinite.
>
> Act 2, Sc 2, L 133–5

All Romeo has to do is renounce his name and he will be able to immerse himself in Juliet's boundless infinite love.

What Juliet offers Romeo is escape from subjecthood and indeed from the symbolic order itself. She holds before him the possibility of losing one's self in the sea of language that so horrified Mercutio in his Queen Mab speech. The problem is that at the same time Juliet's love is fixed on a particular specific object – Romeo. There is therefore a tension between her love as boundless and the requirement to speak it, to make it meaningful, which in turn means participating in the process of symbolisation. Žižek argues that:

> The paradox of symbolization resides in the fact that the object is constituted as One through a feature that is radically external to the object itself, to its reality; through a name that bears no resemblance to the object.[74]

Romeo would not be Romeo were it not for his name. It is this that marks out his space within the symbolic order. Romeo's 'forced choice', his acceptance of who he is on the basis of a radically external object, his name, while it appears unnatural is actually the requirement of subject-hood. One cannot be a subject without accepting that at one level what makes one a subject is one's arbitrary inscription into the symbolic order – the acceptance of one's name as who one is. Juliet's desire to love romeo not Romeo, however, is not simply naive. It represents a real desire to escape the forced choice of subjecthood. It is an act of resistance – a refusal comparable to Antigone's when faced by Creon's tyranny. Juliet's love is caught between a pure fixity and endless expansiveness. In theoret-ical terms the love Juliet offers Romeo is aimed at 'the kernel of the real'.[75] It is doomed to fail but this is not because of the feud but rather because it is predicated on an infantile but seductive desire to love beyond vio-lence of language, beyond reality, beyond even fantasy – a desire to love in the Real.

Romeo and Juliet's love ends in the horror of the Capulets' crypt. In particular, at the end of *Romeo and Juliet* Shakespeare confronts the audi-ence with the cost of love in Verona. When Juliet thrusts Romeo's dagger into her body for it to rust and asks to die she makes literal many of the sexual puns that have littered the rest of the play. Daggers are no longer puns for penises and to die is to die not to have an orgasm. This literalisa-tion of the play's sexual puns subverts the status of nothing as misogynis-tic pun within the play. In *Romeo and Juliet* nothing signifies both the banal reduction of the female body to a sexual object, or indeed to be more accurate a 'hole', and the feminine as an ever expanding field of lin-guistic productivity and excess. When at the end of the play Shakespeare insists on making the sexual puns that filled that first half of his drama literal he confronts the audience with their complicity in the world of Gregory, Sampson and Mercutio, their desire for a nothing that is at once banal and complex, fixed and ever expanding, a golden statue and a story of woe.

Shakespeare's drama consistently circles around the idea of nothing, not simply as regards its relationship to the female body but in more gen-eral terms. There are two key nothings for Shakespeare. One is the misog-ynist nothing of Lear, Othello and Leontes which sustains their senses of self by displacing on to the feminine the burden of subjecthood. The other nothing that Shakespeare is centrally concerned with is the nothing of the audience's desire. It is this nothing that puts into circulation Shake-speare's drama as something to be watched, listened to and consumed. This nothing can only be 'seen' through effects – specifically in terms of its embodiment in the money that the audience pays to make the play happen. In these terms *Much Ado About Nothing* can be taken as the title not simply of one of Shakespeare's plays but of his entire output. All his plays are, at one level, much ado about nothing – the audience's desire, textualised, embodied and acted on stage, for them to see, hear and consume.

The ending of *Romeo and Juliet* refers to this nothing in its banal grudging offer of reconciliation and closure. It is the audience that needs this. It is they who have paid for a specific commodity, a play comprising "two hours' traffic". What Shakespeare shows us at the end of *Romeo and Juliet* is two communities reassembling themselves through the textuali-sation and concretisation of Romeo and Juliet's love in a golden statue and the story of woe. Žižek argues that "a shared lie is an incomparably more effective bond for a group than the truth".[76] At the end of *Romeo and Juliet* the Prince, Montague, Capulet and the audience share the lie that Romeo and Juliet's death has produced some kind of closure. This lie is effective because, like all successful ideologies, it battens on to a gen-uine trans-ideological desire, on and off stage, for closure. Shakespeare, however, by creating a link with the beginning of the play with his emphasis on the protagonists' names suggests that this closure is at best partial and at worst a delusion. It only works if one ignores the real issues that caused the tragedy – the extent to which Queen Mab, far from being an aberrant figure, represents a something that is at the heart of the sub-ject – a nothing whose denial is the real source of violence and death in *Romeo and Juliet.*

New Historicist criticism treats the truths produced by a play like *Romeo and Juliet* within the boundaries of history. Juliet's love, Mercutio's horror, Romeo's name can all be made meaningful by weaving and link-ing them into a historical narrative – a deep description of early modern culture. Žižek's work represents a complete departure from this form of historicism. He writes that:

> The Real *qua* Thing is not 'repressed', it is foreclosed or 'primordially repressed' ... its repression is not a historical variable but is constitutive of the very order of symbolic historicity. In other words, the Real *qua* Thing stands for that X on account of which every symbolization fails – in its

very unhistoricity, it sets in motion one new symbolization after another.[77]

It is this insistence on the unhistorical nature of his ideas that most clearly separates Žižek's thought from prevailing forms of historicist and postmodern criticism. And it is precisely its claim to be true, beyond historical or cultural contexts, that makes it so useful for literary critics – particularly in relation to a writer like Shakespeare. Žižek's work allows one to study the theoretical and aesthetic truths of Shakespeare's work; it enables literary critics to become literary critics again and engage in their duty to study works of literature as spaces for thought capable of producing ethical truths.

Conclusion: the burden of criticism

Žižek's work is often criticised for its repetitive quality. And this is in many ways a justified criticism. In all his works the same basic structures and concepts are applied to produce truths. It is, however, a mistake to accuse Žižek of repetition since it is precisely this quality that marks the ethical nature of his work. The criticism that Žižek repeats himself reflects a situation in which intellectuals have lost sight of what it means to be committed – to stake one's critical analysis on one particular discourse or theory. In the present intellectual market place there is a kind of stoic purity in Žižek's refusal to embrace endless different critical perspectives. Mas'ud Zavarzadeh comments that:

> The textual 'undecidability' produced in the ludic cultural studies classroom cultivates subjectivities that are so complex, subtle, and multifaceted they are unable to accept any single site as the site of 'truth' for themselves and others.[78]

The rejection of the idea of truth is what generates the accusation that the repetitive quality of Žižek's work is a flaw. Underlying this critique of his work is an assumption that what signifies 'good' critical work, in literary criticism and cultural studies, is wit, playfulness, a degree of analytical panache and theoretical daring. The retreat from truth claims within literary criticism and cultural studies has gone hand in hand with the emergence of the star critic: the person whose work may not make truth claims but is exciting, easy to read and witty.

In their study *Empire* Michael Hardt and Antonio Negri have nothing but scorn for the idea that truth has had its day. They comment that:

> The postmodernist epistemological challenge to 'the Enlightenment' – its attack on master narratives and its critique of the truth – ... loses its liberatory aura when transposed outside the elite intellectual strata of Europe and North America. ... In the context of state terror and mystification, clinging to the primacy of the concept of truth can be a powerful and necessary form of resistance.[79]

Hardt and Negri go on to argue that 'truth will not make us free, but taking control of the production of truth will'.[80] For Žižek holding on to the concept of the truth is the duty of the Left, in particular in the face of the new reactionary fundamentalism – in all its forms. If his work is repetitive, complex and in places banal – so are truths.[81] Shakespeare's writing seems a world apart from that of Žižek, Negri and Hardt, but he shares to the full their concern with the production of truth. His plays were designed to entertain and to earn him a living. They reflect the historical time in which they were produced. But they are also complex works of literature that construct themselves as spaces for thought intended to participate in the liberatory struggle that is the production of truth.[82]

Shakespearean Fantasy and Politics is a theoretical engagement with Shakespeare's work. It draws on the work of a range of critical thinkers, primarily Žižek, in order to examine the ways in which Shakespeare during the course of his writing career developed his thought in relation to the status of the theatre, language, politics and ethics. There is a broad chronological structure to the book which reflects its over-arching argument which is that Shakespeare's early plays exhibit a confidence in the power of the theatre which slowly drains from his work until in *Othello* he seems disgusted with himself, his theatre and above all his audience. The book argues, however, that in his late Jacobean plays Shakespeare articulates a new theatrical ethics that answers the doubts so radically expressed in *Othello*. Chapter 1 examines Shakespeare's first tetralogy – *Henry VI Parts 1, 2, 3* and *Richard III*. It argues that in these plays Shakespeare reflects on the status of history as a discourse and advances the theatre as a site for the ethical production of historical knowledge. Chapter 2 looks at Shakespeare's late Elizabethan comedies, while Chapter 3 discusses two of his explicitly political plays, *Julius Caesar* and *Coriolanus*. Both these chapters argue that in the plays Shakespeare wrote at the turn of the century there is a growing sense of unease over the ethics of the theatre. Persistent and nagging questions hover over these plays. Does being a successful playwright mean behaving like Antony? Like Don John? What does the audience desire? What does it will? The analysis of *Othello* in Chapter 4 is the theoretical centre of the book. The final chapter looks at *Cymbeline* and *The Winter's Tale*. In these plays Shakespeare finds an answer to his earlier scepticism. He rewrites Antony as Paulina and Iago becomes Autolycus.

Notes

1   Theodor Adorno, *Aesthetic Theory*, trans. Robert Hullot-Kentor (London: 1997), p.6.
2   One reason for Shakespeare's continuing popularity is the Shakespeare industry – academic, theatrical, cultural and heritage. For an excellent discussion of this important aspect of modern Shakespeare studies see Graham Holderness, *Cultural Shakespeare: Essays in the Shakespeare Myth* (Hatfield: 2001).
3   For New Historicism see two statements from the beginning and end of its emergence as a school of literary criticism: H. Veeser, *The New Historicism* (New York: 1989); and Catherine Gallagher and Stephen Greenblatt, *Practicing New Historicism* (Chicago: 2001). It is interesting to note the extent to which these volumes, despite the over ten years that separate them, are still in basic agreement in terms of what New Historicism is and, perhaps more importantly, what it produces.
4   David Scott Kastan, *Shakespeare after Theory* (New York: 1999), p.31.
5   Mark Poster, 'The Question of Agency: Michel de Certeau and the History of Consumerism', *Diacritics*, 22 (1992), pp.94–107, p.96.
6   Peter Uwe Hohendahl, 'A Return to History? The New Historicism and its Agenda', *New German Critique*, 55 (1992), pp.87–104, p.103.
7   Joan Copjec, *Read my Desire: Lacan against the Historicists* (Cambridge, MA: 1995), p.7.
8   Richard Terdiman has criticised the tendency of New Historicist criticism to self-reflective formalism. He comments that: "… while in deeply salutary ways New Historicism rediscovers the complexities of social and cultural systems and the contestation and subversion that ceaselessly stress, typically these dynamics of alterity are finally represented as recuperated and detoxified by the system itself. In this way, despite the brilliance of its analyses, New Historicism risks falling into a subtle, ultimately airless functionalism, an organicism of the text of power or of dominant discourse." Richard Terdiman, 'The Response of the Other', *Diacritics*, 22 (1992), pp.2–10, p.7.
9   Julian Markels comments that: "In their disinclination to engage either with the total work of art or the total configuration of its ideological context, the New Historicists are also methodologically, systematically disinclined to give hurt even when the subject is ideology and power. In that respect their *apercus* can often seem like mere new bottlings, with eye-catching Foucauldian labels, for the innocuous old monologisms of critics like Dover Wilson." Julian Markels, '*King Lear*, Revolution, and the New Historicism', *Modern Language Studies*, 21 (1991), pp.11–26, p.25.
10 Slavoj Žižek, 'Cultural Studies versus the "Third Culture"', *South Atlantic Quarterly*, 101 (2002), pp.19–32, p.24/5.

11 This reliance on out-dated historical concepts is partly a result of New Historicism's relatively uncritical appropriation of the work of Michel Foucault. Heather Dubrow has commented that: "Foucault is often credited with one of the principal moves of new historicism, the anecdote, but another of his rhetorical strategies, his propensity for sweeping generalisations, has had a deeper and less benign influence on new historicism." Heather Dubrow, 'The Newer Historicism', *Clio*, 25 (1996), pp.421–38, p.429.

12 There are any number of equally valid examples, such as absolutism, a meaningless concept in relation to the English monarchy in the early modern period but one that is consistently deployed by New Historicist critics as a descriptive term in relation to the kingship of James VI and I.

13 Paul Delaney, '*King Lear* and the Decline of Feudalism', *PMLA*, 92 (1977), pp.429–40.

14 For a representative sample of recent work on *King Lear*, all of which despite their very different approaches to Shakespeare's play reproduce the argument that it reflects a real change in the way English society was organised during the early modern period, see William Zunder, 'Shakespeare and the End of Feudalism: *King Lear* as *Fin-de-Siècle* Text', *Shakespeare Studies*, 78 (1997), pp.513–21; Tamise Van Pelt, 'Entitled to be King: The Subversion of the Subject in *King Lear*', *Literature and Psychology*, 42 (1996), pp.100–12; Jerald W. Spotswood, 'Maintaining Hierarchy in *The Tragedie of King Lear*', *Studies in English Literature*, 38 (1998), pp.265–80; and Lyell Asher, 'Lateness in *King Lear*', *Yale Journal of Criticism*, 13 (2000), pp.209–28.

15 Indeed this feat was itself only arguably achieved by two other of the fourteen monarchs who came to the throne in the period 1450 to 1688 – Henry VIII and Charles I. At least James was not a child, woman, usurper or Catholic nor did he have to obscure the process by which he succeeded unlike Henry VI, Edward IV, Richard III, Henry VII, Edward VI, Mary, Elizabeth, Charles II and James II.

16 John Morrill, *The Nature of the English Revolution* (London: 1993), p.5.

17 Susan Reynolds, *Fiefs and Vassals: The Medieval Evidence Reinterpreted* (Oxford: 1994), p.11.

18 Ibid., p.11.

19 The problematic nature of the construction of the medieval period and its narrative function in the work of many Renaissance scholars has been critiqued often since about 1990 by medievalists. Unfortunately it seems to have had little or no effect if the articles I read when preparing this study are any guide. On the medieval period and its place in the work of Renaissance critics see David Aers, 'A Whisper in the Ear of Early Modernists: Or, Reflections on Literary Critics Writing the "History of the Subject"', in *Culture and History 1350–1600: Essays on English Communities, Identities and Writing*, ed. David Aers (Hemel Hempstead: 1992), pp.177–202; and Lee Patterson, 'On the Margin: Postmodernism, Ironic History, and Medieval Studies', *Speculum*, 65 (1990), pp.87–108.

20 Lee Patterson points out that: "The fact is that the Middle Ages has from the beginning served the post-medieval Western historical consciousness as one of the primary sites of otherness by which it has constituted itself." Lee Patterson, 'Critical Historicism and Medieval Studies', in *Literary Practice and Social Change in Britain 1380–1530*, ed. Lee Patterson (Berkeley, CA: 1990), pp.1–14, p.2.

21 Magisterial here refers to the ruling classes in early modern England, the gentry, aristocracy and intellectuals. All these groups possessed power at one level on the basis of their right to speak and be heard within the polity. Of course at another level they all held power because they owned or had access to a disproportionate amount of the country's wealth and, in particular, land.

22 John Selden, '*Jani Anglorum Facies Altera*', 1610, in *Tracts Written by John Selden*, trans. Redman Westcot (London: 1683), p.47/8.

23 Ibid., a.2 (iv).

24 Ibid., p.10.

25 Ibid., p.36.

26 Richard Halpern in one of the most interesting and provocative recent readings of *King Lear* has suggested that the play "is largely about the divorce between the signs and the material realities of royal power ...". Selden's fantasy of a world in which there was no separation in the law between saying and doing is another response to Halpern's semiotic divorce. See Richard Halpern, *The Poetics of Primitive Accumulation: English Renaissance Culture and the Genealogy of Capital* (Ithaca, NY: 1991), p.220.

27 Selden, 1683, p.95.

28 For example, see Arthur B. Ferguson, *Clio Unbound: Perception of the Social and Cultural Past in Renaissance England* (Durham, NC: 1979), p.51.

29 Sir Henry Spelman, 'The Original, Growth, Propagation and Condition of Feuds and Tenures of Knight-Service in England', in *The English Works of Sir Henry Spelman* (London: 1723), p.2.

30 Ibid., p.2.

31 Ibid., p.2.

32 Ibid., p.5.

33 Ibid., p.5.

34 Ibid., p.5.

35 And one that is clearly related to the political conflicts of the reigns of James I and Charles I.

36 Spelman, 1723, p.46. It is worth noting that one of Spelman's concerns here is that someone might adopt the kind of hermeneutics implicit in William the Conqueror's alleged separation of the law's use from its appearance in terms of his text and misread either his words or their meaning.

37 For an important discussion of this aspect of humanism see David Norbrook, *Poetry and Politics in the English Renaissance* (Oxford: 2002).

38 Ferguson, 1979, p.117.

39 This discussion draws directly on Althusser's discussion of invisibility in *Reading Capital*. Althusser comments that: "In the development of a theory the invisible of a visible field is not generally *anything whatever* outside and foreign to the visible defined by that field. The invisible is defined by the visible as *its* invisible, *its* forbidden vision ..." Louis Althusser, 'From Capital to Marx's Philosophy', in *Reading Capital*, Louis Althusser and Étienne Balibar (London: 1997), pp.11–70, p.26.

40 On the idea of the social as inherently antagonistic see Ernesto Laclau and Chantal Mouffe, *Hegemony and Socialist Strategy: Towards a Radical Democratic Politics* (London: 1985).

41 On Tudor history writing see F.J. Levy, *Tudor Historical Thought* (San Marino, CA: 1967).

42 Thomas Blundeville, *The True Order and Methode of Wryting and Reading Hystories* (London: 1574), B.i.

43 Ibid., F.i.

44 Richard Knowles comments that in *King Lear*: "Not only is the chronology of background events vague, the events themselves and their resistance to rational explanation are consistently hidden from our view." Richard Knowles, 'Cordelia's Return', *Shakespeare*

Quarterly, 50 (1999), pp.33–50, p.49.

45 All quotes from Shakespeare's work in this book are from the most recent Arden edition. To avoid unnecessary footnotes line references will be given in the body of the text. The text of *King Lear* is a matter of considerable debate. In this study I defer to the far greater expertise of the editors of the Arden Shakespeare in terms of editorial questions. For a judicious reading of the issues raised by the various different versions of *King Lear* see Graham Holderness and Naomi Carter, 'The King's Two Bodies: Text and Genre in *King Lear*', *English*, 45 (1996), pp.1–31.

46 For a detailed discussion of Elyot's work see Tom Betteridge, *Literature and Politics in the English Reformation* (Manchester: 2004), Ch. 1.

47 On early modern models of kingship see John Guy, 'Tudor Monarchy and its Critiques', in *Tudor Monarchy*, ed. John Guy (London: 1997), pp.78–110.

48 For a recent discussion of Shakespeare's use of Harsnett's text see Amy Wolf, 'Shakespeare and Harsnett: "Pregnant to Good Pity"?', *Studies in English Literature*, 38 (1998), pp.251–64.

49 Harsnett claims that his theatrical popish enemies desecrate graves and attempt to corrupt the past. He writes that: "Those famous renowned Worthies of her Majesties privie Counsel whose bodies sleepe in peace … how our infernal tragedians have disturbed their rest, prophaned their happy memory, violated their tombs, and called forth their spirits like the Witch of Endor, making them tennis-balls for their devils to bandy on their stage …" Samuel Harsnett, 'A Declaration of Egregious Popish Impostures', in *Shakespeare, Harsnett, and the Devils of Denham*, ed. F.W. Brownlow (London: 1993), p.321.

50 For the relationship between the right of inspection and the production of text see Marie-Françoise Plissart and Jacques Derrida, 'Right of Inspection', *Art and Text*, 32 (1989), pp.20–97.

51 The Petrarchan nature of Goneril's words also accounts for the way they construct the experience of linguistic failure in erotic terms.

52 Timothy Murray argues that "Lear's ghastly decline stems from the horrific expanse of Cordelia's 'nothing'. The fear that Lear feels at his daughter's nothing is a sign of his refusal to face his own nothing/lack. It is this denial that drives the tragedy of the play." See Timothy Murray, *Drama Trauma: Spectres of Race and Sexuality in Performance, Video, and Art* (London: 1997), p.41.

53 David M. Bergeron points out that for Lear what is finally important "is what he will be able to say – to speak – about his daughter's love". David M. Bergeron, 'Deadly Letters in *King Lear*', *Philological Quarterly*, 72 (1993), pp.157–76, p.161.

54 In these terms the myths of papistry and feudalism can be related to the paradox at the centre of courtly love in which, as Slavoj Žižek argues, "*external hindrances that thwart our access to the object are there precisely to create the illusion that without them, the object would be directly accessible …*". Slavoj Žižek, *The Metastases of Enjoyment: Six Essays on Woman and Causality* (London: 1994), p.94.

55 Dan Brayton comments that in "the world of *King Lear*, calamity lies in the wilful misreading of the hidden …". Dan Brayton, 'Angling in the Lake of Darkness: Possession, Dispossession, and the Politics of Discovery in *King Lear*', *English Literary History*, 70 (2003), pp.399–426, p.403.

56 Howard Dobin has suggested that the Fool's "prophecy is sheer nonsense, foretelling things that have always been true or will never be true". But is not truthful nonsense one of the languages of liberation? Howard Dobin, *Merlin's Disciples: Prophecy, Poetry,*

and Power in Renaissance England (Stanford, CA: 1990), p.195.

57 See Charles Hobday, 'Clouted Shoon and Leather Aprons: Shakespeare and the Equali-tarian Tradition', *Renaissance and Modern Studies*, 23 (1979).

58 David Scott Kastan comments that while it is difficult to gauge the politics of *King Lear* "Edgar's counterfeiting may well remind even the bourgeois audience of the modern theatre of the reality of human misery that waits outside and remind us as well that perhaps it need not be so". David Scott Kastan, 'Is There a Class in this (Shakespeare-an) Text?', *Renaissance Drama*, 24 (1993), pp.101–21, p.116.

59 Jonathan Dollimore argues, "The timing of these two deaths [Lear's and Cordelia's] must surely be seen as cruelly, precisely, subversive: instead of complying with the demands of formal closure – the convention which would confirm the attempt at recuperation – the play concludes with two events which sabotage the prospect of both closure and recuperation." Jonathan Dollimore, *Radical Tragedy: Religion: Ideology and Power in the Drama of Shakespeare and his Contemporaries* (New York: 1989), p.203.

60 Robert Bacon claimed that history was in some ways the least authored of all forms of writing stating that: "History of all writings deserveth least taxation, as that which holdeth least of the author, and most of the things themselves." Robert Bacon, 'The History of the Reign of K.Henry the Eighth, K.Edward, Q.Mary, and Part of the Reign of Q.Elizabeth', in *The History of the Reign of King Henry VII*, ed. Brian Vickers (Cam-bridge: 1998), pp.209–14, p.209.

61 David Scott Kastan suggests that "Lear's reiterated howl is as much a passionate imper-ative as a pained ejaculation. In a world where death is the ultimate reality one must – and perhaps can only – howl at the agonising absurdity of existence." See David Scott Kastan, *Shakespeare and the Shapes of Time* (London: 1982), p.105.

62 This is a paraphrase of Timothy Murray's suggestion concerning the status of Cordelia's nothing. See Note 52.

63 Claire Colebrook, *New Literary Histories: New Historicism and Contemporary Criticism* (Manchester: 1997), p.220.

64 Hohendahl, 1992, pp.87–104, p.103.

65 Slavoj Žižek, *The Ticklish Subject: The Absent Centre of Political Ontology* (London: 1999), p.51.

66 Brian Nical, 'As If: Traversing the Fantasy in Žižek', *Paragraph*, 24 (2001), pp.140–55, p.147.

67 Slavoj Žižek, *The Sublime Object of Ideology* (London: 1989), p.169.

68 Ibid., p.164.

69 The tension in this final couplet is between the linguistic order of the verse and the 'sound' of woe. This can be related directly to Žižek's suggestion that: "The problem is … always the same: how are we to prevent the voice from sliding into a consuming self-enjoyment that 'effeminitizes' the reliable masculine Word?" The Prince seeks to impose closure at the end of *Romeo and Juliet* but Queen Mab speaks in and through his woe. See Slavoj Žižek, 'Re-visioning "Lacanian" Social Criticism: The Law and its Obscene Double', *Journal for Psychoanalysis of Culture and Society*, 1 (1996), pp.15–25, p.21.

70 Slavoj Žižek, *The Indivisible Remainder: An Essay on Schelling and Related Matters* (London: 1996), p.43/4.

71 Žižek comments that: "The counterpart to [the] process of subjectivization, the encounter of the real in its senselessness, however, is not a 'process without the subject,' but *the subject itself*: what subjectivization renders invisible is *die Versagung*, its void –

subjectivization is a way to elude the void which 'is' the subject, it is ultimately a defence mechanism against the subject." The Queen Mab speech descends into a kind of madness because during its course Mercutio loses himself in the protean quality of his own language – he encounters the senselessness of real at the heart of himself. Slavoj Žižek, *Enjoy Your Symptom! Jacques Lacan in Hollywood and Out* (New York: 1992), p.186.

72 Žižek, 1994, p.178.

73 Žižek, 1992, p.51.

74 Žižek, 1994, p.47.

75 Renata Salecl and Slavoj Žižek, 'Introduction', in *Gaze and Voice as Love Objects*, ed. Renata Salecl and Slavoj Žižek (Durham, NC: 1996), pp.1–4, p.3.

76 Slavoj Žižek, 'Fantasy as a Political Category: A Lacanian Approach', *Journal for Psycho-analysis of Culture and Society*, 1 (1996), pp.77–85, p.83.

77 Žižek, 1994, p.199.

78 Mas'ud Zavarzadeh, 'Pun(k)deconstruction and the Postmodern Political Imaginary', *Cultural Critique*, 22 (1992), pp.5–46, p.17.

79 Michael Hardt and Antonio Negri, *Empire* (Cambridge, MA: 2000), p.155.

80 Ibid., p.156.

81 For a witty and pertinent defence of difficult critical writing see Judith Butler, 'Values of Difficulty', in *Just Being Difficult: Academic Writing in the Public Arena*, ed. Jonathan Culler and Kevin Lamb (Stanford, CA: 2003), pp.199–215.

82 The relationship between the emergence of literature as a space for thought and democracy is a key component in the political thought of Jacques Derrida, who states that he is "not able to separate the invention of literature ... from the history of democracy. Under the pretext of fiction, literature must be able to say anything ...." Derrida's whole agenda is predicated on the creation of philosophical spaces of thought but it is important to note that at its heart is a clear commitment to what he terms the discourse of emancipation. He writes: "Emancipation is once again a vast question today and I must say that I have no tolerance for those who – deconstruc-tionist or not – are ironical with regard to the grand discourse of emancipation. This attitude has always distressed and irritated me. I do not want to renounce this dis-course." Jacques Derrida, 'Remarks on Deconstruction and Pragmatism', in *Decon-struction and Pragmatism*, ed. Chantal Mouffe (London: 1996), pp.77–88, p.80 and p.82.

CHAPTER ONE

The self and history:
Richard III *and* Richard II

I N   H I S   E A R L Y   H I S T O R I E S Shakespeare stages the relationship between theatre, history and the self. In *Henry VI Part 1* Joan la Pucelle (Joan of Arc) embodies a radical subversion of history. The emergence of Richard of Gloucester (later Richard III) as a central figure in *Henry VI Part 3* marks the extent to which Shakespeare in his first tetralogy slowly transmutes the chronicle history of his sources into a fantastical narrative centred upon one man's evil.[1] *Richard III* is an Althusserian essay on compulsory selfhood which concludes with the sudden dramatic appearance, on stage in spectral form, of historical truth and justice. The Ghosts of Richard's victims that appear at the end of *Richard III* disrupt the play's narrative, blasting the continuum of history.[2] In *Henry VI Parts 1, 2* and *3* and *Richard III* Shakespeare sets himself the task of, in Étienne Balibar's phrase, "thinking the materiality of time".[3] In particular, what marks these plays is a constant tension between history as narrative and as a record of injustice and violence. At one level the first tetralogy stages the cost of writing over, playing through, the truth of history. Figures like Pucelle and Richard represent the dispersal and dissolution of the materiality of time in the wash of narrative. *Henry VI Parts 1, 2* and *3* and *Richard III* stage the seduction of the truth of history and its triumphant return. In *Richard II*, however, Shakespeare's confidence in the ability of the theatre to generate historical truths has greatly lessened. In this later play Shakespeare stages the cost of the textualisation of history to satisfy the audience's desire for sad stories and tragic tales.

This chapter is in three parts. The first section examines the historiography of *Henry VI* plays. In particular, it discusses the relationship between history and selfhood. The central part of this chapter examines the historical ethics of *Richard III*. The final section of this chapter looks at *Richard II* and argues that in this play Shakespeare's relative optimism concerning the use of the theatre to produce historical truth as evidenced in his early plays has been replaced by an anxiety that history is doomed to failure – destined to forever lose itself in 'once upon a time'.

The self and history

It has become a critical commonplace that the self and subjectivity can best be understood within a historical context. This is particularly so within literary and cultural studies where there has been the constant production of works focusing on the emergence of the medieval/modern/postmodern self. In the field of Shakespeare studies Hugh Grady has recently argued that:

> ... every self is an outcome of complex psycho-historical processes, and while the selves of specific cultures and societies share socially constructed discourses and ideologies, they are by no means identical or interchangeable, differing significantly through both historical change and individual variations within historical epochs. Our accounts of the history of the self should accordingly be nuanced and open to the complexity of historical and individual differences.[4]

Grady's argument in this passage is uncontentious and in many ways exemplifies current thinking within literary and cultural studies as regards the relationship between the self, subjectivity and history. It is, however, problematic in a number of ways. The idea of a 'psycho-historical process' is at least potentially oxymoronic. At one level psychoanalysis is radically a- even anti-historical. It claims to produce truths, in particular regarding the subject, that are not subject to history: truths which, if they are not eternal, are at least so fundamental to humanity as to make the use of them as the basis for any imaginable historical narrative either banal or meaningless. In this context writing a history of the self is problematic since at one level it requires writing over or ignoring that which is of the subject and is beyond the scope of history. If one accepts that there is an element of the self that is trans-historical any histories of the self will be founded upon the same theoretical block or strut. They will constantly produce historical narratives founded upon an endlessly repeated trans-historical point of non-discussion. Grady's argument that the selves in history will be inevitably complex, and that any history of the self needs to be sophisticated and nuanced, reflects this bind since why should this be the case? There is an argument, particularly if one accepts the ahistorical nature of the subject, that any history of the self is likely to be banal and reductive, that it will consist of nothing more than a constant reproduction of 'once upon a time' narratives in which the modern self, complex, self-reflective, autonomous, etc., emerges from a trans-historical kernel beyond history's scope. Indeed one could argue that this is precisely what literary criticism has incessantly produced in the last twenty years since Stephen Greenblatt's ground-breaking *Renaissance Self-Fashioning*.[5]

It is the ahistorical kernel at the heart of the self that is at the centre of Slavoj Žižek's construction of the subject. Žižek argues that:

> … if we subtract all the richness of the different modes of subjectivization, all the fullness of experience present in the way individuals 'live' their subject-positions, what remains is an empty place which was filled out with this richness; and this original void, this lack of the symbolic structure *is* the subject, the subject of the signifier. The *subject* is therefore to be strictly opposed to the effect of *subjectivation*: what the subjectivation masks is not a pre- or trans-subjective process of writing but a lack in the structure, a lack which is the subject.[6]

This is a complex idea. What Žižek is arguing is that the subject as a universal category has to be understood before subjectivity. In other words the I that signifies, in fact is, the subject has to exist before the process of subjectivation. The place the individual self occupies within the symbolic order precedes their existence so that to be a subject is to be caught in the bind of having an autonomous self which at its most fundamental level is based on a forced choice. This is because at one level the self has to emerge within and through language and that therefore its autonomy is based on a prior acceptance of the 'choice' to embrace language – the I who the subject will be. Judith Butler comments that:

> To persist in one's being means to be given over from the start to social terms that are never fully one's own. These terms institute a linguistic life for the 'one' who speaks prior to any act of agency, and they remain both irreducible to the one who speaks and the necessary conditions of such speech.[7]

The subject has to announce its autonomy in language. It has to use the worn, tarnished tools of others, their words, to make itself. The subject therefore shares, indeed exemplifies, language's inherent failure to be complete or whole since it is split between the need to claim autonomy and the necessity of making this claim with shared social tools. The subject's dependency on language undermines the claim to be an autonomous subject at the moment of its enunciation.[8] The subject can only claim subjectivity by accepting that at a fundamental level its autonomy and individuality are partial and compromised.

When Žižek asks the question, "What kind of monster remains when we subtract from the subject the wealth of self-experience that constitutes subjectivity?" he raises a question that fundamentally problematises any attempt to write a history of the self.[9] The monster that is left once one has subtracted from the subject all the details of selfhood is precisely the kernel of ahistorical lack that histories of the self consistently avoid: the trans-historical reductive kernel of the subject that sustains the wealth of detail that is the historical self.[10] Shakespeare, as a sophisticated Lacanian, stages in his first tetralogy the costs in terms of historical truth and justice of fixing the gaze of history on the fantasy of the historical self. In particular, the figures of Pucelle and Richard embody alternative fantastical versions of monstrosity – the subject as plurality or singularity – which both have the effect of endangering history as a record of truth and therefore a basis for justice.

Henry VI Part 1 opens in the middle of an act of state mourning with the Duke of Bedford on stage bemoaning the death of Henry V:

> Bed: Hung be the heavens with black, yield day to night!
> Comets, importing change of times and states,
> Brandish your crystal tresses in the sky,
> And with them scourge the bad revolting stars,
> That have consented unto Henry's death –
> Henry the Fifth, too famous to live long!
> England ne'er lost a king of so much worth.

Act 1, Sc 1, L 1–7

Bedford's words conjuror up the image of a nightmare world of perpetual night, of pain and death. They are clearly at one level a prophecy of the violence and tyranny that will fill the rest of the tetralogy. The immediate agent of English trauma in *Henry VI Part 1* is Joan la Pucelle. It is she who leads the victorious French armies against the English. Shakespeare portrays Pucelle's defeat of Lord Talbot, the representative of English chivalry, as a direct consequence of her witchcraft which in turn he relates to her feminine subversion of history. Pucelle tells the French nobles that:

> Puc: Glory is like a circle in the water,
> Which never ceaseth to enlarge itself
> Till by broad spreading it disperse to nought.
> With Henry's death the English circle ends;
> Dispersed are the glories it included.
> Now am I like that proud insulting ship
> Which Caesar and his fortune bare at once.

Act 1, Sc 2, L 133–9

Pucelle imagines the space of history as a boundless pond or lake in which the great man is a stone creating the ripples that are the matter of historical record, the glory that slowly disperses over time. Her self-portrayal as a ship, however, places her outside her own logic of the historical. Unlike Henry V and his ilk, Pucelle floats on the space of history. She is not swallowed up by its lack of fixity, its fluidity, but is instead empowered by its boundless liquidity.

For Pucelle, a 'proud insulting ship', traditional history is doomed to failure, caught between the desire to celebrate the glorious deeds of its heroes and the requirement to immerse them in time/water. Pucelle's radical historiography can clearly be related to her transgression of social and gender norms. Phyllis Rackin comments that:

> Joan's masculine dress ... is the sign of the uncanny. It associates sexual ambiguity with the dangers that lurk at the boundaries of the known, rationalised world of sexual difference and exclusion constructed by patriarchal discourse, the inconceivable realities of female power and authority that threatened the idealised world of masculine longing constructed by Shakespeare's historical myths.[11]

Pucelle's status as the uncanny, however, is not simply or indeed even primarily based on her disruption of gender differences. If her transgressive qualities were confined to the field of gender it would be relatively easy to recuperate her within existing historical paradigms. What makes Pucelle such a subversive figure is that she reflects the ahistorical material monstrosity at the heart of Shakespeare's historiography. She represents the power of the water to disperse glory; *and* a voracious French femininity in opposition to English masculinity; *and* the denied but constitutive principle of historical narration – the extent to which traditional history depends on the creation of narratives that obscure a basic lacuna at the heart of the historiographic project.

Michel de Certeau argues that:

> Historiography (that is, 'history' and 'writing') bears within its own name the paradox – almost an oxymoron – of a relation established between two antinomic terms, between the real and discourse. Its task is one of connecting them and, at the point where this link cannot not imagined, of working *as if* the two were being joined.[12]

Pucelle marks the violence of history's *as if*. She threatens the history of English glory not simply because she defeats Talbot and his colleagues but far more seriously because in her person she embodies the temptation of placing the historical subject at the centre of the historical gaze. There is clearly a relation between Pucelle's image of the space of history as a pond disturbed by the ripples of glory and Shakespeare's theatre; the ripples of Pucelle's pond are the same as the lines of Shakespeare's historical drama. The boundless fluid space of history can be read as time/text – ultimately it is the sea of historical texts that disperses and ironically erodes to nothing the deeds of history's heroes. Lurking within Pucelle's image of history is the danger, which Shakespeare's first tetralogy constantly returns to, that the theatre by narrating the fall of the stone into the space of history, putting Talbot on stage, is complicit in the repetitive erosion of historical truth, in particular that staging history will expose its fictionality – its reliance on *as if*.

As a deeply theatrical character Pucelle participates in the theatre's potentially radical deconstructive historiography. Jean Howard and Phyllis Rackin comment that: "Despite her lack of ideological authority, Joan's vivid voice and energetic theatrical presence provide the basis for a serious challenge to the logocentric, masculine historical record."[13] Shakespeare constantly flirts with Pucelle's ability to expose the *as if* at the heart of history as if inviting the audience to embrace their complicity with her historical agenda. Her presence is like Lear's nothing – a nothing that haunts the play, emptying out historical meaning. For example, when

Talbot and his warrior son are killed, Sir William Lucy visits the victorious French army to request their bodies. Lucy is challenged to name the person he seeks among the dead and answers with a list of Talbot's titles:

> Cha: … tell me whom thou seek'st
> Lucy: But where's the great Alcides of the field,
> Valiant Lord Talbot, Earl of Shrewsbury,
> Created for his rare success in arms
> Great Earl of Washford, Waterford, and Valence,
> Lord Talbot of Goodrig and Urchinfield,
> Lord Strange of Blackmere, Lord Verdun of Alton,
> Cromwell of Wingfield, Furnival of Sheffield
> The thrice victorious Lord of Falconbridge
> Knight of the noble Order of Saint George,
> Worthy Saint Michael, and the Golden Fleece,
> Great Marshal to Henry the Sixth
> Of all his wars within the realm of France?

Act 4, Sc 7, L 59–71

Pucelle's response to Lucy's request for the bodies of Talbot and his son is typically dismissive:

> Puc: For God's sake, let him have them; to keep them here,
> They would but stink and putrefy the air.

Act 4, Sc 7, L 89–90

Lucy's speech comprises the matter of traditional Tudor history. It is a record of Talbot's glory as embodied in his chivalric titles. Shakespeare's history in *Henry VI Part 1* is an explication and enactment of this historical record. In this play Shakespeare materialises on stage the glorious Talbot of Lucy's speech. No sooner has the playwright achieved this feat of historical resurrection, however, than it is radically threatened by Pucelle's reduction of Talbot to a meaningless lump of rotting flesh.

History, as de Certeau argues, depends on a moment of *as if* at its heart. It is this that Pucelle's dismissal of Talbot's body as a monstrous and stinking thing endangers. This is because at one level the audience is being invited to draw a parallel between Talbot's 'historical' body and that of the actor lying on stage in such a way as to emphasise the latter over the former. In other words Pucelle is effectively inciting the audience to suspend the *as if* of Shakespeare's dramatic history – to privilege the theatrical over the historical. This is particularly so since the creation of history from Lucy's list of abstract titles is a product of the play's theatricalisation of history – the creation of a 'real' person whose wealth of particular experiences answers the question that is left hanging at the end of Lucy's speech. History is produced at the moment when Talbot's self is filled out with meaning – when the abstract word Talbot and all his equally abstract titles are filled with particular details. Pucelle's response to this filling out of history is to reduce it back again to an ahistorical thing – a lump of flesh.

Pucelle dies cursing the English nobility that has condemned her:

> Puc: May never glorious sun reflex his beams
> Upon the country where you make abode;
> But darkness and the gloomy shade of death
> Environ you, till mischief and despair
> Drive you to break your necks or hang yourselves!

> Act 5, Sc 4, L 87–91

This curse echoes and even confirms Bedford's opening lamentation. But why should this be the case? Clearly something has gone seriously wrong if a figure as aberrant as Pucelle has become the echo, indeed the progeny, of an English hero like Bedford. She becomes his daughter and like that other founding figure of aberrant daughterhood, Antigone, Pucelle repeats, embodies and embraces the words of her 'father'.[14] Pucelle's citation of Bedford's prophecy creates a dangerous moment of narrative hiatus in which a prophecy becomes a curse. It reflects the image of her as a proud ship sailing across history and in the process raises again the dangerous possibility of the *as if* of history emerging on stage. What has been the point of the play if at its end it is simply back where it began?

This is not to suggest, however, that *Henry VI Part 1* is some kind of postmodern celebration of the failure of history, of the impossibility of producing historical truth. The image of history produced by Pucelle does seem to push in this direction with its emphasis on the fluid and protean quality of the space of history – its status as an ever expanding and dissolving sea of text and time. But at the centre of Pucelle's image, ignored and written over by her, is the stone, the fact, the source of history's ripples. Pucelle can dismiss Talbot's body as a stinking lump of flesh but Shakespeare's theatre will stage the constant return of the stone of truth to history's narrative. Indeed by putting Talbot on stage *Henry VI Part 1* opens up the possibility of creating a space of history that is bound – the theatrical event as the one place, far more so than the printed page, where Talbot's glory can be historised without dispersal.

At the end of *Henry VI Part 1* Pucelle is led off stage to be burnt. This does not, however, banish her dangerous and aberrant status. Instead in *Henry VI Parts 2* and *3* a number of other characters inherit her power to disrupt the norms of history. Figures like Queen Margaret and Jack Cade at one level are simply historical actors – stones falling into the lake of Shakespeare's history. They are also, however, like Pucelle, signs of the potential failure of history. This is particularly the case with Cade whose rebellion is at once historical and provocatively Elizabethan. It is as if Shakespeare was seeking to emphasise the extent to which the issues that caused Cade's revolt, utopian fantasies, the consciousness of injustice and political scheming, were still potent sources of popular disorder in the 1580s. It is, however, the figure of Richard of Gloucester who most obviously inherits Pucelle's aberrant mantle. As the historical narrative seems to break down in *Henry VI Part 3* under the weight of meaningless battles and the piles of the slain Richard's presence becomes more and more powerful – as if the collapse of traditional history leads to his emergence as a potential source for historical meaning, if not truth or justice.

In Act 3 Scene 2 of *Henry VI Part 3* Richard engages in the first of his many attempts to explain himself to the audience. In this speech Richard constructs himself, or rather his body, as "a chaos, or unlick'd bear-whelp – That carries no impression like the dam" (Act 3, Sc 2, L 161-2). Richard goes on to claim that this lack of fixity is a source of political strength, boasting that:

> Rich: I can add colours to the chameleon,
> Change shapes with Proteus for advantages,
> And set the murderous Machiavel to school.
> Can I do this, and cannot get a crown?
> Tut! Were it further off, I'll pluck it down.

Act 3, Sc 2, L 191–5

Richard presents himself to the audience as a natural actor. He does so against an implicit norm which is marked by fixity and order – a non-performative normal sense of self. Richard's changeability only makes sense as a source of power on the basis of this difference. If everyone possessed his ability to play a part then his boasting would be meaningless. But is this not the case? Are not all selves at one level performative? Subjectivity is based on the subject accepting the forced choice of their place within the symbolic order. Can a subject name themselves? Who does the naming? What Shakespeare depicts in Richard is a character who constantly boasts of being able to change but whose basic and fundamental identity, the one imposed on him by history, evil villain, is completely beyond his power. Richard's soliloquies, in *Henry VI Part 3* and *Richard III*, despite their wit and complexity, consistently return to the same knot or problem – the relationship between Richard's self and his body.

In the final act of *Henry VI Part 3*, after he has murdered the saintly but hopeless Henry VI, Richard again turns to the audience to explain his actions. It is at this point that he articulates most clearly the fantasy at the heart of his sense of self:

> Rich: ... since the heavens have shap'd my body so,
> Let hell make crook'd my mind to answer it.
> I have no brother, I am like no brother;
> And this word 'love', which greybeards call divine,
> Be resident in men like one another,
> And not in me: I am myself alone.

Act 5, Sc 6, L 78–83

Richard's words seem to announce a form of modern subjectivity. 'I am myself alone' is a claim to complete individuality. The problem is that immediately preceding this speech Richard told Henry VI, as he killed him, that "For this, amongst the rest, was I ordain'd" (Act 5, Sc 6, L 58). There is a basic tension between 'myself alone' and 'for this I was ordained'. Richard consistently constructs his body as the source of his power and the cause of his history and in the process seeks to write over the radical implications of 'for this I was ordained'. The truth is that Richard's claim to exceptionality is bogus. Its repetition is, however, the price that Richard pays to indulge in the fantasy of escaping the forced choice of subjectivity. Richard's insistence on staging the tension between self and body appears to be an attempt to avoid the reality of his status as a historical subject. In other words by constantly constructing the problem of his identity around the knot of self/body Richard performs his avoidance of the extent to which the real problem is the relationship between subjectivity and language.

But this is not the end of the matter. In order to understand the nature of Richard's relationship to history it is necessary to return briefly to Pucelle. As has been suggested In *Henry VI Part 1* there is a relationship between the theatre's and Pucelle's potential to expose the *as if* of history. Richard shares in this potentiality. As Pucelle remakes herself from peasant girl to prophetic warrior she effectively places performance, the endlessly plastic self, at the centre of history and in the process endangers the whole status of historical knowledge. Richard's announcement to the audience that he is an actor repeats Pucelle's strategy – but even more brazenly. In the process he forces the audience to ask 'If the actors of history are just actors then what is history?' Is it anything more than a second-hand account of their performances? Is history simply a 'once upon a time' narrative, recounting the sophisticated and nuanced performances of people like Pucelle and Richard? At another far more radical level, however, it is precisely Richard's and Pucelle's embodiment of theatrical power that prevents the emergence of historical *truth* from the wreck of *as if*. Pucelle and Richard represent the temptation to fill in the radical ahistorical truth of history with fantasy – with the subject as theatrical, complex and performed.

It is as an embodiment of the theatrical possibility within history, and in particular the fantasy of history as performance, that Richard tempts the audience to forget the materiality of time – that history is founded upon facticity, the stone, that cannot be simply written over or washed away. The dramas of selfhood that his soliloquies are, with their wealth of expression, presence and acts of denial, work to fill out the fundamental lack at the heart of the subject *and* history. Richard constantly generates signifiers around his body and its relationship to his self as a way of producing meaning. He theorises the deformed nature of his body in order to explain his selfhood as an ambitious violent person – an aberrant figure outside the norms of society/history. In the process he creates a historical narrative that attempts to write over and obscure the truth of history as a record of his crimes. Richard's drama works because it enables the audience to avoid confronting the truth that history is not a narrative to be consumed and enjoyed – it is not a 'once upon a time story' of great deeds – or indeed the emergence of the modern self. Richard makes his body the fantastical something that enables the reality of his selfhood to emerge as a way of hiding the nothing at the heart of history.

What is it that remains of history once all the particular details have been stripped away? The truth of history is in the now. Historical justice has to take place in the present. The Ghosts of Richard's victims are not interested in narrative or selfhood; or rather they are only to the extent to which they produce justice. The *Henry VI* plays prepare the way for *Richard III* by staging the collapse of historical narrative into a pile of dead bodies. What rises from the wreck of history at the end of *Henry VI Part 3* is the aberrant form of Richard Gloucester.

Richard III *and Althusser*

There are two key aspects to Louis Althusser's understanding of the subject that Shakespeare pre-empted in *Richard III*. Althusser argued that subjects are the products of ideology. In particular, he created the drama of interpellation to explain how subjects are hailed into ideology and therefore subjecthood.[15] Althusser writes:

> ... I only wish to point out that you and I are *always already* subjects, and as such constantly practice the rituals of ideological recognition, which guarantee for us that we are indeed concrete, individual, distinguishable and (naturally) irreplaceable subjects.[16]

Althusser's most famous example of a 'ritual of ideological recognition' is when the subject is hailed by a policeman in the street. It is the subject's acceptance of their part in this ideological ritual that for Althusser is the moment of subjectivisation. The key moment for Althusser's theory of the subject is when the subject accepts themselves as hailed – as a subject 'called' or interpellated by ideology. There is, however, a lacuna in Althusser's theory which is that it appears to be based upon a moment of theoretical slippage. If the subject acknowledges its subjecthood at the moment of interpellation – who or what hears the call of ideology? Mladen Dolar comments that, in Althusser's schema:

> One becomes a subject by suddenly recognising that one has always been a subject: becoming a subject always takes place retroactively – it is based on a necessary illusion, an extrapolation, an illegitimate extension of a later state into the former stage. A leap – a moment of sudden emergence – occurs.[17]

Dolar argues that Althusser's account of how the subject is produced is based on a moment of theoretical collapse due to its reliance on the existence of a subject that hears the policeman's call before interpellation takes place. This leads Dolar to suggest that at one level the ideological formation of the subject always 'fails' – is never complete, final or whole.

Althusser argued that "an ideology always exists in an apparatus, and its practice, or practices. This existence is material".[18] He went on to suggest that: "the category of the subject is only constitutive of all ideology insofar as all ideology has the function (which defines it) of 'constituting' concrete individuals as subjects".[19] Tudor history, particularly as it is portrayed in *Richard III*, is a textual practice or apparatus constituting individuals as subjects. Above all in the person of Richard, Shakespeare reflects on the historical production of the subject of history. In particular, he stages the ideological process whereby a kind of history ends up becoming fixated by the subject at its heart. Shakespeare's Richard is a radically textual figure. This is partly because, despite all Richard's references to his body, the source of his power is his ability to deploy the metaphoric potential of language. Richard's textual status is also, however, a product of his origin in Sir Thomas More's self-knowing textualisation of history in his *History of Richard III*.[20] Against the practice of written chronicle and humanist history, exemplified in the figure of Richard, however, Shakespeare sets up the materiality of the theatre as the privileged site for historical truth; it is theatrical history that in *Richard III* reveals the failure of traditional history as a material ideological process hailing its subjects into its narrative frame.

Richard III opens with Richard's famous speech, 'Now is the winter of our discontent'. During the course of this soliloquy Richard tells the audience that:

> Rich: Since I cannot prove a lover
> To entertain these fair well-spoken days,
> I am determined to prove a villain,
> And hate the idle pleasures of these days.

> Act 1, Sc 1, L 28–31

There are two key aspects to these lines – two moments of rejection. Richard states that he cannot play the part of a lover to provide entertainment. In the process he effectively rejects the desire of the audience to be entertained. Indeed given that one could read 'idle pleasures' as a clear reference to the theatre at one level Richard in this speech is expressing his disdain for Shakespeare's drama. Richard's other moment of rejection in this speech is directed at history itself. His claim that he is going to 'prove a villain' is an attempt to turn the forced choice of history into an act of will. Richard cannot but prove a villain but the fantasy that he is articulating in this opening speech is that the concrete subjectivity that history as a practice has imposed on him is actually his free choice. It is as though Richard not only refuses to hear history's hail but that also he claims to be self-hailing, self-constituting. This moment therefore very clearly harks back to the claim Richard made at the end of *Henry VI Part 3*, "I am myself alone".

Richard's opening speech concludes with him telling the audience that he has spread plots, dreams and libels abroad, "About a prophecy, which says that 'G', Of Edward's heirs the murderer shall be" (Act 1, Sc 1, L 39–40). Richard is so pleased with himself at this moment that he fails to see that in fact his libels are true. A G will murder Edward's heirs since he is their murderer and he is the Duke of Gloucester. In these lines Richard is claiming a degree of agency that in practice he does not have. Indeed his earlier boasts, that he will choose to play a villain and that he cannot play the part of lover or entertain, are equally empty. In this opening speech Shakespeare creates the temptation that will flow throughout *Richard III* – that of allowing one's gaze to become fixed and fixated on Richard's performance to the extent that one stops seeing the truth of history.

This is not to suggest that Shakespeare depicts it as easy to resist Richard's blandishments. In particular, the seduction scene between Richard and Anne can be seen as an extended reflection upon the complicity of the audience in Richard's performance. The scene opens with the entry of Henry VI's corpse. Anne also enters as one of the mourners. She goes on to curse Richard as Henry VI's murderer:

> Anne: O, cursed be the hand that made these holes;
> Cursed the heart that had the heart to do it;
> Cursed the blood that let this blood from hence.
> More direful hap betide that hated wretch
> That makes us wretched by the death of thee
> Than I can wish to adders, spiders, toads
> Or any creeping venom'd thing that lives.

Act 1, Sc 2, L 14–20

Anne's curse on Richard, of which these lines are only a part, is profoundly violent. This is perhaps not surprising given that Richard killed her husband and father-in-law. It is also, however, strangely excessive as though Anne is desperately trying to find the words that can contain Richard sufficiently to curse him properly. It is as if Richard's chameleon character has in some way infected Anne's language so that as she seeks to name the object of her hate she finds she cannot find the words. The object of Anne's curse seems to generate more and more words that do not quite match or contain him – Richard's chaos cannot be reduced to words.

It is this infection of her language by Richard's protean quality that in the end leads to Anne's seduction. The actual moment when Anne gives in to Richard is marked by Shakespeare through a change in verse form:

> Anne: I would I knew thy heart.
> Rich: 'Tis figur'd in my tongue.
> Anne: I fear me both are false.
> Rich: Then never was man true.

> Act 2, Sc 2, L 196–9

It is, however, a mistake to see this as the moment of seduction since as has been suggested at one level Anne has already been seduced by Richard before the scene even starts. When Richard first appears Anne asks:

> Anne: What black magician conjures up this fiend
> To stop devoted charitable deeds?

> Act 2, Sc 2, L 34–5

By constructing Richard as a fiend and his milieu as black magic Anne implicitly accepts Richard's claims to empowerment through performance – through his ability to play a part since the black magician who is ultimately responsible for Richard's appearance on stage is Shakespeare himself. Anne's opening characterisation of Richard suggests that the only way to make sense of him is through the use of tropes and metaphors. She calls him a 'devil' and a 'dreadful minister of hell'. The latter in particular, with is carnivalesque reversal of religious norms, places Richard within a fantastic metaphoric context and reflects the extent to which Shakespeare's play is a self-conscious critical engagement with More's *History of Richard III*.[21] Anne associates Richard with metaphors and tropes. In the process she unwittingly places him in Pucelle's proud insulting ship coasting across the pond of history. Indeed Richard's own use of metaphors, and the way he incites other characters to produce them, reflects his embodiment of a metaphoric principle that endangers history by filling it with texts that simply refer to other texts in an ever expanding self-referential circle. At the end of this scene Richard celebrates his seduction of Anne with the audience:

> Rich: Was ever woman in this humour woo'd
> Was ever woman in this humour won?
> I'll have her, but I will not keep her long.
> What, I that kill'd her husband and his father:
> To take her in her heart's extremest hate,
> With curses in her mouth, tears in her eyes,
> The bleeding witness of her hatred by
> Having God, her conscience, and these bars against me –
> And I, no friends to back my suit at all
> But the plain devil and dissembling looks –
> And yet to win her, all the world to nothing!

> Act 2, Sc 2, L 232–42

Richard's seduction of Anne depends on his ability to make her forget the past, most radically and materially as embodied on stage in the bleeding corpse of her father-in-law. Henry VI's body is a stone of history that needs to be obscured in order for Richard's seduction to work. Richard fills Anne's historical gaze with language – poetic, witty, metaphoric language – and in the process ensures that she loses sight of Henry's corpse.

It is not, however, only Anne that is seduced by Richard in this scene; the audience is also his target. At the beginning of the play Richard told the audience that he could not play a lover or entertain, and within a scene of making this claim he is doing both. He woos Anne for explicitly political reasons but implicitly because he can despite all that is stacked against him. Commenting on this scene Steve Larocco argues that: "Through his command of the metaphoric mobility of language, Richard fashions an imaginary realm in which laws and nature and the stasis of grief yield before the captivating, monstrous onslaught of seduction."[22] Richard's seduction of the audience exploits their desire for entertainment, but also for a historical narrative that makes sense – which is meaningful. Richard as monstrous, as brazen, seductive performer, offers himself as the perfect object of the audience's historical gaze. He is a monster, a performer and a villain. His soliloquies constantly incite the audience to understand his sense of self, and in particular its relation to his body, as the source of the play's meaning. Even before Richard appears, Anne is effectively in his power. Her opening curse reflects the extent to which she has already accepted the fantasy of Richard's exceptional villainy, his status as a thing whose meaning pushes at the boundaries of language. The audience are in the same state as Anne. They believe, or at least the play offers this as a possibility, that Richard's monstrous evil, his complex tortured sense of self and powers of seduction can explain the drama's history.

Richard's speech celebrating his seduction of Anne ends with a strange coda, 'all the world to nothing'. The most obvious, and undoubtedly correct, reading of this phrase is that Richard is claiming that his seduction has rendered the world to nought – that in the face of all the facts he still managed to seduce Anne. The problem with Richard's thinking here, of which he is at this moment clearly unaware, is that if his seductive power has made the world nothing then it is itself meaningless – nothing. The only thing that makes the seduction of Anne meaningful is the dead body of Henry VI lying on stage. Richard's ability to conjure up imaginary worlds, to exploit the possibilities of language, ultimately produces nothing – or more accurately an imaginary world of nothings.[23]

Richard seeks to fill up the stage with totalising metaphoric language. He does this most obviously and effectively by exploiting his own sense of self to generate signifiers that seem to spin out endlessly as he stages, for the audience's pleasure, a drama of historical subjectivity that obscures the truth of history. In particular, Richard offers himself as an endlessly adaptable origin of historical narrative motivation. Once he becomes king, however, his powers clearly and dramatically start to wane. It is as though he is no longer free to create imaginary worlds and wield the power of seduction. This process reaches its apogee with the appearance of the Ghosts of Richard's victims on stage the night before the Battle of Bosworth. What the Ghosts represent is the return of the materiality to history. It is as though the stones of the past suddenly explode from the depths of narrative history to erupt on stage. The effect of the Ghosts on Richard is to completely undermine his sense of self:

> Rich: What do I fear? Myself? There's none else by;
> Richard loves Richard, that is, I and I.
> Is there a murderer here? No. Yes, I am!
> Then fly. What, from myself? Great reason why,
> Lest I revenge. What, myself upon myself?

Act 5, Sc 3, L 183–7

What is breaking apart here appears to be Richard's sense of self, but this is an illusion. What is really collapsing is the idea of the historical subject. Richard's speech enacts the collapse of the narrative of the play at least as far as it has been motivated by the monstrous subjectivity at its heart. It is a specific kind of historical reading or interpretation that breaks apart in these lines. For example, the phrase 'I and I' is strictly speaking nonsense. What Richard is trying to express here is something that ends up producing this repetitive nonsensical phrase. Richard's 'I and I' marks the moment when he can no longer produce signifiers around his sense of self, he can no longer fill the space of history with metaphoric totalising language. The Ghosts have robbed him of this ability. And they have done so by enacting a return of metonym to the field of historical gaze – a return that can clearly most effectively take place on stage.

The Ghosts represent what does not hear the siren voice of narrative history – that which is in history once all the particular details have been stripped away. The Ghosts are monstrous but not in the sense that Richard is. His monstrosity, certainly as he presents it to the audience, is something to be gazed at, interpreted, consumed and enjoyed. The monstrosity of the Ghosts lies in their spectral materiality. They are insubstantial and yet they represent the material truth of history – the stones that Richard and Pucelle seek to wash away. The Ghosts stick in the throat of history as 'once upon a time' – history to be consumed and enjoyed. The first Ghost to appear to Richard and Richmond is that of Prince Edward:

> Ghost of Pr. Ed. to K. Rich: Let me sit heavy on thy soul tomorrow.
> Think how thou stab'st me in my prime of youth
> At Tewkesbury; despair therefore, and die.
> To Richmond: Be cheerful, Richmond, for the wronged souls
> Of butcher'd princes fight in thy behalf;
> King Henry's issue, Richmond, comforts thee.

Act 5, Sc 3, L 119–24

Richard uses his skill with language, his ability to exploit the metaphoric possibilities of speech to create a world of nothing – to smooth the ripples of history and place himself as a proud ship at the centre of the audience's historical gaze. He thinks, and constantly claims, that this achievement is his alone, but in fact it is a product of the kind of historical subject that he is. Richard's totalising metaphoric occupation of the space of history reflects the way in which traditional narrative history interpellates its subjects – the extent to which it is based on the temptation to see the self as the object of investigation and explanation. Edward's Ghost tells Richard that he will 'sit heavy on' Richard's soul. But these lines are not directed solely at Richard; they are also aimed at the audience. The image of sitting heavily *on* Richard's soul reflects the metonymic nature of the Ghosts – they are not metaphors. Despite their spectral form they embody the material weight of the past – the stone at the heart of history. The Ghosts represent in their calls for justice and vengeance an understanding of historical truth that is outside time or text – a truth of history that exists in the now. This is why they expressly construct their effectiveness, negative and positive, in terms of emotions. Edward's Ghost tells Richard that it will drive him to despair while making Richmond cheerful. This is not, however, a confession of weakness since what it represents is a radical understanding of the location of the truth of history, that it operates in the now at the level of material struggle – the truth represented by the Ghosts is felt on the battlefield.

Richard III ends with a restoration of order and the defeat of tyranny. In particular, the appearance of the Ghosts reflects the extent to which in this play Shakespeare claims that the theatre is the privileged space for the production of historical truth. While the kind of metaphoric evil that Richard represents is always a danger in historical texts, staging history creates the possibility of resisting Richard's temptations and seductions. *Richard III* celebrates the ability of the theatre to produce historical truth. This relatively optimistic conclusion is, however, overshadowed by the disturbing possibilities that Shakespeare hints will result from Richmond's victory. The seductive power that Richard exploited and embodied is still a theatrical possibility. What is to stop a Don John or an Iago exploiting it for their evil ends? Nothing. Indeed even more disturbing is the sense at the end of *Richard III* that Richard's death also leads to the end of theatre. This is particularly troubling given the religious language that Richmond uses to legitimate his actions.[24]

There is a sense at the end of *Richard III* that Richmond's triumph will not only defeat Richard's illegitimate theatre centred on his monstrous performance but have the same effect on the theatre of the Ghosts – that the ethical possibilities opened up by the end of the play will be closed down along with Richard's defeat.

Richard II *and sad tales*

In *Richard II* the collapse of legitimate rule is portrayed as a fall into the textual practice, the discursive apparatus, of history. With the losing of his power Richard feels himself dissolving into a historical self that he recognises he is and is not. History in *Richard II* becomes a totalising metaphor greedily reducing everything in its path to narrative. In particular, Richard's disposition creates a situation in which Pucelle's ripples completely wash away the stones of history – all that is left is 'once upon a time'. There are, moreover, no ghosts in *Richard II*. Instead the lack of stability felt by Richard becomes the play's norm. There are no real words or kings any more, just metaphors, actors in a narrative of history. The reality has been lost in a realm with an empty monarch, a king of nothing, and history's *as if* has been reduced to an empty formalist gesture. It no longer matters if the oxymoron at the heart of the historical endeavour is exposed since history itself no longer has any real purpose – it has become a sad tale signifying nothing.

Richard II opens with a Richard who appears to be fully in control of the situation. This is, however, an illusion. Richard is a failing king at the beginning of *Richard II* and his failure has a particularly linguistic quality.[25] Alexander Leggatt points out that one of the play's most striking features is its pervasive self-consciousness about language.[26] Richard's failings as a monarch relate directly to the fact that he is uncounselled.[27] As a monarch he should be the still centre of the commonwealth – hearing counsel from all quarters before making any decision. Instead, according to his detractors he has surrounded himself with fawning flatterers:

> Gaunt: Though Richard my life's counsel would not hear,
> My death's sad tale may yet undeaf his ear.
> York: No, it is stopped with other flatt'ring sounds,
> As praises, of whose taste the wise are fond,
> Lascivious metres, to whose venom sound

> The open ear of youth doth always listen;
> Report of fashions in proud Italy
> Whose manners still our tardy-apish nation
> Limps after in base imitation.

Act 2, Sc 1, L 15–23

What is noticeable in this exchange is the extent to which the failure of counsel is given a specifically poetic spin. Richard will not hear Gaunt's sad tale because his ear is full of poetry, 'lascivious metres'. York's critique of Richard's rule creates a symbolic relation between it and that of Henry VIII since it was during the latter's reign that Petrarchan poetry, the original Italianate form, became one of the dominant forms of court writing.[28] York's words, however, also create a disturbing sense that Richard's ears have been literally filled with venom as if the language of his flatterers possesses a strange material quality. Richard's failure to listen to counsel leaves him in the same imaginary world as that which Richard III created to seduce Anne – although in this case the seduction is self-willed.

Not surprisingly the end result of Richard's failings as a monarch is rebellion. Bolingbroke, the future Henry IV, rebels in order to protect his inheritance. Richard's response when confronted with the success of Bolingbroke's rebellion is to turn to history:

> Rich: For God's sake let us sit upon the ground
> And tell sad stories of the death of kings –
> How some have been depos'd, some slain in war,
> Some haunted by the ghosts they have deposed,
> Some poisoned by their wives, some sleeping killed
> All murdered. For within the hollow crown
> That rounds the mortal temples of a king
> Keeps Death his court; and there the antic sits
> Scoffing his state and grinning at his pomp,
> Allowing him a breath, a little scene
> To monarchize, be feared, and kill with looks ...

Act 3, Sc 2, L 155–65

The movement of this passage seems to be from sad tales to the theatre but in practice the sad tales are already theatrical. This is not only because of the reference to *Richard III*, but also because of the self-referential nature of this moment. Is not the play *Richard II* a sad tale? Are not the audience paying to see precisely the fantasy of monarchical vulnerability imagined in the second part of this passage? The movement of all Richard's speeches from the moment he loses power is inward, not only in terms of his own sense of self but also as regards theatre. Richard as king and actor experiences the second half of *Richard II* as a self-regarding journey which is ultimately entirely sterile. There is no self-knowledge at the end of Richard's musing, nor any sense of theatrical closure. *Richard II* peters out with Bolingbroke, now Henry IV, marked out as a man caught in a bloody metaphoric act of penance endlessly washing Richard's blood from his hands:

> Bol: I'll make a voyage to the Holy Land,
> To wash this blood off from my guilty hand.
> March sadly after; grace my mournings here
> In weeping after this untimely bier.

> Act 5, Sc 6, L 49–52

The scene where Richard gives up the crown to Bolingbroke can be read as a dramatisation of what is left of the subject without subjectivity. Žižek writes that:

> The object becomes One through the appendage of some completely null, self-obliterating Being, *le peu de réalité* of a couple of sounds – the fly that makes the elephant – as with the Monarch, this imbecile contingent body of an individual that does not merely 'represent' the State *qua* rational totality but constitutes it, renders it effective.[29]

The tragedy that forms the heart of the moment when Richard as king gives away all that makes him king is that all he is left with is his contingent body, which without the appendage that made it meaningful, the title King, becomes meaningless. But at the same time Bolingbroke cannot fully become king while Richard exists as a material remainder – a left-over piece of kingship. Richard gives away his entire kingship but he cannot give Bolingbroke that which was of his kingship but external to him. Richard cannot stop being king even as he gives his kingship to Bolingbroke. Like Romeo, Richard cannot renounce his name, his place in the symbolic order, since it is not his to give, to renounce. Names define who we are and are radically and arbitrarily beyond our power, imposed on us from outside but defining our selfhood. Richard gives all that he has to Bolingbroke but is still left with something:

> Rich: I give this heavy weight off my head,
> And this unwieldy sceptre from my hand,
> The pride of kingly sway from out my heart;
> With mine own tears I wash away my balm,
> With mine own hands I give away my crown,
> With mine own tongue deny my sacred state,
> With mine own breath release all duteous oaths.
>
> Act 4, Sc 1, L 204–10

It is only as a king that Richard can give away his kingship, only as a king that his tongue has the power to release his subjects from their oaths of allegiance. Anne Righter comments that, "When … Richard appears before Bolingbroke to renounce his throne, he is no longer a king. Neither, on the other hand, is he anything else. He has not position, virtually no existence. He is a kind of nothing."[30] Richard gives away everything but is still left with something. What this thing is remains unclear but Richard's reaction to seeing it in a mirror shows that it is clearly monstrous:

> Rich: I'll read enough
> When I do see the very book indeed
> Where all my sins are writ, and that's myself
> *Enter one with a glass*
> Given me that glass, and therein will I read.
>
> …
>
> A brittle glory shineth in this face –
> As brittle as the glory is the face!
> *Dashes the glass against the ground*
> For there it is, crack'd in an hundred shivers.
>
> Act 4, Sc 1, L 273–89

Richard is being pressed to read a 'book' of his crimes as an act of public confession. He finally agrees but asks for a mirror so that he can see "what a face I have, Since it is bankrupt of his majesty" (Act 4, Sc 1, L 266–7). Richard's desire at this moment can be related directly to Althusser's drama of interpellation but with a twist. Richard was a monarch – hailed by ideology to be a, if not the, concrete subject within a very material ideological apparatus. Once he gives up the throne, however, Richard's subjectivity is stripped of its support. It is dissolved and fractured. It is this nothing that Richard sees in the mirror. The breaking of the glass is not an act of denial but is rather Richard's attempt to make the self he sees in the mirror correspond to the subject he now is.

There is, however, no place left for Richard to turn to sustain his sense of self – he cannot be 'hailed' since the person he was is no more. There no longer is someone to be called Richard II. In his place there is only a shadow, a player king or rather a player playing at not being a king. The fate of Richard after his deposition reflects the perspicacity of Dolar's critique of Althusser, for what Richard is left with in this scene is precisely what escapes interpellation – the subject before the hail, before being fitted into an ideology apparatus. This is why the more power Richard loses the more he talks and the more incessant becomes his association with theatrical images. It is as though after Richard is stripped of his kingship he falls back into language. In particular, his speech becomes decidedly more poetic and metaphoric as the play goes on. By the end of the play Richard's transformation into a poet appears to be complete:

> Rich: I have been studying how I may compare
> This prison where I live unto the world;
> And, for because the world is populous
> And here is not a creature but myself,
> I cannot do it. Yet I'll hammer't out.
> My brain I'll prove the female of my soul,
> My soul the father, and these two beget
> A generation of still-breeding thoughts;
> And these same thoughts people this little world,
> In humours like the people of this world;

> Act 5, Sc 5, L 1–10

Richard here is depicted as a poet imagining a world of people. He is therefore in many ways back in the state that he was in at the beginning of the play. The only, but of course crucial, difference is that now he is creating his own imaginary world rather than relying on flattery and 'lascivious metres'. It is he who is the flatterer and who produces his own poetry. This escape into a poetic realm is, however, an illusion since even within this fictional world Richard is haunted by his loss of kingship:

> Rich: Sometimes am I king,
> Then treasons make me wish myself a beggar,
> And so I am. Then crushing penury
> Persuades me I was better when a king;
> Then am I king'd again, and by and by
> Think that I am unking'd by Bolingbroke,
> And straight am nothing. But whate'er I be,
> Nor I, nor any man that but man is
> With nothing shall be pleas'd, till he be eas'd
> With being nothing.

Act 5, Sc 5, L 32–41

Richard constantly seeks to explain what he is once he loses the crown. The problem is that he keeps coming back to the idea that he is nothing – but what does this mean? Can a person be nothing? In his prison cell Richard forces his mind to conjure up a world of 'still-breeding thoughts'. One reading of this phrase is that it refers to the imagination. Richard's imaginary creations, like those of a poet, become people that in turn generate more and more thoughts/people. But this phrase could also reflect the extent to which *Richard II* as a play is concerned with the status of language and in particular history. Richard's abilities as a poet are far-reaching. He can populate his prison cell with people. He can also imagine himself to be a king and then not. In his thoughts Richard can be endlessly king'd and unking'd. But none of this is real. Richard's fantasy world is entirely fantastic and this is his nothing – to paraphrase Žižek the monstrous thing left to Richard once he has been stripped of everything is lascivious language, the fantasy that his flatterers poured into his ear.

What makes this scene so particularly disturbing is its sterile and solipsistic image of writing. What is the point of Richard's poetry? Certainly he has generated an enormous amount of material for audiences and critics to pore over and enjoy deciphering. Indeed Richard is one of Shakespeare's most prolix characters in terms of self-analysis. Richard III consistently offered himself as an object to be interpreted and explained, but Richard II offers much more material – but is not all this detail just the imaginary thoughts of a poet? Is not Richard just the stuff of Shakespeare's mind? And is not the temptation here to allow the lascivious metres that are Richard II, the material words spoken by an actor, clog the ear of history so that the truth can no longer be heard? As Richard more and more fills the stage with signifiers about himself, what happens to history? What becomes of the truth of the past? Perhaps it is in Richard's sense of self, but this seems to be either a thing of nothing or (and) a thing of subtle and nuanced complicity. And thereby hangs the danger. Richard consistently offers himself as an object for the historical gaze, as a fit subject for a sad tale, for 'once upon a time'. His endlessly self-reflective words, which are profoundly poetic and therefore rewarding in terms of analysis, fill the space of history just as surely as Richard III's do when he seduces Anne.

In one of those small scenes that often mean so much in Shakespeare's drama a Scrivener comes on stage in *Richard III* to comment on the irony that he began writing Lord Hastings's indictment eleven hours ago, "And yet within these five hours Hastings liv'd / Untainted, unexamin'd, free, at liberty' (Act 3, Sc 6, L 8-9). The Scrivener goes on to ask:

> Scriv: Who is so gross
> That cannot see this palpable device?
> Yet who's so bold but says he sees it not?
> Bad is the world, and all will come to naught
> When such ill-dealing must be seen in thought.

Act 3, Sc 6, L 10–14

The Scrivener's final line is a condemnation of Richard III's rule as a time when evil could only be thought and not made public. It is also, however, a subtle valorisation of the theatre as a place where evil can be seen – in *Richard III* this point is made again and much more pointedly with the Ghosts. In *Richard II*, however, it is Richard II's thoughts that populate the stage – particularly as the play draws towards its strangely flat end. Shakespeare's confidence in the power of the theatre to produce historical truth has been replaced in *Richard II* with a historical cynicism that simply gives the audience what they want – a sad tale, a history of the self, a 'once upon a time' in which justice has no place.

Conclusion

Shakespeare's histories theorise the ethics of writing history. In his early plays there is a sense that the theatre can generate historical truths. In

Richard II, however, history seems to have become a postmodern game in which one narrative can simply be swapped for another. This is not to suggest that *Richard III* is more accurate in historical terms than *Richard II*. It is, however, to argue that the former expresses a desire for a history that escapes the totalising seductive power of 'once upon a time'. Paul Ricoeur argues that: "… the historian is moved by the vow to do justice to the past. The relation of historians to the past is first of all that of an unpaid debt in which they represent us all, we the readers of their works."[31] Shakespeare's problem is that he realises that the audience do not want to do justice to the past – they do not want to be confronted with the fact that oppression and injustice are the banal norms of the past. History as a sad tale, populated by Richard's imagination, can be endlessly re-written and turned into ever more exotic narratives. Richard II, in the scene when he is waiting to die, takes on the spectral form of a postmodern historian seeing the truth of the past as a purely relative thing – matter to be narrated, commodified and sold. In the process, however, the idea of the truth of the past itself disappears. Terry Eagleton comments that:

> … if the past is just an indeterminacy of which we can make what we will, there's nothing whatsoever to be angry about. This is one reason why poststructuralists tend on the whole to be pleasantly tolerant, even occasionally euphoric people. What there is to be angry about when we survey the contemporary political scene, history as the present, is exactly that the narratives of most people within it already have the finality and determinacy conferred on life by death even before they have died. If Marxism seems to those enamoured of difference and heterogeneity to tell the same tedious story, I'm afraid that's because that's the way history is. Nothing really happens in history …[32]

It is postmodern euphoria that fills Richard's imaginary world, 'all the world to nothing'. The unpaid debt that the present owes to the past is far easier and less painfully paid with the false gold of narrative history – the once upon a time stories of the history of the self or the death of feudalism.

Historical truth takes place in the present and the only thing that prevents it from being tedious, from, in the Ghost's words, weighing on the souls of the living, is an awareness of its presence in the now. Commenting on the temptation of historicism Žižek argues that:

This ... is the point where the Left must not 'give way': it must preserve the traces of all historical traumas, dreams and catastrophes which the ruling ideology of the 'End of History' would prefer to obliterate – it must become itself their living monument, so that as long as the Left is here, these traumas will remain marked. Such an attitude, far from confining the Left within a nostalgic infatuation with the past, is the only possibility for attaining a distance on the present, a distance which will enable us to discern signs of the New.[33]

There is no way to access the Real of the past – all that one has is what passes as its reality, history, and the fantasies that give this reality consistency. This does not mean, however, that the only option is to give up and allow history to become the play-thing for those like Richard III for whom it is simply a story, a text, to be told, retold, distorted and destroyed. The pursuit of historical truth means keeping the stone's fall alive and creating, as Shakespeare does in *Richard III*, moments when the tedious truth of history is imagined as a call for justice in the now.

Notes

1. In his first tetralogy Shakespeare welds together chronicle history with the humanist historiography of Sir Thomas More's *Richard III*. Typically, however, Shakespeare chooses to leave the welds rough and obvious for all to see. On Tudor history writing in general see Tom Betteridge, *Tudor Histories of the English Reformations 1530–1583* (Aldershot: 1999); and F.J. Levy, *Tudor Historical Thought* (San Marino, CA: 1967).

2. This is a paraphrase of Walter Benjamin's claim that: "The historical materialist leaves it to others to be drained by the whore called 'Once upon a time' in historicism's bordello. He remains in control of his powers, man enough to blast open the continuum of history." Walter Benjamin, 'Theses on the Philosophy of History', in *Illuminations*, ed. Hannah Arendt, trans. Harry Zohn (London: 1973), pp.245–55, p.254.

3. Balibar uses this term to refer to the understanding of time within Marxist thought as filled with sensuous human activity. Étienne Balibar, *The Philosophy of Marx*, trans. Chris Turner (London: 1995), p.81.

4. Hugh Grady, 'On the Need for a Differentiated Theory of (Early) Modern Subjects', in *Philosophical Shakespeares*, ed. John J. Joughin (London: 2000), pp.34–50, p.41.

5. See Stephen Greenblatt, *Renaissance Self-Fashioning: From More to Shakespeare* (Chicago: 1980). One should note that the narrative told in works like Greenblatt's of the emergence of the modern self is also open to serious historical critique. See David Aers, 'A Whisper in the Ear of Early Modernists: Or, Reflections on Literary Critics Writing the "History of the Subject"', in *Culture and History 1350–1600: Essays on English Communities, Identities and Writing*, ed. David Aers (Hemel Hempstead: 1992), pp.177–202.

6. Slavoj Žižek, 'The Object as a Limit of Discourse: Approaches to the Lacanian Real', *Prose Studies*, 11 (1988), pp.94–120, p.96.

7 Judith Butler, *The Psychic Life of Power: Theories of Subjection* (California: 1997), p.197.

8 Joan Copjec comments that: "The fact that it is materially impossible to say the whole truth – that truth always backs away from language, that words always fall short of their goal – *founds* the subject." Joan Copjec, *Read my Desire: Lacan against the Historicists* (Cambridge, MA: 1995), p.35.

9 Slavoj Žižek, 'Introduction: Cogito as a Shibboleth', in *Cogito and the Unconscious*, ed. Slavoj Žižek (Durham, NC: 1998), pp.1–8, p.7.

10 Žižek comments that: "… every version of historicism relies on a minimal 'ahistorical' formal framework defining the terrain within which the open and endless game of contingent inclusions/exclusions, substitutions, renegotiations, displacements, and so on, takes place". Slavoj Žižek, 'Class Struggle or Postmodernism? Yes, Please', in *Contingency, Hegemony, Universality: Contemporary Dialogues on the Left*, ed. Judith Butler, Ernesto Laclau and Slavoj Žižek (London: 2000), pp.90–135, p.111.

11 Phyllis Rackin, *Stages of History* (London: 1990), p.200.

12 Michel de Certeau, *The Writing of History*, trans. Tom Conley (New York: 1988), p.xxvii.

13 Jean Howard and Phyllis Rackin, *Engendering a Nation* (London: 1997), p.58.

14 On Antigone see Judith Butler, *Antigone's Claim: Kinship between Life and Death* (New York: 2000).

15 For Althusser's theory of the subject see Louis Althusser, *Lenin and Philosophy and Other Essays*, trans. Ben Brewster (London: 1971).

16 Louis Althusser, *Essays on Ideology*, trans. Ben Brewster (London: 1971), p.46/7.

17 Mladen Dolar, 'Beyond Interpellation', *Qui Parle*, 6 (1993), pp.75–96, p.76.

18 Althusser, *Essays on Ideology*, 1971, p.40.

19 Ibid., p.45.

20 For More's self-consciously textual historiography in this work see Daniel Kinney, 'Kings' Tragicomedies: Generic Misrule in More History of Richard III', *Moreana*, 86 (1985), pp.128–50.

21 More's *History of Richard III* is centrally concerned with the textuality of history and the process through which the historical is produced out of the textual scraps of the past. It was the primary source of Shakespeare's play, albeit mediated through Hall and Holinshed.

22 Steve Larocco, 'Contentious Intimations: John Donne, *Richard III*, and the Transgressive Structures of Seduction', *Exemplaria*, 7 (1995), pp.237–67, p.246.

23 Roland Barthes suggested that: "In the historical discourse of our civilisation, the process of signification is always aimed at 'filling out' the meaning of History. The historian is not so much a collector of facts as a collector and relater of signifiers; that is to say, he organizes them with the purpose of establishing and filling the vacuum of pure, meaningless series." Richard offers and embodies the possibility of filling the historical gaze with himself as a monstrous self whose monstrosity guarantees the endless production of signifiers to fill history. Roland Barthes, 'The Discourse of History', trans. Stephen Bann, *Comparative Criticism*, 3 (1981), pp.3–20, p.16.

24 Maurice Hunt has pointed out the strange resemblance that Shakespeare creates at the end of the play between Richmond and Philip II of Spain. See Maurice Hunt, 'Ordering Disorder in *Richard III*', *South Central Review*, 6 (1989), pp.11–29, pp.25–6.

25 For a fascinating discussion of the linguistic qualities of Richard's kingship see Madhavi Menon, '*Richard II* and the Taint of Metonymy', *English Literary History*, 70 (2003), pp.653–76.

26 Alexander Leggatt, *Shakespeare's Political Drama: The History Plays and the Roman Plays* (London: 1988), p.74.

27 For the importance of counsel as an ideal in Tudor political praxis see John Guy, 'Tudor Monarchy and its Critiques', in *Tudor Monarchy*, ed. John Guy (London: 1997), pp.78–109.

28 For the political implications of the emergence of Petrarchan poetry during the reign of Henry VIII see James Simpson, *Reform and Cultural Revolution 1350–1547* (Oxford: 2002).

29 Slavoj Žižek, *The Metastases of Enjoyment: Six Essays on Woman and Causality* (London: 1994), p.47.

30 Anne Righter, *Shakespeare and the Idea of the Play* (London: 1962), p.111.

31 Paul Ricoeur, *The Reality of the Historical Past* (Milwaukee: 1984), p.26.

32 Terry Eagleton, 'History, Narrative and Marxism', in *Reading Narrative: Form, Ethics, Ideology*, ed. James Phelan (Columbus, OH: 1989), pp.272–82, p.277.

33 Slavoj Žižek, *For They Know Not What They Do: Enjoyment as a Political Factor* (London: 1991), p.273.

CHAPTER TWO

Reading with desire: Twelfth Night, A Midsummer Night's Dream, As You Like It *and* Much Ado About Nothing

I N *Twelfth Night* William Shakespeare explores the ethics of his art. In particular, in this play Shakespeare constructs a number of alternative and competing interpretative models – the hysterical, the perverse and the ethical. *Twelfth Night* consistently foregrounds the production of meaning, the different ways in which characters read themselves, each other and their world. It is this emphasis that disrupts any attempt to read the play in terms of simple oppositions, carnival versus law, comic sub-plot versus courtly love triangle or social criticism versus the play of desire. In *Twelfth Night* reading through and with fantasy is the norm. The play's sub-title, 'What You Will', reflects the extent to which in this play Shakespeare is centrally concerned with desire. After all at one level *Twelfth Night*'s sub-title can be read as a simple, banal even, statement of intent – an advert designed to drum up an audience by assuring them that the play will give them what they will. This is, however, to read 'you' as referring to the audience. In practice the phrase 'what you will' raises radical questions of identity and meaning. Who is 'you'? What do they desire? What do they desire of me? What do you desire me to be? 'What you will' can also be read as a warning – be careful what you wish for. When Othello is seeking proof of Desdemona's adultery, Iago advises him to interpret the evidence on the basis of 'what you will'. *Twelfth Night* offers the audience the possibility of producing, and reducing, meaning through wilful reading – producing meaning in order to satisfy one's hysterical or perverted desire. It incites us as an audience to read like Malvolio and crush Shakespeare's work so that it reflects back to us what we desire. In the process it foregrounds the relationship between desire and meaning, and the role of fantasy in mediating between these two concepts/states/terms/words – call them what you will.

This chapter is in two parts. The first part applies Slavoj Žižek's Lacanian understanding of fantasy to a number of Shakespeare's late Elizabethan comedies. In these plays Shakespeare displays an anxious concern over the status and ethics of his art. The relative confidence of *Richard III* is replaced by a nagging sense of failure. Despite the pleasure engendered by works like *As You Like It* and *A Midsummer Night's Dream* these late Elizabethan comedies are haunted by a fear that they are no more than much ado about nothing – the expenditure of a mass of words, wit and skill ultimately simply to satisfy the audience's voyeuristic desire for something. The second part of this chapter discusses the relationship between carnival and law in *Twelfth Night*. It then moves on to examine the different models of interpretation that Shakespeare presents to the audience in this play – hysterical, perverse and ethical, or Orsino, Malvolio and Viola.

Fantasy in Shakespeare

In his study, *The Plague of Fantasies*, Žižek contends that the normal relationship between fantasy and reality should be reversed. Instead of assuming an existing reality that fantasy deviates from he argues for a realm of the fantastic that is prior to, and constitutive of, reality. Žižek's argument is based on the Lacanian idea that the place of subjects within the symbolic order depends on an acceptance of a fantasy that produces reality – in other words it is the fantastical that enables the emergence of reality from the Real. Brian Nical comments that in Žižek's thought:

> The function of fantasy is to fill the void created by the real. It creates a space, a kind of blank screen on which the subject's desires can be projected. In this way, fantasy *realizes* desire – not in the sense of satisfying it, but by bringing it out in the open, giving it a shape.[1]

Fantasy allows desire to take shape. In the process it enables the subject to make sense of the world – to make a reality. The crucial point is that in Žižek's thought fantasy is not something separate from, external to or following behind reality – it is the fantastical that makes reality possible.

In the opening section of his work *The Plague of Fantasies* Žižek produces a sustained discussion of the seven aspects or veils of fantasy. In particular, in this study Žižek relates the fantastical to the same issues of interpretation and desire that Shakespeare addresses in his late Elizabethan plays. For both thinkers the relationship between the law, transgressive pleasures and fantasy is central – is there liberation in the fantastical or simply the desire that sustains the existing social order? Law versus fantasy, law and fantasy, fantasy making law – which is it to be? Which is the truth?

Desire is a central issue in *As You Like It*. In particular, as numerous critics have pointed out, the figure of Rosalind – a boy playing a girl who dresses as a boy and adopts the name of Zeus's gay lover and then when she (he) meets Orlando, the man Rosalind (Ganymede) loves, offers to play the part of Rosalind the girl (boy) who is the object of Orlando's desire – functions as a complex erotic trope. Rosalind's eroticism is, however, in some ways profoundly textual. This is despite Shakespeare's exploitation of the erotic possibilities produced by the male body hidden within but also constitutive of Rosalind as an object of desire. Valerie Traub has suggested that: "Throughout the play, what makes erotic contingency possible is a simple conjunction: 'if'. Indeed, Touchstone's discourse on the virtues of 'if' can serve as an index of the play's entire erotic strategy ...."[2] Rosalind functions within the field of gender as a constant provocation. She incites the production of erotic ifs – if he were a girl, if she were a boy, if I were a boy, if we were a girl. At times there seems to be no limit to the amount of play in Rosalind's performance of gender and the possibilities that it creates. The limitless quality of the erotic potential of Rosalind is a product of Shakespeare's textualisation of the body – the boy playing Rosalind cannot actually become her but he can as an embodied text or a walking metaphor (although importantly not as a metonym).[3] Rosalind's transgressive effect on gender norms can be illustrated by examining the mock wedding scene when Rosalind playing Ganymede playing Rosalind 'marries' Orlando:

> Ros: Come, sister, you shall be the priest and marry us. Give me your hand Orlando. What do you say sister?
> Orl: Pray thee marry us.
> Cel: I cannot say the words.
> Ros: You must begin, 'Will you, Orlando – '
> Cel: Go to. Will you, Orlando, have to wife this Rosalind?
> Orl: I will.

Ros: Ay, but when?
Orl: Why now, as fast as she can marry us.
Ros: Then you must say, 'I take thee Rosalind for wife'.
Orl: I take thee Rosalind for wife.
Ros: I might ask you for your commission; but I do take thee Orlando for my husband.

Act 4, Sc 1, L 118–32

It is not simply that at this moment Orlando thinks Rosalind is a boy called Ganymede playing the part of Rosalind that accounts for the transgressive nature of this scene. There is also Celia's usurpation of the role of priest and the suggestion that having staged a wedding the next thing on Rosalind's/Ganymede's agenda will be the honeymoon. In this context the fact that throughout this scene the women are on top reflects the perspicacity of Traub's argument. Rosalind generates erotic possibilities. She incites the audience to indulge in the production of multiple endless sexual ifs.

It is, however, a mistake to see this in entirely positive terms. Rosalind's generation of erotic possibilities takes place within a clearly defined sexual economy. Žižek comments that "a fantasy constitutes our desire, provides its co-ordinates; that is, it literally 'teaches us how to desire'".[4] In *As You Like It* Rosalind has the literal job of teaching Orlando to desire. This is why she creates the fantasy figure of Rosalind as portrayed by Ganymede. Rosalind teaches Orlando to fill his desire with play, and in particular witty language – with endless and erotic ifs. Indeed she instructs him to embrace the fantasy of Ganymede's Rosalind in order to prepare him for the reality. In this case Shakespeare makes literal the dependence of reality on fantasy – it is the fantastical courtship of Orlando and Rosalind that allows the emergence of the reality. Rosalind also, however, has to teach the audience to desire. Or to put it more accurately she has to teach them to enjoy and embrace the deferment of desire as a form of endless textual interpretation. As with *Twelfth Night* the title of *As You Like It* reflects the extent to which in this play Shakespeare is commenting upon the status of his drama as a commodity. If 'if' can be related to Rosalind then so can 'It' – the 'it' which is open to the constant play of 'if'. She is the thing that the audience like because in her person she will offer all of them what they want. The only cost is that they accept the fantasy of erotic play that she embodies. When Rosalind first meets Orlando in the forest they are already in love. Why does she not simply tell him who she is? Because, while that might satisfy the audience's proper public commitment to heterosexual union, it would frustrate their desire for 'if' and 'it' – for the play of erotic possibilities offered specifically by Rosalind in this play but in general by Shakespeare's theatre.

In *As You Like It* Shakespeare plays with the audience. He constantly creates moments when the fantasy might collapse and give the audience what they ought to want, heterosexual union, but not yet. The fantasy at the heart of this play is, however, not simply the erotic possibilities generated by Rosalind. Nor is it that of a privileged space in which desire can have free play. The lesson that *As You Like It* ultimately teaches its audience is that their fantasy of the free play of desire requires an arbitrary, harsh, law in order for it to emerge – a world in which its are fixed and there are no ifs. It is Duke Frederick's court that provides Arden's coordinates. The same logic can be seen in *A Midsummer Night's Dream*. In this play Shakespeare constructs a division between Theseus's court with its formality, order and law, and the forest where love and desire run free (and mad). At one level the important point to make about this separation is Shakespeare's concern to highlight the extent to which it is compromised. Court and forest look and sound like different places but at the same time share many characteristics. It is as though Shakespeare is tempting his audience to understand *A Midsummer Night's Dream* as a clash between two worlds as a way of making it meaningful while at the same time subtly mocking this reductive reading.

At another level, as with *As You Like It*, the title of *A Midsummer Night's Dream* gives the game away. The dreamlike quality of much of this play is dependent upon the harsh reality of Theseus's world. It is not drama as a dream that is the fantasy in this play – but drama as law. This point can be related to Žižek's suggestion that "the original question of desire is not directly 'What do I want?', but 'What do *others* want from me? What do they see in me? What am I to others?'"[5] In Shakespeare's late Elizabethan comedies the answer to these questions offered to the audience is that "the others want me to be someone whose desire is posed between the free play of erotic possibilities, of if, of the dream, and the law". I am to the others the person whose desire summons up Duke Frederick's and Theseus's courts in order to enjoy the freedom of Arden and the forest – this is what I am to others. In these terms *As You Like It* should be re-titled 'As You Like Me To Like It'.

The pleasure incited by *A Midsummer Night's Dream* is to enjoy the world of the forest as the opposite of the court. The fantasy that this play offers the audience is that it is the law as embodied by Theseus that makes the drama happen not the desire of the audience to consume – to satisfy their desire by paying the admission fee that ultimately produces the drama of *A Midsummer Night's Dream*. In the process the reality of the audience's financial responsibility for the play's existence – it is their money that makes it happen – is obscured. The ordered formal world of Theseus protects the audience from acknowledging the entirely functional and banal nature of their relationship to the play – it turns their material desire, the admission fee, into the nothing that makes the play happen but can only be seen in its effects. The ultimate fantasy that preoccupies Shakespeare in his late Elizabethan comedies is that his plays are something more than commodities produced to be brought and sold to the audience. The anxiety and fear that runs through these plays is a product of Shakespeare's awareness that this is indeed a fantasy – that he, like Rosalind, is simply an 'it' producing endless 'ifs', nothings, for the audience to consume as they will.

Žižek argues that 'fantasy is the primordial form of *narrative*, which serves to occult some original deadlock'.[6] Shakespeare's late Elizabethan comedies can be read as narratological essays that consistently address the relationship between consumption and desire. In *As You Like It* Rosalind's deferment of the heterosexual union between her and Orlando seems designed to foreground the production of narrative. It is her creation of a detour that produces a central strand of the play's story, or rather creates the space for a number of different stories to emerge.[7] In *A Midsummer Night's Dream* Puck acts as an internal author of the play's narrative – as a *Vorstellungsrepräsentanz* (representative of representing). Puck's role is to produce narrative; he operates as an embodied textual device or literary trope making the play happen but at the same time constantly embodying the dangerous possibility that the created artificial nature of the play will be exposed.

At the end of the play Puck has a strange and disturbing speech:

> Puck: Now the hungry lion roars,
> And the wolf behowls the moon;
> Whilst the heavy ploughman snores,
> All with weary task fordone.

Now the wasted brands do glow,
Whilst the screech-owl, screeching loud,
Puts the wretch that lies in woe
In remembrance of a shroud.
Now it is the time of night
That the graves, all gaping wide,
Every one lets forth his sprite
In the church-way paths to glide.
And we fairies, that do run
By the triple Hecate's team
From the presence of the sun,
Following darkness like a dream,
Now are frolic; not a mouse
Shall disturb this hallow'd house.
I am sent with broom before
To sweep the dust behind the door.

Act 5, Sc 1, L 357–76

There is a tension in this speech between its nursery rhyme form and its nightmarish content. It is as though Puck here is stressing the arbitrariness of language, the extent to which the relationship between form and content is entirely arbitrary. Puck's speech reflects all the violence and fear that has been kept at the edges of the play. Its emphasis on the tension between form and content also reflects the violent imposition of order in the play's verse. In particular, it expresses the denied violence of the iambic pentameter with its ideological claims to naturalness and authority.[8] It also reflects the arbitrariness of the play's conclusion, the extent to which the need for a conclusion is a product not of the play's natural story but of its status as a commodity that offers its audience specific, if ultimately frustrated, satisfactions. The dust that Puck sweeps behind the door, which he hides but does not destroy, is the original deadlock that the narrative of the play works around and through without ever actually addressing. It is, to paraphrase Žižek, 'that which remains of the reality of the play after it is deprived of its support in fantasy'.[9] Puck's dust, in its obscene disavowed materiality, dirt to be swept behind the door so that it remains a hidden but noted element of the play's world, is the money that materialises the audience's desire in the form of the entrance fee – the actor's wage and author's fee. At the centre of *A Midsummer Night's Dream* is not the audience's erotic desire, and the original deadlock is not the law or Theseus – it is the audience's desire to consume and the status of the play as a commodity.[10]

It is the law of the commodity that is installed at the heart of Shakespeare's late Elizabethan comedies. This is not to suggest, however, that these plays are in any sense not erotic comic masterpieces. They had to be in order for Shakespeare to make a living. It is to argue that at this stage of his career Shakespeare's writing is beginning to indicate a profound ambiguity about its own ethical status. In particular, there is a concern in these plays that selling erotic fantasies means being a pornographer; creating texts that allow audiences to simultaneously indulge their desires while avoiding any responsibility for them. This fear is articulated very clearly in *Much Ado About Nothing*. The basic tension in this play is between its courtly love plot and its male characters' obsessive fear of being cuckolded. This does not mean, however, that courtly love and cuckoldry are not linked in this play. Instead Shakespeare goes out of his way to show the extent to which the reality of the play's lovers is sustained by the fantasy figure of the cuckold. Žižek suggests that: "… 'fantasy' designates an element which 'sticks out', which cannot be integrated into the given symbolic structure, yet which, precisely as such, constitutes its identity".[11] *Much Ado About Nothing* ends with the required heterosexual union of the main participants. But at this very moment of closure Benedick re-installs the fantasy figure of the cuckold – that which sticks out of the play's love plot but at the same time provides its matter:

> Bene: Come, come, we are friends. Let's have a dance ere we are married, that we may lighten our own hearts and our wives' heels.
> Leon: We'll have dancing afterward.
> Bene: First, of my word! Therefore play, music. Prince, thou art sad; get thee a wife, get thee a wife! There is no staff more reverend than one tipped with horn.
> *Enter Messenger.*
> Mess: My lord, your brother John is ta'en in flight,
> And brought with armed men back to Messina.
> Bene: Think not on him till tomorrow; I'll devise thee brave punishments for him. Strike up, pipers!
> *Dance. [Exeunt]*

Act 5, Sc 4, L 116–26

Despite appearances to the contrary the resolution at the end of *Much Ado About Nothing* is profoundly and provocatively arbitrary. This is not to suggest that it in any way undermines the status of the heterosexual marriages which the play deploys in an entirely conventional way to produce closure. *Much Ado About Nothing* ends by stressing the extent to which the reality of its love plots is built upon the fantasy figure of a cuckold. It does so through Benedick's perverse return to the discourse of cuckoldry after the resolution of the play's romance story lines. The evocation of the cuckold's horn at the end of *Much Ado About Nothing* reflects the extent to which the public formal narrative of the play's plot is based upon a fantastical element, the discourse of cuckoldry, which is at once alien to the world of romance and its denied logic.

This point can, however, be pushed further since *Much Ado About Nothing* ends not with Benedick's dig at the Prince to get horns but with his promise to devise brave punishments for Don John. Why does a love comedy end with an image of torture? Who is 'thee' in Benedick's line? Clearly at one level it is simply the other characters on stage. In these terms Benedick is simply promising to torture Don John for his crimes against them. But there is also a sense that Benedick's 'thee' includes the audience. In particular, there is something deliberately clumsy about Don John's spectral appearance at the end of the play. Has he not been summoned up largely to provide a tidy ending for the audience? And therefore is it not the audience who have the largest investment in his torture? After all, as with *Othello*, there is a sense that the closure of *Much Ado About Nothing* is flawed by the failure of its villain to confess – Don John like Iago denies the audience the pleasure of hearing him explain his actions. One is left asking why summon Don John up if this only serves to remind the audience that the play lacks 'proper' closure? That one never really finds out why Don John stages his corrupt play? Why he chooses to undermine the romance between Claudio and Hero with a piece of theatre?

Don John is a tangential figure in *Much Ado About Nothing* and at the same time crucial to the play's plot. In particular, while this is a play about love there is nothing of the lover about Don John. He does not even stay on stage to see his plans come to fruition. Having arranged for Claudio to be tricked by a piece of crude play-acting he leaves the stage with his place being taken by his minions, Conrade and Borachio. Despite this there is a level at which Shakespeare creates a clear parallel between himself and Don John. After all it is Don John's play that seduces Claudio and Don Pedro into thinking Hero has been unfaithful. He is therefore at one level the 'author' of the entire second half of *Much Ado About Nothing*. The 'nothing' in the title of the play can be read as Don John's play – it is a nothing that creates much ado. Nothing is also, however, a reference to the voyeuristic logic of the pun on vagina/nothing – the voyeur's simultaneous desire to see nothing and the fear of nothing to see. Jean E. Howard has pointed out that:

> ... a characterological focus on Don John as origin of evil can obscure the extent to which the assumptions about women upon which his trick depends are shared by other men in the play. The trick at the window silently assumes and further circulates the idea that women are universally prone to deception and impersonation. ... Don John lies about Hero, but his lie works because it easily passes in Messina as a truthful reading of women.[12]

Don John's play, like Shakespeare's, works because it exploits misogynist assumptions, desires and fears about women – the fantasies that sustain the reality of woman. Don John's drama produces much ado about nothing by exploiting an existing male fear of nothing as a source of female power and male disempowerment. Women, and their nothing, suck men in and then strip them of their power to leave them helpless, horned objects of ridicule. The fact that Don John uses existing male fantasies to dramatically create a new reality does not, however, explain his actions. These still appear entirely arbitrary. He does evil because he is evil. Don John reflects Shakespeare's awareness that the ultimate truth of his drama was its status as a commodity – a something sold to satisfy the hidden desire of the audience, their no-thing. The tension between romance and cuckoldry in *Much Ado About Nothing* works to create a narrative that avoids the truth that it is the audience's desire to consume, and perhaps specifically to consume plays that allow them to indulge their voyeuristic desire for nothings, that is the much ado that produces nothing – the nothing that is Shakespeare's play.[13]

The nothing of *Much Ado About Nothing* is also, however, love. The radicalism of Shakespeare's critique of his art in these late Elizabethan comedies is revealed most clearly in his approach in these works to love. This can be illustrated by looking at the moment in *As You Like It* when the erotic possibilities produced by If/Rosalind appear in danger of spinning out of control:

Phebe: Good shepherd, tell this youth what 'tis to love.
Silvius: It is to be all made of sighs and tears;
And so am I for Phebe.
Phebe: And I for Ganymede.
Orlando: And I for Rosalind.
Rosalind: And I for no woman.
Silvius: It is to be all made of faith and service;
And so am I for Phebe.
Phebe: And I for Ganymede.
Orlando: And I for Rosalind.
Rosalind: And I for no woman.
Silvius: It is to be all made of fantasy,
All made of passion and all made of wishes
All adoration, duty, and observance,
All humbleness, all patience, and impatience,
All purity, all trial, all observance;
And so am I for Phebe.

Act 5, Sc 2, L 83–98

Silvius teaches the others that being in love means being in a state of incompletion, to be constantly seeking fullness, to lack. The repetition of the word 'all' marks the extent to which to describe love in the way Silvius attempts to is an endless futile task. The 'all' will never be full or complete. It is this desire to fill love with matter, with meaning, that creates the fundamental difference between the loves of Rosalind and Silvius. As has been suggested a key element in Rosalind's love is the production of narrative around, through and over desire. Silvius's love, which is an excessive parodic version of courtly Petrarchan love, is instead marked by fixity. His lover is trapped in desire's gaze. Žižek points out that in courtly love:

> … *external hindrances that thwart our access to the object are there precisely to create the illusion that without them, the object would be directly accessible* – what such hindrances thereby conceal is the inherent impossibility of attaining the object.[14]

Silvius's pæan to unrequited love works to defer the emergence of the act of love. It puts off indefinitely, until there are no more alls to be filled, the moment when the subject has to risk all in love. Renata Salecl comments that: "There is no love outside speech: non-speaking beings do not love. ... Love emerges out of speech as a demand that is not linked to any need."[15] The love that Silvius seeks to describe is precisely one that escapes language. He wants to find the words, the phrase, which will fill up love, make it complete and therefore, ironically, destroy it. This is because there can be no completion, no finality, within language. Love cannot be fixed. Silvius's attempt to fully describe love is doomed to be endless and this is its attraction since it therefore operates to sustain the fantasy of a love that escapes the play of signification – Juliet's love outside and beyond language. If there is one fantasy that causes tragedy in Shakespeare's drama it is this. Othello, Leontes and Lear all desire a love beyond language and this leads them to destroy the very thing that they desire.

Rosalind's response to Silvius's endless litany to love's lack is ultimately violent and dismissive:

> Rosalind: Pray you, no more of this, 'tis like the howling of Irish wolves against the moon.
>
> Act 5, Sc 2, L 110–11

At first sight Rosalind's description of the preceding exchange seems bizarre. Silvius's love lesson, and the contributions of Phebe, Orlando *and* Rosalind, is provocatively poetic. The way he introduces themes that are then repeated by the other characters gives this moment a harmonious, even choral, texture. So why does Rosalind describe it as like 'the howling of Irish wolves against the moon'? The most obvious reading is that Silvius's love lesson is, in Rosalind's eyes, complete nonsense, as purposeless as howling against the moon. While this is clearly right, there are, however, two further crucial points to be made about this line. The fact that it is Irish wolves that Silvius, Phebe and Orlando resemble introduces a disturbing racist sub-text to this moment. Ireland for Elizabethans was a site of violence and papistry but also of temptation and wealth. The racial specificity of Rosalind's wolves raises the disturbing prospect that their howling may not be nonsense. This worrying possibility is linked to the poetic implications of characterising Silvius's love lesson as meaningless, animalistic, as nonsensical noise. As with Puck's song at the end of *A Midsummer Night's Dream* the implication of Rosalind's words is that the relationship between form and content is entirely arbitrary.

It is as though at this moment the erotic possibilities created around

Rosalind have escaped the world of fantasy and become reality. In the process their essentially arbitrary and violent nature is revealed. A similar process takes place around the figure of Duke Frederick whose sudden conversion from evil reflects the extent to which the world of the law is dependent on that of fantasy and not vice versa. Frederick's embodiment of the law depends on the existence of a fantasy state of erotic play in Arden, and the redundancy of the latter with the multiple marriages at the end of the play renders the former equally redundant. It is as if Shakespeare is saying we don't need the law as an external element now we have installed it at the heart of Arden. Rosalind's howling Irish wolves emerge at precisely the point where the detour she creates in the love plot between her and Orlando is coming apart. In these terms one can suggest a final twist to the reading of Rosalind's characterisation of Silvius's love lesson. Are not the Irish wolves representative of the collapse of Rosalind's fantasy of love? Žižek suggests that: "In order to be operative, fantasy has to remain 'implicit', it has to maintain a distance towards the explicit symbolic texture sustained by it, and to function as its inherent transgression."[16] In other words once the erotic possibilities of 'if' become the norm in Arden they can no longer be transgressive and instead require sustaining by a fantasy of their own – the nightmare of Irish wolves filling love with an arbitrary mix that is harmonious in formal terms but at the level of meaning simply noise.[17] Or to put it more accurately the danger raised by the normalisation of erotic play is that love as a real possibility is driven from the stage.

This disturbing possibility is stalled by the emergence of Hymen at the end of the play but, as with all of Shakespeare's late Elizabethan comedies, the conclusion to *As You Like It* is far from unproblematic. In particular, the sudden change of tone with the appearance of the god Hymen seems designed to emphasise the artificial nature of the play's closure. This is particularly so since although at one level Hymen's role is to perform the miracle that resolves all the play's complicated love stories in practice the god's role is entirely redundant. There is no need for Hymen to appear given that all that needs to happen is for Rosalind to take off her disguise, or at least two of them, and the play can end in a form of heterosexual closure. The redundancy of Hymen is, however, precisely the point since he introduces again the possibility of 'if'. Indeed it is no coincidence that Hymen's appearance follows on immediately from Touchstone's speech praising the virtue of 'if'.

The fantasy that Hymen protects is of a realm of erotic possibilities that appears to transgress the law but in practice sustains it. Hymen's function is to place the dangerous possibility created by the normalisation of Rosalind as an erotic 'if' safely back into the realms of the fantastical. In the process the god protects the audience from having to acknowledge the extent to which *As You Like It* is a commodity whose value depends on its ability to present multiple 'its' to the audience to be voyeuristically consumed.

In the epilogue to *As You Like It*, however, Shakespeare reflects again on the status of his art. Rosalind ends her epilogue by making an explicit erotic offer to the audience:

> If I were a woman, I would kiss as many of you as had beards that pleased me, complexions that liked me, and breaths that I defied not; and, I am sure, as many as have good beards, or good faces, or sweet breaths, will, for my kind offer, which I make curtsy, bid me farewell.
>
> Epilogue, L 214–20

At one level this offer appears to be simply playful. Of course Rosalind is not a woman so the offer to kiss those who have beards is nothing more than a joke. However, it is important to note that not only is beard a pun on female pubic hair but also that Rosalind's offer can be related directly to one of the jests contained in *A Hundred Merry Tales* – allegedly one of Queen Elizabeth's favourite books:[18]

> A yonge gentylman of the age of xx yere some whate dysposyd to myrth and game on a tyme talkyd with a gentylwoman which was ryght wise and also merry. This gentyll woman as she talkyd with hym happened to loke uppon hys berde / which was but yong and growen some what uppon the over lyppe and but lyttyl growen beneth as all yonge mennys berdys co[m]monly use to growe sayd to hym thus. Syr ye haue a berde above and none beneth. And he herynge her say so / sayd in sporte / mistress ye haue a berde benethe and none aboue / mary quod she / then set the one agaynst the other / which answere made the gentylman so abashyd that he had not one worde to answer.[19]

Rosalind as a girl offers to kiss all the men in the audience and as a boy she makes the same offer to the women. The source of the young gentleman's unease over the gentlewoman's provocative invitation for him to bring his beard to hers, to give her oral sex, is, however, also present in the Epilogue to *As You Like It*. One assumes that Rosalind's offer is like the howling of Irish wolves just a piece of nonsense, but what if it were real? What if at the end of *As You Like It* the audience were offered the chance to make their desires real? What if Rosalind – character and actor – really were an 'it' to be consumed? Indeed is this not actually the case? Even worse, does not Rosalind's reduction of the audience to their beards, their desirability as objects to be kissed, suddenly reverse the whole logic of the play – it is as though at this moment it is the audience who have become 'it', the 'ifs' that Rosalind will weigh up, consume and discard.

What prevents a literal consumption of Rosalind is our obscene libidinal investment in the consumption of her as a voyeuristic object. The last thing the audience want is for 'it' to speak, for 'if' to become a reality.[20] *As You Like It* plays with the audience's desire while knowing that all along what the audience want above all is to passively enjoy indulging their desire for an it/law that will excuse their if/fantasy.

Shakespeare's late Elizabethan comedies are haunted by the fear that the theatre is all that its critics said it was – a whorehouse, a place where the bodies of actors were put on display to be consumed by a hungry audience seeking only to satisfy their base desires. In all these plays, and particularly *Twelfth Night*, however, Shakespeare does articulate a defence of his art – but it is one that is tentative and unsure.

Carnival, reading and ethics in Twelfth Night

One of the main concerns of *Twelfth Night* is the ethics of desire. In particular in this work Shakespeare explicitly creates three divergent perspectives on desire – the hysterical, perverse and ethical. The hysteric, Orsino, wallows in the fantasy of love in order to postpone what he publicly desires – the embrace of the Other. The pervert, Malvolio, sacrifices his enjoyment for a greater good – he celebrates the law's prohibition of his desire. Viola, and indeed in quite different but linked ways, Antonio and Feste, adopts a truly ethical approach to desire by remaining faithful to it.[21] This triad can also be related to the different forms of reading that Shakespeare stages in this play, in particular the flawed, wilful and selfless. And finally the symbolic structure of *Twelfth Night* can also be seen in terms of these three categories. At one level there is the law whose most obvious representative is Malvolio. Running alongside the law is its obscene carnival support – the fantasy that appears to transgress the law but is in fact that which allows it to emerge. This fantasy, in *Twelfth Night*, is embodied primarily in the stalled relationship between Orsino and Olivia. At first sight it appears the carnivalesque state of Illyria is a product of Orsino's love sickness and Olivia's transgressive status as an independent unmarried young woman. It soon becomes clear, however, that it is precisely the stalled nature of their relationship that allows the law to function. Finally there are a number of characters whose place within the play places them between the law and its carnivalesque support. Viola makes a truly ethical decision to remain true to her love even though she knows it is hopeless. Feste represents a world of proverbial wisdom ultimately quite incompatible with the linked worlds of courtly love and carnivalesque excess. Antonio embodies humanist male friendship, *amicitia*, and finds there is no place for him within *Twelfth Night*'s concluding celebration of heterosexuality.

Twelfth Night opens with Orsino on stage playing Silvius's role of a Petrarchan lover:

> Orsino: If music be the food of love, play on,
> Give me excess of it, that, surfeiting,
> The appetite may sicken, and so die.
> That strain again, it had a dying fall:
> O, it came o'er my ear like the sweet sound
> That breathes upon a bank of violets,
> Stealing and giving odour. Enough, no more;
> 'Tis not so sweet now as it was before.
>
> Act 1, Sc 1, L 1–8

Orsino's love, like Silvius's, is marked by a lack that all the sound in the world cannot fill. Indeed what Shakespeare makes clear in these opening words is that Orsino not only is caught in a state of stalled desire but also derives enjoyment from this stalled state. Orsino's relationship to love can therefore be understood as profoundly hysterical. He pretends to be caught in a stalled state of desire while in practice embracing this forced choice as a way of postponing an encounter with what he really fears – enjoyment/*jouissance*. In these terms his relationship to Olivia can be read as fantastical. Žižek comments that: "… fantasy provides a *rationale* for the inherent deadlock of desire: it constructs the scene in which the *jouissance* we are deprived of is concentrated in the Other who stole it from us".[22] Fantasy allows one to tell a story in which the impossibility of escaping the logic of desire is turned into narrative and therefore placed back into space and time. In Orsino's chase the narrative he latches upon is the hackneyed one of courtly love. He raises Olivia to the status of the prohibited Other and in the process creates a fantastical explanation for his constitutive lack. Orsino, however, goes further than this when he embraces the role of Petrarchan lover which not only does he know Olivia hates but which is also constitutively frustrated.

Throughout *Twelfth Night* Shakespeare emphasises the extent to which Orsino is committed to hysterical reading. In particular, Orsino's misreading of Olivia, and later Viola, is predicated on the need to maintain his performance as a desiring male in order to stall the emergence of *jouissance*.[23] One therefore needs to reverse the common-sense reading of Orsino's relationship with Olivia. It is not that Orsino misreads Olivia and that therefore he is frustrated. Rather it is in order to occlude his frustration, his sense of lack, that Orsino misreads Olivia to create a fantastical courtly love narrative that explains away the inherent deadlock of desire.

One should note that in many ways Olivia, like Orsino, reads as a hysteric. It is therefore no surprise that she so fundamentally misreads Viola:

> Olivia: I prithee tell me what thou think'st of me.
> Viola: That you do think you are not what you are.
> Olivia: If I think so, I think that same of you.
> Viola: Then think you right; I am not what I am.
> Olivia: I would you were as I would have you be.
> Viola: Would it be better, madam, than I am?
> I wish it might, for now I am your fool.

> Act 3, Sc 1, L 140-6

Viola's responses to Olivia in this exchange are noticeable for their brevity and accuracy. It is the character playing a role and wearing a disguise who knows the truth. Olivia, however, is portrayed by Shakespeare as incapable of knowing either Viola or herself. She has been playing the role of the stern mistress but now appears suddenly to be about to embrace its opposite – that of desiring lover. Of course this opposition is entirely illusionary. Olivia as lover of Viola is as hysterical as her role as Orsino's Petrarchan lady. Like Orsino Olivia would rather live with her fantasy and renounce the world than risk an encounter with the Other with all that that might entail.

If Orsino and Olivia can be seen as hysterics then Malvolio is clearly a pervert. This means, however, that his relationship to the world of the play is far more problematic than Orsino's or Olivia's. This is because there is a correlation between hysteria's production of narrative to forestall *jouissance* and requirements of the theatre for a complex two-hour love plot. The pervert's constant attempts to be totally under the law and therefore the object of the Other's desire, however, ultimately threaten the play's very existence. Perversion, in Žižek's sense, involves an erasure of any space for play or narrative as the pervert seeks to fully become an instrument of the Other. Shakespeare, however, goes out of his way to place the figure of the pervert at the centre of his play. Malvolio becomes a fulcrum around which Shakespeare simultaneously mounts a defence and critique of his art.

In the box tree scene, Act 2 Scene 5, Malvolio's desire for social advancement, the desire of Toby and his cohorts to be revenged on Malvolio and the audience's desire to be entertained are all staged. In particular, it is the desire of the audience to be an audience that protects the lubricious, albeit conventional, nature of the scene. The box tree scene opens with Malvolio fantasising that he has married Olivia and become Count Malvolio. What Shakespeare depicts here is the extent of Malvolio's commitment to the desire of the Other – to what the Other desires of him.[24] This might seem a perverse reading since this scene appears to be all about Malvolio's desire – for Olivia, for social advancement and for order. But to concentrate on these aspects of the scene is to ignore the extent to which the box tree scene is a profoundly meta-theatrical moment. The central desire it interrogates is that of the people who make it happen – the desire of the audience. The opening of box tree scene serves the purpose of making the following comic action plausible. But for whose benefit is this plausibility? Opening the box tree scene with Malvolio already fantasising about marrying Olivia is designed to satisfy the audience's desire for plausible explanations. Indeed Malvolio's first response to the forged letter reflects the extent to which Shakespeare in this scene is questioning the ethics of his audience – the kind of desire or will they bring to his art, the law they impose.

Malvolio is drawn to Maria's letter because it is written in Olivia's hand, but the bawdy pun, "these be her very C's, her U's and her T's, and thus she makes her great P's" (Act 2, Sc 5, L 88-9), indicates the extent to which it is his sexual desire for Olivia that motivates his reading of the letter. In particular, Malvolio's collapse of Olivia's hand into her cs, us and ts and the making of her great ps suggests a fantasy of the female sex as a direct counterpart of the phallic pen. At this point, however, Shakespeare is also questioning the audience's own investment in the kind of wilful sexual reading Malvolio performs here. After all it is the audience that have to supply the 'n' that makes the joke 'funny'. They have to fill in the gap or lack in Malvolio's words/fantasy. Sir Andrew's response to Malvolio's speech is important in this context: "Her C's, her U's, and her T's: why that?" (Act 2, Sc 5, L 91). This line indicates Andrew's naivety, and his curiously asexual nature, but his question is actually rather insightful. At one level the answer is clearly that ultimately Malvolio picks out these letters since they reflect what really interests him about Olivia. The other answer to Andrew's 'why that?', however, is that this kind of bawdy pun is what the audience wants; it is what they will/desire.[25]

Having established that Malvolio reads in a very particular way it is no surprise that Shakespeare goes on to illustrate the effects of his reductive approach to reading upon the letter's contents. Malvolio consistently reads Maria's trick entirely in terms of his own desires. He notes that the first part of the letter is poetry but ignores the implications of this in terms of its interpretation. His only thought is to make the text work. This means for Malvolio making it satisfy his desire. But it is important to note that this is also what Sir Toby and his cronies want and what the audience desires. The audience to Malvolio's fall, on stage and off, don't want him to worry about the letter's poetry or even worse to reject it as a piece of nonsense. There is, however, no danger of this. Maria, the playwright of this scene, knows her audience well. She knows that Malvolio will treat her letter, with its mixture of poetry and prose, in an entirely reductive instrumentalist fashion. He will construct her trick as a riddle, a desire filled crossword, whose complexity is designed simply to give its reader the pleasure of finding (making) order in its web of words. The fact that Malvolio finally resorts to 'crushing' the text of the letter in order to make it relate to him shows his haste and fear of any deferment of desire. In complete opposition to Orsino Malvolio rushes to obey the law – to become the object of the Other's (audience's) desire.[26]

At the end of the scene Toby tells Maria that she has put Malvolio into an intoxicated dream. At one level, however, the audience know that from the scene's opening Malvolio was already drunk, already in a dream. Indeed Maria's trick only works because of Malvolio's existing fantasy.

The entire box tree scene is therefore at one level redundant. It perhaps affects the moment of Malvolio making a fool of himself, but not whether he does so. The purpose of the box tree scene is to provide Sir Toby, Sir Andrew, Fabian and the audience with entertainment; with the satisfaction of seeing the moment when Malvolio gives in to his fantasy.

But is it simply Malvolio's fantasy that is staged at this moment? This is a particularly pertinent question given that the box tree is an image of the Elizabethan theatre. Malvolio is the actor, first in his own fantasy but later in the play written for him by Maria. Sir Toby, Sir Andrew and Fabian are Malvolio's audience and as such represent the real audience on stage. There is, however, something a little odd about the specific characters that Shakespeare chooses to put in the box tree auditorium. Why is Maria not there? Where is Feste? The reason these characters are not included in the on-stage audience at this moment is that the image of the theatre presented in the box tree scene is very specific. It is an image of the theatre as imagined in the works of those Elizabethan and Jacobean writers who criticised the theatre as a home of immorality and disorder.[27] In the box tree scene a steward fantasises about social and sexual advancement while being watched by an audience made up of a dissolute knight, his foolish companion and a servant who clearly has no compunction about taking time out of his working day to watch a fool strutting about on stage. The theatre of the box tree scene is bawdy and comic. Its only real purpose is to provide its audiences, on and off stage, with the pleasure of watching the come-uppance of a fool.

At one level the box tree scene can be seen as Shakespeare's response to his critics. They dismissed his theatre as bawdy, lower class and immoral so he constructs an image of just such a theatre and places one of them, a prig and kill-joy, at its centre. Shakespeare clearly understood perfectly the voyeuristic logic of Elizabethan anti-theatrical writing with its constant gothic incitement of its readers to enjoy the pleasure of being shocked and appalled at, while secretly enjoying, the immorality of its image of the theatre. 'What you will' in this context relates to the suppressed desire of anti-theatre writers, their desire, constantly expressed in their works, for a theatre obsessed with sex and watched by low-lifes, decayed knights and lazy servants.

There is, however, another form of wilful reading that Shakespeare critiques in *Twelfth Night*. Lorna Hutson has pointed out that despite the emphasis in much recent criticism of *Twelfth Night* on the body in practice Shakespeare's play is a relatively chaste version of the various Italian plays that are its sources. Hutson comments that:

> ... a glance at the Italian or Roman models of any comedy by Shakespeare will reveal how consistently he chastened their arguments, displacing deep in his depiction of female 'character' the signs of an inclination towards sexual betrayal that in his originals were explicit sexual acts.[28]

Twelfth Night is a 'chaste' play built on wanton foundations, but one which offers a certain kind of reader, the well-read, learned readers whose business it is to read texts for their hidden sub-texts, writers, censors and critics, the pleasure of working through the play's top-soil in order to evacuate and enjoy its the hidden depths. These readers can 'read' the other texts that make up *Twelfth Night*, not only its Italian sources but also its reference to medical texts, courtly love poetry, etc.[29] Not for these readers the bawdy pleasures of Sir Toby's theatre. They can enjoy Shakespeare's play as a sophisticated, self-knowing reflection on sex, desire and the body. But actually this kind of reading simply ends up in the same place as that of Malvolio. The learned, just as much as the fool and drunk, end up crushing the text in order to make it produce its hidden sexual depths. What you will in this context is the desire for an apparently chaste text that allows its readers to enjoy its cs, us and ts – and the pleasure of supplying its missing ns. It is a text moreover that protects the audience from acknowledging their voyeuristic desire to consume through the production of Malvolio – the perverse scapegoat who embraces his role as the object of the Other's/audience's desire.

In *Twelfth Night* Shakespeare reflects upon the tendency of early modern English culture to resolve or answer social antagonism through the creation of religious scapegoats. Žižek has suggested that one of the basic operations of any ideology is the construction of a point of fantasy that gives consistency to the rest of the symbolic order, for example the figure of the Jew in Nazi discourse or the Communist in 1950s America. Žižek argues, in relation to Nazi Germany, that: "Society is not prevented from achieving its full identity because of Jews: it is prevented by its own antagonistic nature, by its immanent blockage, and it 'projects' this internal negativity into the figure of the 'Jew'."[30]

In *Twelfth Night* it is Malvolio who plays this role. He is the scapegoat exiled at the end of the play as though this will solve the problems and questions that the play raises. This is particularly so given that the play hints that Malvolio is a Puritan. After all Shakespeare's culture was in the process of developing the term Puritan to explain away social and political tension when he was writing *Twelfth Night*. In Malvolio Shakespeare is saying to his audience, 'You want a scapegoat; well, here he is, made to your order, made to satisfy your desire for a closure that is neat, fixed and does not raise any awkward questions.' But will getting rid of Malvolio stop people crushing texts to make them fit their desires? Where does this desire to dominate a text come from, to consume it and make it one's own? Will excluding the Puritan from the stage mean that the theatre is freed from the dictates of its audience? That it no longer needs to give the audience what it wants? What they will?

Twelfth Night is at one level a profoundly perverse text. It offers itself to the audience on the basis of what you will – it will be, or more properly will produce, whatever will meet the audience's desire. The perverse logic of 'what you will' echoes throughout the play and in particular can be associated with the play's central character – Viola. As a boy actor dressed as a girl who assumes a male disguise does she not, like Rosalind, function as an erotic trope open to a range of interpretations? It is significant, however, that in *Twelfth Night* Shakespeare creates a range of characters, including Viola herself, that seek to find a place outside or critical of the audience's desire to consume, figures like Feste and Antonio that do not 'fit' and who, like Viola, ultimately do resist the perverse logic of the play – its desire to be the instrument of the audience's pleasure, to give them what they will.

Feste has been interpreted as representing popular wisdom and carnival humour. There are, however, a number of significant problems with this reading which can be illustrated by looking briefly at the song with which Feste ends the play. Feste's song appears at one level to be an appropriately bawdy conclusion to *Twelfth Night* but only if one approaches it as an extended musical riddle – as if it were a text left by Shakespeare/Maria for audience members to crush until it resembles something in them. In this song Feste reflects on the nature of language and wisdom. For example, the phrase 'For the rain it raineth every day' (Act 5, Sc 1, L 391) appears on first sight to be a simple tautology – what can the rain do but rain? These words can also be read as a statement of the inevitability of fate, of fortune's circular nature. The tension between the formal linguistic qualities of this phrase, that it is based on a tautological statement, and the ideas that it expresses, fortune's or nature's freedom from humanity's control, however, suggests that this song is less a conclusion than a provocation to the audience to think further on the relationship of language to reality. Feste's song creates a proverbial space for thought. Although Feste is credited with the song it would clearly be problematic to view him, even in fictional terms, as the song's author. Feste's song, or perhaps more accurately the song he sings, refers to a world of proverbial learning, exemplified in Shakespeare's time by Erasmus's *Adages*, in which authorship is replaced by the collective production of wisdom. The mistake to make with this song is to see it as representing a carnivalesque, non-courtly, non-textual world, and to therefore see its linguistic complexity as a reflection of the extent to which this carnival world was a magisterial literate fantasy. This reading, however, relies on an anachronistic understanding of the relationship between oral and textual learning in early modern England.[31] Adam Fox has recently commented that:

> One of the fascinating and defining characteristics of English society in the early modern period is the way in which oral, scribal, and printed media fed in and out of each other as part of a dynamic process of reciprocal interaction and mental infusion.[32]

Fox's argument is that in early modern England there was no simple or even meaningful separation between print and speech. In Feste's song Shakespeare ends *Twelfth Night* with a text that resists the simple binary oppositions, law/carnival, learning/wisdom, and instead embodies an image of an interpretative community united in the non-perverse, non-hysterical pursuit of meaning. In particular, like Puck's speech at the end of *A Midsummer Night's Dream*, Feste's song creates a space for the audience to see the radical arbitrariness of language.[33] This in turn creates the possibility, however unlikely this may be, of the audience's investment in the play's status as a commodity being exposed as equally arbitrary and provisional.

Viola's name, viol being the name of a musical instrument and therefore suggestive of harmony, gives a broad hint of the role that Viola is destined to perform in the play. It is, however, noticeable that her initial effect on the world of *Twelfth Night* is to further increase the confusion and disharmony. So in what ways does Viola produce or embody harmony? A key moment in the presentation of Viola's character is at the end of Act 2 Scene 2 when she realises that Olivia has fallen in love with her:

> Viola: As I am man,
> My state is desperate for my master's love:
> As I am woman (now alas the day!)
> What thriftless sighs shall poor Olivia breathe?
> O time, thou must untangle this, not I,
> It is too hard a knot for me t'untie.

Act 2, Sc 2, L 35-40

It is difficult to think of a more different response to the frustration of one's desire than that between Malvolio and Viola. The former seeks to make the world fit his fantasy and when confronted with Maria's letter does not hesitate to crush the text to make it say what he wants (or rather what he thinks the Other/audience wants him to will). There is no sense in which Malvolio is prepared to wait or defer his desire. Viola, however, renounces control over the resolution of her blocked frustrated position. In the process Shakespeare constructs Viola's love as the only true love in the play.[34] Žižek comments that:

> Only a lacking, vulnerable being is capable of love: the ultimate mystery of love, therefore, is that incompleteness is, in a way, higher than completion. On the other hand, only an imperfect, lacking being loves: we love because we do *not* know all.[35]

Shakespeare's drama is full of men who destroy their world in the pursuit of a complete knowledge of the person they love. Viola's acceptance of her lack is, however, not simply a question of resignation. In particular, unlike Orsino and Olivia she resists the temptation to produce a hysterical narrative in order to write over and obscure her incompleteness. Instead she makes the ethical decision to live with her lack. Žižek comments that Lacan's

> ethical injunction not to compromise on one's desire ... in no way condones the suicidal persistence in following one's Thing: on the contrary, it enjoins us to remain faithful to our desire as sustained by the Law of maintaining a minimal distance towards the Thing – one is faithful to one's desire by maintaining the gap which sustains desire, the gap on account of which the incestuous Thing forever eludes the subject's grasp.[36]

Viola maintains this gap by remaining true to her love but placing its achievement in the arbitrary hands of Time. When she tells Orsino that the fate of her love is a blank she performs a genuinely ethical act by sacrificing her desires, but not renouncing them, for the person she loves (Act 2, Sc 4, L 111).[37] The problem, however, for Viola and Shakespeare is that the audience is incapable of such an ethical decision. They, like Orsino, cannot live with lack. Their relationship to *Twelfth Night* as consumers means that they need to see the play as complete and whole – as a commodity that will satisfy their desire. And in the end this pressure leads to the heterosexual closure, with the requisite hint of other erotic possibilities (Orsino's insistence on Viola remaining Cesario until the marriage) that scars all of Shakespeare's late Elizabethan comedies.

Shakespeare confirms the ethical status of Viola's love in the figure of Antonio. The defining characteristic of Antonio in *Twelfth Night* is his friendship with Sebastian. Ironically Antonio's love is most powerfully expressed when he mistakes Viola for Sebastian and thinks that the latter has betrayed their friendship.

> Ant: This youth that you see here
> I snatch'd one half out of the jaws of death,
> Reliev'd him with such sanctity of love;
> And to his image, which methought did promise
> Most venerable worth, did I devotion.
> …
> But O how vile an idol proves this god!
> Thou hast, Sebastian, done good feature shame.
> In nature there's no blemish but the mind
> None can be call'd deform'd but the unkind.
> Virtue is beauty, but the beauteous evil
> Are empty trunks, o'er-flourished by the devil.

Act 3, Sc 4, L 368-79

One of the things being articulated here is Antonio's feeling that he and Sebastian shared a true friendship of the kind placed at the centre of humanist political thought, in particular in Sir Thomas Elyot's *The Governour*. In this text friendship or *amicitia*, which Elyot says can only exist between learned virtuous men, protects those who possess it from tyranny, particularly tyrannous love, and the future's wiles.[38] Elyot's idealised friendship is based on the mutual recognition of virtue. He argues that only good men can be true friends and their virtue can be known by the absolute match between their inner qualities and outward behaviour.

Central to Antonio's attack on Sebastian is that his outward beauty is not matched by his corrupt inner self. What Antonio is articulating in this speech is his anger at his own failure to properly *read* Sebastian, that Sebastian's 'beauteous evil' hid the fact that he was an 'empty trunk'. In theoretical terms Antonio's complaint is that the signifier Sebastian failed to match the signified. This suggests, however, a possibility of a friendship between men in which there is a complete match between sign and meaning, inner self and outward behaviour. Indeed it is significant that Antonio's accusations against Sebastian, at this stage in the play, are entirely unfounded. It is only when Sebastian marries Olivia and in the process accepts playing a role in the fantasy of the Other, Olivia and the audience, that the real betrayal takes place. This suggests that the person Antonio really loves is not Sebastian, but a Sebastian prepared to resist the perverse logic of the play – in other words Sebastian as Viola/Cesario.

Conclusion

The box tree scene in *Twelfth Night* stages concerns about the status of his art that Shakespeare articulated in his other later Elizabethan comedies. Is not Maria's trick a classic example of much ado about nothing? In the box tree scene, however, something quite specific happens to Malvolio's desire. It is not fundamentally altered but it is given a specific spin. He starts the scene fantasising about social and sexual advancement through Olivia. Maria's letter, however, focuses on the latter. Certainly she does exploit Malvolio's desire to be more than a steward but it is Olivia's cs, us and great ps that Maria uses to trap Malvolio. The trap that Maria's trick sets the audience, and indeed literary critics, is to assume that the truth of Malvolio's desire can be produced by simply reversing this process – that Malvolio's social aspirations are a cover for his hopeless sexual desire for Olivia. In the world of *Twelfth Night*, however, barred sexual desires are the norm. What makes Malvolio a potentially radical figure is the extent to which his sexual desires have an explicit social component. It is this which makes him a truly aberrant figure and means he has to be expelled from the stage.[39] Malvolio as a lusty, sex obsessed steward fits easily into the world of 'what you will'. Or rather he does if 'what you will' is kept safely locked in the audience's commodified world in which the scope of will appears to extend no further than the erotic.[40]

Similar issues are raised in *Much Ado About Nothing* where it is the

Watch who prevent tragedy. Why is this? What do the Watch have that the other characters do not? Certainly they are no wiser. Indeed they 'understand' the truth of Don John's plot without even knowing all its details. What they reflect is a commitment to the solution of sexual and poetic problems in the social field. In other words the Watch embody a set of nothings, social solidarity, popular wisdom and justice, that can prevent the tragedy which the personal sexualised nothings of their betters come close to producing.

Andrew Hadfield has commented on the way in which Shakespeare criticism has turned its back on the explicitly political in favour of an emphasis on questions relating to identity and selfhood.[41] *Twelfth Night* reflects the danger of this move since the politics of this play are precisely located at the intersection between self, desire and the social. All the time the critical gaze is fixed on issues relating to Malvolio's sense of self or the erotics of the play it cannot see the politics of *Twelfth Night* which amount to a compete rejection of the binary opposition law/carnival and an insistence on an image of friendship that in its material textual practice seeks to imagine and create a space resistant to Petrarchan tyranny and carnival excess.[42] Viola's love, Feste's wisdom and Antonio's friendship are all aspects of Shakespeare's Erasmian commitment to the communal production of proverbial wisdom; reducing them to figures representing the erotic possibilities of cross-dressing, a fantasy 'folkish' world or an apolitical homoeroticism strips *Twelfth Night* of its politics and locates it firmly within the perverse hysterical world of Orsino, Olivia and Malvolio.

Notes

1   Brian Nical, 'As If: Traversing the Fantasy in Žižek', *Paragraph*, 24 (2001), pp.140–55, p.147.
2   Valerie Traub, 'Desire and the Differences It Makes', in *The Matter of Difference: Materialist Feminist Criticism of Shakespeare*, ed. Valerie Wayne (Hemel Hempstead: 1991), pp.81–114, p.104.
3   This distinction is important since, as I will argue in the next chapter, it is Brutus's failure to distinguish between Caesar as a metonym for Rome's greatness and as a metaphor that ultimately leads to Caesar's death.
4   Slavoj Žižek, *The Plague of Fantasies* (London: 1997), p.7.
5   Ibid., p.9.
6   Ibid., p.10.

7   It is important to note that many of the stories produced by Rosalind's detour exist only as possibilities – the most obvious being the story of Orlando's and Ganymede's love.

8   Commenting on the emergence of the iambic pentameter as a dominant and authoritative form in English poetry during the sixteenth century Anthony Easthope suggests that: "Pentameter can be seen as a mechanism by which the poem aims to deny its production as a poem, a mechanism therefore [that] promotes commodity fetishism." In these terms one could see texts like Puck's speech as attempts to run the mechanism backwards – to show to the audience what their poetry as a commodity is made of. Anthony Easthope, *Poetry as Discourse* (London: 1983), p.67.

9   Slavoj Žižek comments that it is possible to see clearly the extent to which fantasy is on the side of reality in those moments when "the subject undergoes a 'loss of reality' and starts to perceive reality as an 'irreal' nightmarish universe with no firm ontological foundation; this nightmarish universe is not 'pure fantasy' but, on the contrary, *that which remains of reality after reality is deprived of its support in fantasy*'. Žižek, 1997, p.66.

10 The nothing of the audience's desire to consume can be read in Lacanian terms as the symptom of Shakespeare's drama. Žižek comments that: "This, then, is a symptom: a particular, 'pathological', signifying formation, a binding of enjoyment, an inert stain resisting communication and interpretation, a stain which cannot be included in the circuit of discourse, of social bond network, but is at the same time a positive condition of it." Slavoj Žižek, *The Sublime Object of Ideology* (London: 1989), p.75.

11 Slavoj Žižek, *Enjoy Your Symptom! Jacques Lacan in Hollywood and Out* (New York: 1992), p.89.

12 Jean Howard, *The Stage and Social Struggle in Early Modern England* (London: 1994), p. 60/1.

13 Carol Cook comments that: "[*Much Ado About Nothing's*] explicit representation of masculine fantasy and delusion trades on, and partakes of, the process it explores. Or should we say it exposes the process it trades on? The mode of representation that makes possible the play's main plot – a mode in which women are ciphers – is implicated in that plot, obliquely revealing the underlying sexual values and assumptions that motivate the unfolding of the drama." Carol Cook, '"The Sign and Semblance of Her Honour": Reading Gender Difference in *Much Ado About Nothing*', in *Shakespeare and Gender: A History*, ed. Deborah Barker and Ivo Kamps (London: 1995), pp. 75-103, p.100.

14 Slavoj Žižek, *The Metastases of Enjoyment: Six Essays on Woman and Causality* (London: 1994), p.94.

15 Renata Salecl, *(Per)Versions of Love and Hate* (London: 1998), p.17.

16 Žižek, 1997, p.18.

17 Žižek comments that 'the moment we subtract from a discursive field its "distortion," the field disintegrates ("dequilts")'. The disintegration of the language of love at this moment in *As You Like It* is marked by the emergence of the tension between the formal harmony of this moment and Rosalind's claim that it is as meaningful as the howling of Irish wolves. The distortion that is disintegrating is the idea of erotic play as transgressive. Žižek, 1992, p.103.

18 See Garrett Sullivan and Linda Woodbridge, 'Popular Culture in Print', in *English Literature 1500-1600*, ed Arthur F. Kinney (Cambridge: 2000), pp.265–86, p.274.

19 *A Hundred Merry Tales*, 1526 (London: 1887), c.ii.

20 One is reminded of Luce Irigaray's critique of the idea of women as commodities. Irigaray asks: "… without the exploitation of women, what would become of the social order? What modifications would it undergo if women left behind their condition as commodities – subject to being produced, consumed, valorised, circulated, and so on, by men alone – and took part in elaborating and carrying out exchanges? Not by reproducing, by copying, the 'phallocentric' models that have the force of law today, but by socializing in a different way the relation to nature, matter, the body, language and desire." Luce Irigaray, *This Sex Which Is Not One*, trans. Catherine Porter (Ithaca, NY: 1985), p.191.

21 On the differences between the hysteric and the pervert see Žižek, 1997, pp.32–5.

22 Ibid., p.32.

23 Orsino's behaviour is classically hysterical. Žižek comments that: "… the hysteric perceives himself as a neutral observer, a victim of unfortunate circumstances that are independent of his will – what he cannot accept is the fact that the circumstances whose victim he is can reproduce themselves only through his active participation." See Žižek, 1994, p.177/8.

24 Paul Yachnin suggests that: "Malvolio … is an embodiment of the self-interest and instrumentality of the players' 'service' to the nobility." In these terms one can see that Malvolio's perversity, his desire to be an instrument of the Other's enjoyment, relates directly to the status of the actors, and playwrights, in Shakespeare's theatre, and their instrumental service of the audience's desire to consume – to buy plays, actors and acting. See Paul Yachnin, 'Reversal of Fortune: Shakespeare, Middleton and the Puritans', *English Literary History*, 70 (2003), pp.757–86, p.758 and p. 781.

25 M. Keith Booker has argued that carnival in *Twelfth Night* leads to a destabilisation of gender roles and of monological discourse. I would, however, argue that the logic of the box tree scene is that carnival produces monological discourse: what Malvolio attempts to do to Maria's trick is reduce it to a monologue, in other words to turn carnival into the law. See M. Keith Booker, '"Nothing That Is So Is So": Dialogic Discourse and the Voice of the Woman in *The Clerk's Tale* and *Twelfth Night*', *Exemplaria*, 3 (1991), pp. 519–37.

26 Žižek comments that "the pervert's dream is to transform sexual activity into an instrumental purpose-orientated activity that can be projected and executed to a well-defined plan". Malvolio's perversion is such that not only does he want to reduce his erotic desire for Olivia to a plan but he is eager to allow Maria/Olivia to do the planning for him. See Slavoj Žižek, *The Ticklish Subject: The Absent Centre of Political Ontology* (London: 1999), p.322.

27 For how Shakespeare's theatre and in particular his audience were depicted in the antitheatrical writing of the period see Andrew Gurr, *Playgoing in Shakespeare's London* (Cambridge: 1987).

28 Lorna Hutson, 'On Not Being Deceived: Rhetoric and the Body in *Twelfth Night*', *Texas Studies in Literature and Language*, 38 (1996), pp. 140–74, p.151.

29 Malvolio's fall is profoundly textual and reflects the issues that Carla Mazzio discusses in the article, 'The Melancholy of Print: *Love's Labour's Lost*'. In this piece Mazzio comments that: "… it might be said that in representations of lovesickness in sixteenth-century England, the 'melancholic ego' is itself conditioned by the 'bibliographic ego' as lovers and texts entwine in a discourse that conflates love melancholy with the conspicuous proliferation of text in the social world". It is noticeable that Malvolio's desire to crush Maria's text also leads to the production of another text, the one he has

crushed. See Carla Mazzio, 'The Melancholy of Print: *Love's Labour's Lost*', in *Historicism, Psychoanalysis, and Early Modern Culture*, ed. Carla Mazzio and Douglas Trevor (New York: 2000), pp.186–227, p.189.

30 Žižek, 1989, p.127.

31 For a discussion of popular literature in early modern England see Sullivan and Woodbridge, 2000, pp.265–86, p.274.

32 Adam Fox, *Oral and Literate Culture in England 1500–1700* (Oxford: 2000), p.410.

33 Žižek comments that: "From a Lacanian perspective, the object as real is then, in the last resort, just a certain limit: we can *overtake* it, leave it behind us, but we cannot *reach* it." Feste's song, like Puck's speech at the end of *A Midsummer Night's Dream*, emphasises and performs the arbitrariness of the relationship between form and content. In other words these are moments when Shakespeare articulates the limit of language as real. Slavoj Žižek, 'The Object as a Limit of Discourse: Approaches to the Lacanian Real', *Prose Studies*, 11 (1988), pp.94–120, p.110.

34 Stephen Greenblatt comments that: "No one but Viola gets quite what she or he consciously sets out to get in the play, and Viola gets what she wants only because she is willing to submit herself to the very principle of deflection: 'I am not that I play' (Act 1, Sc 5, L 184). She embraces a strategy that the play suggests is not simply an accident of circumstance but an essential life-truth: you reach a desire or at least desirable destination not by pursuing a straight line but by following a curved path." Stephen Greenblatt, *Shakespearean Negotiations: The Circulation of Social Energy in Renaissance England* (Oxford: 1988), p.70/1.

35 Slavoj Žižek, *The Puppet and the Dwarf: The Perverse Core of Christianity* (Cambridge, MA: 2003), p.115.

36 Žižek, 1997, p.239.

37 Viola's love as a blank can be related to Renata Salecl's suggestion that "Love addresses that point in speech where the word fails". Renata Salecl, 'I Can't Love You Unless I Give You Up', in *Gaze and Voice as Love Objects*, ed. Renata Salecl and Slavoj Žižek (Durham, NC: 1996), pp.179–207, p.192.

38 For a discussion of the politics of friendship in *The Governour* see Tom Betteridge, *Literature and Politics in the English Reformation* (Manchester: 2004), Ch. 1.

39 Edward Cahill argues that Malvolio's "true revenge … is his refusal to allow the main plot to be completely resolved before the end of the play". I would argue, however, that this refusal is Malvolio's last gift to the audience since it leaves open, and therefore available for interpretation, the relationship between his sexual and social desires – in other words Malvolio leaves the stage but his parting words construct his desire as an ongoing object for the audience to interpret and consume that does not threaten their voyeuristic investment in the play. See Edward Cahill, 'The Problem of Malvolio', *College Literature*, 23 (1996), pp. 62–82, p.77.

40 Cristina Malcolmson comments that *Twelfth Night* "transfers anxieties about fluid social relations onto gender relations, and solves the problem through its ideal of marriage". This is undoubtedly the case but the reason that there is a problem is the desire of the audience for closure which in turn means that social problems have to be displaced. See Cristina Malcolmson, '"What You Will": Social Mobility and Gender in *Twelfth Night*', in *The Matter of Difference: Materialist Feminist Criticism of Shakespeare*, ed. Valerie Wayne (Hemel Hempstead: 1991), pp.29–57, p.31.

41 Andrew Hadfield, 'Shakespeare and Republicanism: History and Cultural Materialism', *Textual Practice*, 17 (2003), pp. 461–84.

42 For the politics of homoerotic friendship, and in particular its use as a weapon to resist tyranny, see the discussion of the correspondence between the Protestant martyrs, John Careless and John Philpot, written while in prison waiting to be burnt to death for their beliefs in Tom Betteridge, 'The Place of Sodomy in the Historical Writings of John Bale and John Foxe', in *Sodomy in Early Modern Europe*, ed. Tom Betteridge (Manchester: 2012), pp. 11–26.

CHAPTER THREE

Hegemonic struggle: Julius Caesar *and* Coriolanus

When we think, we win. When we emote, they win.
Ex-President Bill Clinton on the Democrats' election prospects,
quoted in the *Observer*, 7 March 2004

SHAKESPEARE'S ROME IS intensely political. From the death of republican Rome in *Julius Caesar* to its birth in *Coriolanus* Shakespeare uses Roman history as a laboratory for staging political ideas. What remains constant in all of Shakespeare's Roman plays, however, is the crises of legitimation that drive Rome's politics. It is these crises that fracture Roman society and the individuals who constitute it. Shakespeare's Rome, at all levels – individual, language and society, is marked by crises of legitimation that can only be solved by either the creation of enabling political spaces or a tyrannical closure of the space of politics. Crisis is the norm of the Roman politics in *Julius Caesar* and *Coriolanus* – in the former it causes betrayal and violence and in the latter it is the basis for the articulation of a republican ideal.[1]

The idea of legitimation crisis was developed by the German philosopher Jürgen Habermas as part of his project to sustain the validity of modernist narratives of enlightenment and liberation. For Habermas, stressing the extent to which political orders require constant legitimation is an essential component in any social democratic critique. He writes that, "*Legitimacy means a political order's worthiness to be recognized. This definition highlights the fact that legitimacy is a contestable validity claim ...*".[2] What Habermas is arguing here is that political orders have to secure recognition as legitimate through continuous public argument; they have to constantly assert their legitimacy in a way that secures a minimum acceptance of their validity by the populace. This creates the possibility or space for contestation and critique. It means that no political order, no matter how secure and natural it appears, can ever dispense with the need to continuously and publicly assert its legitimacy.

Habermas stresses in his work that *all* political orders need legitimation. In particular, he rejects the idea that crises of legitimation only affect modern political orders.[3] Habermas argues that class conflict is the fundamental cause of the deficit of legitimation of all political orders – existing and historical.[4] The basic aim of all legitimating ideologies is to remove as far as possible from the public sphere the social antagonism arising from the unequal distribution of wealth, power and authority within society.[5] In other words all the political orders that have so far existed have ultimately been illegitimate because they have been based upon an unequal, oppressive distribution of wealth, power and authority between classes. Working to remove this fundamental issue from public debate, typically by obscuring it so that its effects within society are misrecognised, is the basic aim of all legitimating ideologies.[6] It is important to note, however, that the need for legitimation reflects the extent to which all legitimating ideologies fail. It is the impossibility of producing a fully legitimate class based political order that produces the need for legitimation. Indeed the ideal of a political sphere that is fully and finally legitimate is a fantasy and one which has serious consequences since ultimately it embodies a desire to close down the space of the political.[7] Brutus and Coriolanus fight and die for a Rome in which the political order is fully and totally legitimate. Their political credos are therefore, at one level, self-defeating. Brutus and Coriolanus are committed to a political negation of politics – they desire a fully transparent legitimate political order and in the process destroy the very ground for their own beliefs.

In Shakespeare's Rome politics, the crisis of legitimation, takes many forms. In *Julius Caesar* the issue for Brutus and Cassius is not the legitimation of the existing political order as such, so much as its inability to cope with Caesar and the political possibilities that he represents. In effect they kill Caesar as part of a conservative attempt to retain the existing political structures. In the process, however, they ironically create precisely the situation that they feared. Brutus and Cassius act to prevent the closure of the political sphere that they fear would be produced by Caesar taking the crown. In the process, however, they not only cause a crisis of legitimation but also the conditions for its resolution in the politics of empire – in precisely the kind of closure that they acted to prevent. In some ways the political conflict in the Rome of *Coriolanus* is a less complex matter than it is in *Julius Caesar*. The issue in *Coriolanus* is the ability of the existing political order to create and sustain an effective community – one capable of maintaining itself against internal and external enemies and threats. In both plays, however, politics is played out around issues of recognition and misrecognition that relate directly to the political legitimacy of Shakespeare's theatre. *Julius Caesar* stages the events that led to the collapse of the Roman republic. In the process it depicts a moment when key figures in Rome no longer trust the existing political order. The result of this is, however, not the emergence of a new legitimate political order but the collapse of the public sphere and the evaporation of political ethics. It is Antony's theatricalisation of politics that produces this closure of the Roman public sphere. In *Coriolanus*, however, a crisis of legitimation produces resolution and the creation of an inherently ethical and theatrical politics.[8]

This chapter is in three parts. The first section looks in detail at Shakespeare's depiction of political struggle in the Rome of *Julius Caesar*. In particular, it examines the struggle for hegemony as waged between Caesar, Antony, Brutus and Cassius in this play. The middle section of this chapter discusses the political ethics of *Julius Caesar*. The final section of this chapter turns to *Coriolanus* and the way in which this play imagines an ethical political order.

Ghosts, politics and hegemony in Julius Caesar

Towards the close of *Julius Caesar* Brutus is visited by a phantom, the Ghost of Caesar. This is a strange, spectral moment. Up to this point in the play Brutus has been presented as a man of reason and logic. Indeed the ghostly presence that visits him in Act 4 Scene 2 seems to have come from another play. Despite appearing in the full view of the audience, and being introduced in a stage direction as 'the Ghost of Caesar', its status is unclear. The few words it speaks to Brutus are opaque in the extreme:

> Bru: Speak to me what thou art.
> Ghost: Thy evil spirit, Brutus.
> Bru: Why com'st thou?
> Ghost: To tell thee thou shalt see me at Philippi.
> Bru: Well; then I shall see thee again?
> Ghost: Ay, at Philippi.
> Bru: Why, I will see thee at Philippi then. *[Exit Ghost]*
> Now I have taken heart thou vanishest.

Act 4, Sc 3, L 279–85

If this phantom is the ghost of the murdered Caesar then it is strange that it claims to be Brutus's 'evil spirit'. But then it is not Caesar's ghost. It is the ghost *of* Caesar – what is left after Caesar himself has gone. But why does it disappear the moment that Brutus 'takes heart'? The prosaic reason is that the Ghost extracts a promise from Brutus that he will see it again at Philippi. If the ghost is Brutus's evil spirit, and its appearance can be related to him losing heart, then what Brutus is promising here is to see his own evil and fear during the battle that will be fought at Philippi. Its is almost as though Brutus is accepting in advance that he will be defeated by those seeking to avenge Caesar's murder. Marjorie Garber comments that "Caesar is more powerful in his absence than his presence".[9] In person Caesar was powerless to defend himself against Brutus's sword but as a ghost it seems he can ensure the defeat not only of Brutus but also of all the other people who took part in his murder.

But is the phantom that appears before Brutus Caesar's ghost? Shakespeare goes out of his way to raise doubts about this. In particular, Brutus himself seems unclear what it is that materialises before him:

> Bru: How ill this taper burns! Ha! Who comes here?
> I think it is the weakness of mine eyes
> That shapes this monstrous apparition.
> It comes upon me. Art thou any thing?
> Art thou some god, some angel, or some devil,
> That mak'st my blood cold, and my hair to stare?

Act 4, Sc 3, L 273–8

There is a tension in this moment that is completely lacking in the similar scene in *Richard III*. There the appearance of the Ghosts on the eve of

Richard's defeat is unambiguous to everyone involved, the characters on stage, the Ghosts themselves and the audience. The meeting between Brutus and the Ghost of Caesar is far more spectral. Does the spirit really appear at all? Or is it simply a trick of the eye? Brutus banishes the Ghost by promising to see it at Philippi but is this believable? Can one trust Brutus's word? After all he initially thought the Ghost was a trick of the light, a failure of his eyesight. Brutus promises to see the Ghost of Caesar, his 'evil spirit', at Philippi. And in a sense he will, since the whole tragedy of *Julius Caesar* is a drama of misrecognition, Brutus's above all. He fails to recognise the reality of the events leading up to Caesar's death. It is Brutus's political vision that fails before and after the assassination. And it is the failure of his foresight that in the end leads to his death and those of his comrades. Brutus cannot see the reality of the political crisis threatening Rome at the opening of the play and it is this failure that leads to the collapse of the republic. *Julius Caesar* depicts the assassination of republican Rome and the chief assassin is Brutus himself.

Brutus's attempt to restore order once the Ghost has exited is undermined by Lucius's words, spoken in a dream, "The strings, my lord, are false." It is in the space created by Lucius's sleep that the phantom appears. What is the significance of Lucius's words? He had been playing the lute when he fell asleep and is dreaming that he is still at his instrument. This creates a parallel between the ghost that Brutus sees and Lucius's dream playing. Dreaming and seeing, false strings and ambiguous ghosts, this is the world that Brutus has created by murdering Caesar – a spectral world of misrecognition, of hollowed-out meaning and discordant notes. To understand how Brutus, the man of reason, ended up in this irrational fantastical state it is necessary to return to the opening of the play and discuss its depiction of Roman politics.

Julius Caesar opens with the tribune, Flavius, ordering the Plebeians to stop celebrating Caesar's defeat of Pompey:

> Flav: Hence! Home, you idle creatures, get you home!
> Is this a holiday? What, know you not,
> (Being mechanical) you ought not walk
> Upon a labouring day, without the sign
> Of your profession?

Act 1, Sc 1, L 1–5

Flavius's words are directed to 'certain commoners' but one cannot help but think that they would also have been applicable to many of Shakespeare's original audience.[10] Indeed no one in the Globe when *Julius Caesar* was first performed, apart from the actors themselves, was labouring. At one level being a member of an audience is to be on holiday – or rather this is one model of audiencehood. One *can* labour when watching a play. Bertolt Brecht argued that good drama should force an audience to work. In particular, Brecht's politics led him to attack what he viewed as the passivity of traditional theatre audiences which he argued:

> … look at the stage as if in a trance: an expression which comes from the Middle Ages, the days of witches and priests. Seeing and hearing are activities, and can be pleasant ones, but these people seem relieved of activity and like men to whom something is being done.[11]

Flavius's concern at the opening of *Julius Caesar* is a political version of Brecht's critique of the state of the audience in traditional theatre. The tribune demands the Plebeians return to their labour because he is worried that they are allowing themselves, in their holiday mood, to become people to whom things are done. Flavius is worried that Plebeians free from labour will be easier to manipulate by Caesar and his followers – that, like Brecht's traditional audience, they will be rendered passive by the consolatory dramas of their masters.

Flavius's concerns are made explicit in the exchange between him and his colleague, Marullus, after the Plebeians have left the stage:

> Flav: Disrobe the images,
> If you do find them deck'd with ceremonies.
> Mar: May we do so?
> You know that it is the feast of Lupercal.
> Flav: It is no matter. Let no images
> Be hung with Caesar's trophies. I'll about
> And drive away the vulgar from the streets;
> So do you too, where you perceive them thick.
> These growing feathers pluck'd from Caesar's wing
> Will make him fly an ordinary pitch,
> Who else would soar above the view of men
> And keep us all in servile fearfulness.

Act 1, Sc 1, L 65–76

Flavius's political credo is dominated by two ideas. Firstly he is committed to the maintenance of the existing political and social order. It is this which makes him insist that the Plebeians wear the signs of their trades. Flavius is convinced that Caesar intends to change the political order, that he has the power to do so, and that the Plebeians are so stupid, so easily seduced by a few cheap theatrical tricks and robed images, that they will feather Caesar's ambition – they will give him the wings to fly beyond the scope of existing Roman politics. This fear illustrates the second central element of Flavius's politics, which is a lack of confidence in the Plebeians. He does not trust the people he is meant to represent. Flavius, like Brecht, looks out over his audience and sees 'idle creatures', people entranced by the performance put on by the powers that be – or in Caesar's case the powers that will be.

This lack of confidence is shared by a number of other characters, and in particular Brutus, Cassius and their fellow conspirators. Shakespeare, however, goes out of his way to depict the Plebeians as a relatively sophisticated active audience. When presented with Antony's king-making drama they participate in his show but at the same time effectively prevent Caesar from becoming king. This event, as reported by Casca, has an almost pantomime feel to it as Caesar and Antony play a game of 'will he won't he' with the crowd. Casca tells Brutus and Cassius that:

> Casca: I saw Mark Antony offer [Caesar] a crown – yet 'twas not a
> crown neither, 'twas one of these coronets – and … he put it by
> once; but for all that, to my thinking, he would fain have had it.
> Then he offered it to him again; then he put it by again; but to my
> thinking, he was very loath to lay his fingers off it. And then he
> offered it the third time by; he put it the third time by; and still as
> he refus'd it, the rabblement hooted, and clapped their chopped
> hands, and threw up their sweaty nightcaps, and uttered such a deal
> of stinking breath because Caesar refused the crown …
>
> Act 1, Sc 2, L 235-45

Casca goes on to give Caesar's performance a specifically theatrical gloss when he assures Brutus and Cassius:

> Casca: If the tag-rag people did not clap him and hiss him, according as he pleas'd and displeas'd them, as they use to do the players
> in the theatre, I am no true man.
>
> Act 1, Sc 2, L 257–60

Political power in Casca's version of Caesar's refusal of the crown is a matter of theatrical performance with Caesar as the central actor milking the applause of his audience. Richard Wilson comments that "Caesar turns politics into theatre".[12] But is it Caesar who turns politics into theatre or Casca? Who introduces the theatrical into what appears on the surface to be a clearly political event? Indeed are not politics always at one level theatrical? What Casca's account constantly pushes towards is an emphasis on the theatricality of this moment as a dangerous evaporation of its political implications. But in fact it is within the report given by Casca that a division is produced between politics and the theatre – or at least between reasoned politics and a reductive view of the theatre as a place of deception and manipulation.

Casca claims that the Plebeians used Caesar like an actor. The implication of this is that he was in their power or at least dependent on their approval. Casca's version of Caesar's rejection of the crown is predicated upon the Plebeians' passivity as the audience to Antony's and Caesar's act which his own account undermines since the Plebeians, unlike the audience in Brecht's traditional theatre, are far from passive. They are active and indeed empowered participants in a moment of political drama. Certainly the show they witness is written and performed by others but its outcome – even in Casca's version – is within their control. Casca, almost despite himself, shows that Caesar will not or cannot take the crown in the face of popular disapproval.

The opening of *Julius Caesar* depicts a Rome in which the status of the political is itself a source of conflict. When Flavius insists on the removal of trophies from Caesar's images and Casca creates a basic conflict between politics and theatre what is being expressed is a lack of confidence in politics and a fear that the political sphere is becoming tainted by the power of the theatre. The ideology that sustains Flavius's and Casca's political credo, which is shared by all the conspirators, and Brutus in particular, is ultimately a form of anti-politics. This is because what drives Flavius and Casca is a desire to close down the political sphere – to place certain possibilities, specifically the idea of Caesar as emperor, beyond public debate. Ironically, but inevitably, this attempt in itself has the opposite effect by making the emergence of the emperors far more likely. Shakespeare is absolutely explicit about this. He creates a direct relationship between Brutus's political credo, his lack of confidence in the people, theatre and politics, indeed his suspicion of anyone or any event that brings these three elements into conjunction, with the emergence of tyranny.

To understand the sophistication of Shakespeare's political thinking in *Julius Caesar* it is useful to place it within a theoretical perspective. Ernesto Laclau has discussed in detail the importance of empty signifiers to political debate. Laclau argues that: "Politics is possible because the constitutive impossibility of society can only represent itself through the production of empty signifiers."[13] Laclau's argument here is complex. It is based upon the idea that all societies are defined by limits that are at once marginal and fundamental, peripheral and central. In *Hegemony and Socialist Strategy: Towards a Radical Democratic Politics* Laclau and Chantal Mouffe argued that "Society never manages fully to be society, because everything in it is penetrated by its limits, which prevent it from constituting itself as an objective reality."[14] What defines a society, gives it form and meaning, is a set of limits that are at once external and internal – placed beyond society and an integral antagonistic part of its totality. In the final instance no society in which wealth and power are unequally distributed can be complete and whole since in the last instance, and in all its instances, it is defined by injustice and oppression. Laclau argues that empty signifiers allow the playing out of the tensions created by the fundamental constitutive failure of society. They create the possibility for the public testing of a society's limits through hegemonic struggle. Empty signifiers are privileged terms, citizen, people, nation, justice, whose lack of fixity in terms of meaning is the prerequisite for political debate – indeed for the existence of a political sphere. Laclau's argument is ultimately based on the necessary non-closure of the political sphere.

In *Julius Caesar* Laclau's empty signifier is the word Rome itself. The dispute between Caesar and his opponents is over the meaning of this word. Does being Roman mean one is a republican? Or is it possible to stay true to the spirit of Rome and support other political arrangements? It is a mistake, however, to talk as if there is a political dispute between Brutus, Cassius and Caesar since these characters never have a real political discussion – and certainly not of the kind that constantly take place in *Coriolanus*. This is primarily because politics in the Rome of *Julius Caesar* is depicted as a conflict between individuals. The dispute, if indeed there really is one, between Brutus, Cassius and Caesar is presented by Shakespeare as matter of identity and selfhood. The problem with Caesar is that his sense of self is such that it embodies a totalising fantasy in which the great leader becomes one with the commonwealth – in which the metaphor of the body politic becomes literal. This literalisation is clearly what Cassius fears. He tells Brutus that:

> Cas: ... [Caesar] doth bestride the narrow world
> Like a colossus, and we petty men
> Walk under his huge legs and peep about
> To find ourselves dishonourable graves.

Act 1, Sc 2, L 134–7

Ironically Caesar seems to share this fantasy. He constantly refers to himself in the third person as if he lacks any private sense of self. Immediately before the assassination Caesar claims: "I am as constant as the northern star" (Act 3, Sc 1, L 60). He goes on to argue that he alone of all men is always the same, never changing, fixed and permanent. Of course, this is nonsense. And Shakespeare goes out of his way to show to the audience that far from being constant Caesar is in a constant state of flux (as are all men) – most obviously in terms of whether or not to go to the Senate. What Cassius fears, and what Caesar aspires to, is the closure of the political system with the fixing or filling of the empty signifier Rome with Caesar.

Putting Cassius's fears and Caesar's desires in these terms, however, reveals that they are groundless. Indeed they are based on a category mistake – Caesar the man cannot become Rome the concept. The whole tragedy of *Julius Caesar* is driven at one level by Cassius's confusion of metaphor with metonym. The difference between these terms can seem very small but in *Julius Caesar* it produces violence and ultimately tyranny. Metaphors are based on the creation of likeness between different objects or people while in metonym the relationship is one of substitution. In classical rhetoric the distinction between metaphor and metonym was understood in terms of analogy versus contiguity – while metonyms are based upon a spatial logic that announces their contingent partial status metaphors depend on a process of analogy in which the metaphoric term becomes that which it signifies. The tension between these two terms is a key element in Laclau's political theory. He writes that:

> ... all hegemony tries to re-totalize and to make as necessary as possible the contingent links on which its articulating power is based. In this sense,

it tends to metaphorical totalization. This is what gives it its dimension of power. It is a power, however, which maintains the traces of its contingency and is, in that sense, essentially metonymic.[15]

This is a complicated idea partly because the distinction between metaphor and metonym in the field of politics, as Laclau himself points out, is unstable. In *Julius Caesar* what Shakespeare dramatises is a political conflict over the idea of Rome in which both Caesar and Cassius attempt to produce metaphoric closure. In Caesar's case this is self-evident in his attempts to collapse the idea of Roman greatness into himself so that he becomes one with it. This is a classic political move and is based on the substitution of a metonymic relationship – Caesar stands for Rome's greatness – with a metaphoric one – Caesar's greatness and Rome's become one. Shakespeare, however, stresses the extent to which the attempt to totalise the metaphoric relationship between Caesar and Rome is entirely political, in other words that it is open to public debate and dispute. Even Caesar and his allies, particularly Antony, seem aware that what they are engaged in is a piece of political theatre which, while it seeks to fill the empty signifier Rome with meaning, knows that such an operation can never be complete or final.

Ironically the people who take this possibility most seriously, and therefore make what they fear a reality, are Cassius, Brutus and their fellows. Why is this? Why do the conspirators see public acts of political theatre, in which Shakespeare goes out of his way to emphasise the audience's active role, as harbingers of tyranny? What is it about the theatricality of politics in the Rome of *Julius Caesar* that produces such anxiety in Brutus and Cassius?

Shakespeare's Rome is a heterogeneous place in which political struggle takes place at a number of different levels. Given this, even the most skilled politician in normal circumstances could not achieve a full or total victory. Indeed men like Antony know this and therefore base their politics on the need for negotiation and debate. Hegemonic struggle is a fact of life in Rome. Yet this is precisely what Cassius and Brutus cannot or will not allow. They desire to win once and for all in the field of politics. In Cassius's case this can be related, as has been suggested, to a fundamental mistake over the nature of Caesar's political agenda. Cassius thinks, probably rightly, Caesar aspires to become emperor and, because he mistakes a metonym for a metaphor, assumes that the only way of combating Caesar's ambition is to kill him. Cassius seeks to produce metaphoric closure by killing Caesar, to prevent for ever the collapse of Caesar's greatness with Rome's, and instead makes it a political reality. The situation with Brutus is slightly different. It is also more crucial to the politics of *Julius Caesar* since, as Cassius himself constantly makes clear, without Brutus's involvement the conspiracy would be powerless. Ironically Cassius places Brutus in relation to the conspiracy against Caesar in exactly the same relationship as he fears Caesar aspires to in relation to Rome. It is Brutus, and he alone, who can give the conspiracy form and consistency. He is the one person who can bring it into being – make it real. Cassius makes Brutus into the conspiracy – into a totalising metaphor for the plot to murder Caesar.

Brutus shares Cassius's interpretative failings. He consistently articulates an anxiety about any form of language that is not, in his terms, plain or transparent. Like Cassius, Brutus cannot recognise the difference between metaphor and metonym in the field of politics. His justification for Caesar's murder is based upon a grotesque hermeneutic inversion. Brutus argues that the only way to break the metaphoric relationship between Rome and Caesar is to kill the man and therefore destroy the metaphor:

> Bru: Let's be sacrificers, but not butchers, Caius.
> We all stand up against the spirit of Caesar,
> And in the spirit of men there is no blood.
> O that we then could come by Caesar's spirit,
> And not dismember Caesar! But, alas,
> Caesar must bleed for it.

> Act 2, Sc 1, L 165–70

The spirit of Caesar is his ambition, his desire to take over, indeed take in, Rome. Brutus wishes to kill the possibility of Caesarean tyranny and the only way he can imagine doing so is killing the man himself – he kills the body that allowed a metonymic relationship to exist between Rome and Caesar and in the process frees the totalising potential of the metaphor from its metonymic brake – Caesar's body.

Brutus's failure of political interpretation is a product of his anxiety over language and in particular any hiatus between word and meaning, word and voice, word and act. When Brutus is confronted with the need to decide whether or not to take part in the conspiracy against Caesar his response is to meditate on the gap between thought and action:

> Bru: Between the acting of a dreadful thing
> And the first motion, all the interim is
> Like a phantasma or a hideous dream:
> The genius and mortal instruments
> Are then in council; and the state of man,
> Like to a little kingdom, suffers then
> The nature of an insurrection.

Act 2, Sc 1, L 63–9

Phantasma in this speech means both vision and spectre. It cuts across the metaphor of the body politic that sustains the second half of this passage. At the level of the individual the gap between thought and action takes spectral form – embodying the moment of hesitation before the act. In terms of the body politic, as far as Brutus is concerned, for it to be caught in a state of hiatus, of debate and struggle over its future course, is akin to it being racked by insurrection. But why should this be the case? Surely there is nothing wrong with a body politic being 'in council'. This speech reflects the extent to which Brutus views the normal state of Roman, and indeed early modern English, politics as an aberration, a constant unruly state of emergency in which different aspects of the body politic struggle to have their voices heard in council.[16]

It is in order to put an end to this insurrection that Brutus acts. Ironically he does so in order to prevent Caesar from making the same decision. Indeed, while Shakespeare only allows us to hear through Casca an account of Caesar's failure to act, he forces us to watch in detail the bloody and violent results of Brutus's action. Clearly at one level *Julius Caesar* is a play in favour of insurrection. It is a play that illustrates the dangers of a political credo that, like Brutus's, sees normal political struggle through a lens distorted by an anti-theatrical prejudice as intolerable. Brutus acts to defend what he regards as the truth of Roman politics and in the process produces precisely the phantasma he sought to banish – tyranny produced through the theatricalisation of politics.

Caesar's funeral

It is perhaps not surprising that it is only after Caesar's death that the real cost of Brutus's anti-politics and Cassius's hermeneutic mistake become apparent. The form that the post-Caesar politics takes is, however, more of a surprise. The problem with *Julius Caesar* as a play is that when Caesar was alive there was no real danger of tyranny since at the crucial theatrical moment when the crown was offered to him the people encouraged him to reject it. With Caesar dead, however, the restraining power of his audience also disappears. This creates the disturbing suggestion that while Caesar lived the theatricality of Roman politics prevented tyranny but once he is dead it embraces, indeed enables, it. Even more disturbing is the sense that pervades the post-assassination section of the play that the political system that emerges from the chaos left by Caesar's death is tyrannical, popular and inherently theatrical.

It is difficult to overemphasise the importance of the comparison that Shakespeare sets up between the speeches that Brutus and Antony make at Caesar's funeral. In particular, Shakespeare incites the audience to see them as totally different while at the same subtly suggesting important similarities. Brutus's speech appears on the surface to be an appeal to reason. He opens by asking the crowd to listen:

> Bru: Romans, countrymen, and lovers, hear me for my cause, and be silent, that you may hear. Believe me for mine honour and have respect to mine honour, that you may believe. Censure me in your wisdom and awake your senses, that you may the better judge.

> Act 3, Sc 2, L 13–17

Brutus is asking here for the Plebeians to be silent, to accept he is a man of honour and to judge his words. However, despite appearances to the contrary, Brutus's intention in this speech is not simply to make a rational defence of his actions and those of his fellow conspirators. He is also attempting to redefine the nature of Roman politics. It is impossible not to notice that the image of the Plebeians implicit in Brutus's opening words corresponds to Brecht's traditional theatre audience. Certainly Brutus explicitly asks the Plebeians to use their judgement but only after they have been told to be silent and acknowledge his honour. Brutus's political theatre is predicated on the silence of its audience. It is also one in which belief and judgement are effectively determined in advance. Brutus does ask the Plebeians to judge his words but at the same time he states that this judgement has to be on the basis of a prior *belief* in his honour.

Brutus's words are also strangely tautological. He tells the Plebeians to hear and to be silent so that they can hear. It is as though Brutus's aim in his speech is to speak a form of public political language that in its plainness and repetition actually requires no real judgement from its audience. Despite asking them to judge his actions from his words, what Brutus effectively demands in this speech is silence, order and passivity. When he actually comes to defend Caesar's murder he continues in this plain repetitive form:

> Bru: As Caesar loved me, I weep for him; as he was fortunate, I rejoice at it; as he was valiant, I honour him; but as he was ambitious, I slew him. There is tears, for his love; joy, for his fortune; honour, for his valour; and death, for his ambition. Who is here so base, that would be a bondman? If any, speak, for him have I offended. Who is here so rude, that would not be a Roman? If any, speak, for him have I offended. Who is here so vile, that will not love his country? If any, speak, for him I have offended. I pause for a reply.
>
> Act 3, Sc 2, L 24–34

It is, however, a mistake to see Brutus's speech here as in any sense clumsy or simple. Rather what is happening here is a claim is being made for a particular version of plain speaking as normative within the Roman public sphere. Brutus's words are based on the creation of a set of political choices that seek to collapse the meaning of Caesar's murder into a particular understanding of what it means to be a Roman. The first thing to note is that Brutus's words immediately assume that desiring to be a bondsman is anti-Roman. This may be the case but it is important to note the extent to which Brutus deploys in this speech the figure of a 'failed' individual, a rude, vile bondsman, to attack those who reject his arguments.

Brutus seeks to create an image of Rome composed of active citizens which he goes on to argue was threatened by Caesar's ambition. In particular, Brutus's words suggest a correlation between those who fail to see the justice of Caesar's murder and Casca's representation of the Plebeians as a passive audience to Caesar's theatre. In effect Brutus is claiming that by murdering Caesar he and his fellow conspirators have banished the possibility of Caesarean theatrical tyranny. And in a sense he is right. Caesar can no longer be a tyrant. If the danger of tyranny was a product of Caesar's ambition, of his theatrical corruption of the Roman public sphere, then it has passed. But of course it has not. The one thing that Caesar's death unambiguously produces is a violent theatrical political tyranny.

The problem with Brutus's politics is that it is based on a profound act of personal misrecognition. Brutus sees the existing Roman political order as creating the possibility for tyranny because of his personal anxieties over the performative nature of language and power. Shakespeare constantly emphasises Brutus's rejection of performance, in either the personal or political sphere, and the extent to which all his actions are drenched in theatricality. This tension is most obvious around the conspiracy. At one level Brutus consistently resists any sense that his actions and those of his fellow conspirators are at all theatrical. It is this which drives him to reject Cassius's suggestion that the conspirators swear an oath of resolution:

> Bru: Swear priests and cowards, and men cautelous,
> Old feeble carrions, and such suffering souls
> That welcome wrongs: unto bad causes swear
> Such creatures as men doubt. But do not stain
> The even virtue of our enterprise,
> Nor th'insuppressive mettle of our spirits,
> To think that or our cause or our performance
> Did need an oath ...

> Act 2, Sc 1, L 128–35

Brutus constructs those who swear as people lacking mettle, superstitious priests, cowards and deceivers – the kind of people that all men doubt. Not surprisingly there is a direct symbolic relationship between the kind of men who have to swear oaths and those rude, vile bondsmen whom Brutus imagines mourning Caesar's death. In Brutus's political credo enterprises that require an oath must be lacking in some basic legitimacy. Indeed people who need to swear must themselves lack something; their sense of self must be in some way flawed or inadequate if they need to add something to their word to make it complete or potent.

It is therefore profoundly ironic that immediately after killing Caesar Brutus embraces Cassius's construction of the murder as a theatrical performance:

> Cas: How many ages hence
> Shall this our lofty scene be acted over
> In states unborn and accents yet unknown?
> Bru: How many times shall Caesar bleed in sport,

That now on Pompey's basis lies along,
No worthier than the dust?
Cas: So oft as that shall be,
So often shall the knot of us be call'd
The men that gave their country liberty.

Act 3, Sc 1, L 111–18

What Cassius does in this exchange is turn murder into performance. This is entirely consistent with his misrecognition of a metonym for a metaphor. Cassius assumes that future performances of Caesar's murder will enact the destruction of the metaphoric collapse of Caesar into Rome and instead they will, as indeed Shakespeare's does to a large degree, restage the death of Caesar as substitute for Rome's greatness – the theatre that Cassius imagines will not celebrate the death of a metaphor but mourn the murder of a man. It is far more difficult to understand why Brutus, the man of reason, who refused to swear an oath because this would undermine his honour, accepts Cassius's theatricalisation of Caesar's murder. How is one to make sense of Brutus's reference to Caesar bleeding in sport when he has just killed the real Caesar? Of course at one level what Shakespeare is doing here is reminding his audience that they are watching a play. At the same time he is engaging in a subtle but devastating critique of Brutus's anti-theatrical political credo. Brutus can never escape the theatre and his desire to do so is itself the matter of Shakespeare's political theatre.

At Caesar's funeral Brutus effectively asks the Plebeians to renounce the pleasures of Brecht's traditional audience. He asks them to stop being vile, rude bondsmen and instead embrace freedom. But this is nonsense. The whole conspiracy is based on a complete lack of confidence in the Plebeians. At Caesar's funeral Brutus treats the Plebeians as if they are capable of reasoned thought – indeed he implies that to be a citizen is to share in his sense of republican stoic honour. But if he had any faith in the people, indeed if he had even listened properly to Casca's account of Caesar's rejection of the crown, he would not have murdered Caesar. It is Brutus's failure to trust the Plebeians that leads him to act for them – to make the decision that he thinks they lack the courage and wisdom to. Shakespeare, however, shows us that this is simply not the case. The Plebeians can and do resist Caesar's ambition. What the conspiracy ultimately expresses, as do all conspiracy theories, is a lack of confidence in the people and in politics. In his heart, despite what he says at Caesar's funeral, Brutus *knows* that the Plebeians are all vile, rude bondsmen, and it is this knowledge that drives his fear of political theatre. It is, moreover, Brutus's own actions that lead to the emergence of the Plebeians as vile, rude bondsmen.[17]

In terms of what I have argued so far it would be possible to regard *Julius Caesar* as a defence of theatrical politics. In particular, all the time that Roman politics in this play takes place in public as a form of theatre tyranny is kept at bay. Once Caesar is dead, however, the theatricalisation of politics becomes far more dangerous and disturbing. In particular, as an audience one is confronted with the problem that it appears that the price of justice for Caesar is tyranny.

It is very easy to fall into the trap of constructing an absolute distinction between Brutus's and Antony's speeches at Caesar's funeral – not least because Shakespeare encourages this reading. The difference between the two speeches, however, is far less than at first appears. The reason that Shakespeare offers the temptation of seeing absolute difference in the place of the reality of a more nuanced reading is that it is at this point in the play that the ability of an audience to use their reason becomes crucial. Antony's speech opens famously with him asking the Plebeians to lend him their ears. Already this opening line reflects the differences and similarities between Brutus's and Antony's orations. Brutus had also opened his speech with a request that the Plebeians listen to him. But his request, indeed his whole speech, constructed itself as a kind of statement, an announcement that demanded its audience acknowledge its validity, believe in Brutus's honour, before they exercise their reason. Antony asks to borrow the Plebeians' ears. Straight away this makes his speech sound more temporary and provisional than Brutus's. This emphasis on the provisionality of his speech, that he only wants to borrow their time, is at the heart of Antony's polemical tactics at Caesar's funeral. Antony locates his speech in the here and now. He steers clear of abstractions and avoids making large political claims. Alexander Leggatt makes an important point when he comments that:

> The power of Antony's funeral oration stems not just from its tricky irony but from the way it overturns Brutus' appeal to abstraction and theory with an appeal to facts. This is what Caesar did, this is his torn mantle, this is his mangled body.[18]

It is, however, not so much that Antony appeals to the facts as that he changes what will count as a fact in post-Caesar Rome. Antony's whole agenda in the funeral scene is predicated upon establishing the meaning of Caesar's murder as the political fact in Rome transcending all others. This has the effect of performing precisely the metaphoric totalisation that Cassius killed Caesar to prevent. Caesar's dead body becomes the truth of Roman politics but in such a way as to close down real political debate. Instead what Antony does is make the pursuit of justice for Caesar the justification for tyranny.

Antony's oration to the Plebeians is an exercise in political rhetoric. His first move is to open up the meaning of the key term in Brutus's speech – honour. He does this by the simple process, in Leggatt's terms, of referring to the facts:

> Ant: You all did see, that on the Lupercal
> I thrice presented him a kingly crown,
> Which he did thrice refuse. Was this ambition?
> Yet Brutus says, he was ambitious,
> And sure he is an honourable man.

> Act 3, Sc 2, L 96–100

Antony's technique here, and throughout his oration, is to create interpretative space around key elements in Brutus's justification for Caesar's murder. He constantly asks the Plebeians questions while at the same time reminding them of 'facts' intended to spin their answer. At the same time he takes words like honour and ambition and questions their meaning. Can one be honourable and a murderer at the same time? Was Caesar ambitious if he turned down the crown three times? At the centre of Antony's oration is the moment when he descends into the Plebeians and asks them to form a ring around him and Caesar's corpse. There is an obvious relationship in this moment between Antony's circle and Shakespeare's Globe – the great political speaker descends from the podium and becomes one with the crowd in a totalising gesture popular with demagogues. Antony ends his oration, having read what he claims is Caesar's will, by inciting his audience to violence and insurrection:

> Ant: ... I have neither wit, nor words, nor worth,
> Action, nor utterance, nor the power of speech
> To stir men's blood. I only speak right on:

I tell you that which you yourselves do know,
Show you sweet Caesar's wounds, poor poor dumb mouths,
And bid them speak for me. But were I Brutus,
And Brutus Antony, there were an Antony
Would ruffle up your spirits and put a tongue
In every wound of Caesar that should move
The stones of Rome to rise and mutiny.

Act 3, Sc 2, L 214–32

The image of putting tongues in Caesar's wounds is a perfect illustration of the way in which Antony has turned Caesar into a metaphor for Roman so that Antony's voice, spoken by the Plebeians, becomes the truth in post-assassination Rome – Roman politics is silenced as Plebeians speak the truth of Caesar's wounds. The power of Antony's performance depends on his adaptation of existing Roman political forms to the new post-Caesar conditions. Caesar's funeral is a restaging of the offer of the crown, only here the Plebeians behave far more like Brutus's, and Brecht's, traditional theatre audience. On the Lupercal they resisted Antony's, and Caesar's, play; here they allow themselves to be entirely seduced by the performance that Antony puts on.

The cost of this transformation of the Plebeians into Brutus's fantasy image of them is illustrated in the next scene when they murder a poet simply because he shares the name of one of the conspirators. What could be more rude or vile? After Caesar's funeral the Plebeians seem to lose all critical judgement and become bondsmen to Antony's political tyranny. The irony of Brutus's entire political agenda, and indeed that of all the conspirators, is that their murder of Caesar creates the conditions for the reduction of the Plebeians to a vile, rude mob no longer capable of exercising any political wisdom.

The ghost that haunts *Julius Caesar* is the confident and reforming status of the theatre in *Richard III*. In this earlier play it is the commons who alone refuse to accept the legitimacy of Richard's tyranny. In *Julius Caesar* the situation is more complex. Whatever Antony's faults, and Shakespeare portrays them in detail, he is no Richard. There is also the problem that without the Plebeians' mob violence Caesar's murder would be unavenged. In *Julius Caesar* justice is produced by an inspired actor manipulating an initially hostile audience. Unfortunately what is also produced is cold-blooded tyranny complete with death lists. The really disturbing aspect of the politics of *Julius Caesar* is, however, that the theatrical politics that secure justice for Caesar appear fully compatible with the rule of the Triumvirs. The implication of this is that there is nothing inherently ethical or legitimate about theatrical politics. People like Antony can use it for good or evil and the theatre will not in itself provide any basis to judge their behaviour. This is not, however, the whole story. As has been suggested Antony's performance does produces a particular model of the theatre turning the Plebeians into precisely the vile mob of bondsmen that Brutus had already fantasised they were. In effect Antony makes the Roman Plebeians into the easily led, irrational and revolting audience that fills the works of the opponents of Shakespeare's theatre – a spectral fantasy of the Globe's audience – or an image of the future. The second half of *Julius Caesar* is haunted by the spectre of theatrical power distorted and corrupted by men like Antony. The tragedy of the play is that men like Brutus fail to see that in political terms the theatre is on their side. It is this act of misrecognition that leads to Caesar's death. The Ghost of Caesar is Brutus's evil spirit because it represents the positive side of public debate and theatrical politics that Brutus has destroyed – leaving in its place a violent world in which politics has been reduced to Antony's gaudy tricks, plots and lies.

Julius Caesar opens with Rome racked by hegemonic struggle. In particular, there is no agreement within the Roman polity concerning the meaning of a number of key terms. The fear that drives Brutus and Cassius is that Caesar's ambition will lead him to take the crown, become emperor, and in the process close down the space of the political. It is, however, their murder of Caesar that leads to the result they dread. This is because while Caesar lived political debate over his meaning was possible. After his death Antony uses the power of the theatre to perform an act of metaphoric totalisation in which Caesar's memory, his spirit, becomes one with the greatness of Rome. The move that Caesar himself as a mortal man made impossible is enabled by his death – now metonym can be turned into metaphor. The effect is to fill the empty signifier Rome with meaning – and in the process Rome's political sphere is closed down and destroyed. Politics becomes a matter of secret meetings and plots where before it had been conducted in public; political theatre is broken into parts – the violence of the mob and the tyranny of the Triumvirs. Politics in *Julius Caesar* is betrayed and reduced by the failure of Brutus and Cassius to recognise that the theatre was their natural and necessary ally in the defence of Roman/English liberty.

Ethical politics in Coriolanus

In *Coriolanus* Shakespeare returns to the issues he staged in *Julius Caesar*.[19] There are, however, a number of fundamental differences between the state of Rome in the two plays. In particular, while in *Julius Caesar* it is the fear of future strife that leads to conflict, in *Coriolanus* there is an explicit internal and external threat. There is a reality to the famine and the danger posed by the Volscians that the possible consequences of Caesar's ambition lack.

Coriolanus, like *Julius Caesar*, opens with the stage occupied by the commons – although significantly in this play called Citizens not Plebeians. But in the later play the mood is far from a holiday. The first action that the audience is confronted by in *Coriolanus* is a riot – or more accurately a popular demonstration. If it were a riot then one would be back into the world conjured up by Antony at Caesar's funeral. The Citizens in *Coriolanus*, however, are not a mob. When Menenius tells them the famous parable of the belly they debate its meaning with him in an orderly and rational way. Menenius's parable is a version of the clichéd metaphor of the body politic. He tells the Citizens that:

> Men: There was a time, when all the body's members
> Rebelled against the belly: thus accus'd it:
> That only like a gulf it did remain
> I'th' midst o'th'body, idle and unactive,
> Still cupboarding the viand, never bearing
> Like labour with the rest, where th'other instruments
> Did see, and hear, devise, instruct, walk, feel,
> And, mutually participate, did minister
> Unto the appetite and affection common
> Of the whole body.

Act 1, Sc 1, L 95–104

It is easy to see Menenius's parable as simple and banal; however, it is neither. This becomes apparent above all in the responses of the Citizens who are happy to participate in the politics of the moment. It is the First Citizen who suggests a sophisticated detailed reading of the parable:

> First Citizen: The kingly crowned head, the vigilant eye,
> The counsellor heart, the arm our soldier,
> Our steed the leg, the tongue our trumpeter,
> With other muniments and petty helps
> In this our fabric ...
>
> Act 1, Sc 1, L 114–18

Menenius, however, has a more specific reading of the parable in mind. He tells the Citizens that:

> Men: The senators of Rome are this good belly,
> And you the mutinous members: for examine
> Their counsels and their cares, digest things rightly
> Touching the weal o'th'common, you shall find
> No public benefit which you receive
> But it proceeds or comes from them to you,
> And no way from yourselves.
>
> Act 1, Sc 1, L 147–53

Menenius's reading of his parable is far more specific than that produced by the First Citizen. It also has the interesting effect of reproducing the logic of official Tudor and Stuart polemical attacks on early modern popular demonstrations.[20] In particular, in common with such works, Menenius argues, against all logic, that the health of the entire commonwealth depends on the work of the ruling class and not the labour of the commons. Menenius's reading of the parable also, however, comes close to suggesting that the Senators' role is inherently material. What else are the implications of arguing that the Senators are the belly? Menenius's argument suggests that the role of the Senators is to eat the labour of others and turn it into action, will and, perhaps most pertinently, words.

The First Citizen's reading of the parable stresses the mutuality of the body politic. Throughout his speech he uses the word 'our' to describe the parts of the commonwealth. This is not to suggest, however, that there is anything anti-communal about Menenius's reading of the parable. What Shakespeare shows us in the first act of Coriolanus is a Roman polity racked by real dangers but which manages to retain a space for political discussion and debate. The argument over the meaning of Menenius's parable allows a playing out of the class tensions that have been caused by the famine. It also enacts the emergence on stage of a new political consensus produced through debate. In particular, the parable in this first scene works as a privileged site for hegemonic struggle.

Menenius and the First Citizen engage in a political struggle around an empty signifier, the body politic, which is made possible by the interpretative space created by the parable. Stanley Cavell has suggested that the parable can be seen as a 'play within the play' and that during the course of the first scene of the play the Citizens effectively accept it as a substitute for the food they lack.[21] He goes on to comment that: "[The play's] incorporation of the parable of the belly I understand to identify us, the audience, as starvers, and to identify the words of the play as food, for our incorporation."[22] Cavell's argument is that the interpretative space created by the parable leads to the production of words which in turn symbolically fill the starving Citizens, and the audience of the Globe. However Shakespeare's audience clearly were not starving. The hunger that the parable satisfies is therefore not so much material as political. It is a hunger or desire to be part of a meaning-producing community – in other words precisely the desire that Iago exploits in *Othello*. Menenius, however, is no Iago. Nor is he an Antony. The main result of his parable, particularly as it is enacted on stage, is to create a pause in the action, a space for debate and council. The implication of this is that Shakespeare in this first scene is arguing for the political efficacy of his work – that drama can create a space for political debate, even in times of internal and external danger, which is necessary for the good of the commonwealth.

Menenius's reading of the parable in these terms has another more radical implication. The temptation in terms of interpreting the idea of the Senators as the belly is to stress, as I did above, the negative implications of their consumption of the commons' labour. They eat real food, the product of others' material labour, and produce nothing – or rather all they produce is words, commands and orders. But to create a contrast between the Senators' material eating and what they produce is to fail to fully engage with the parable since one of the things it suggests is that the definition of labour within the commonwealth is itself something to be discussed. Why should one see the production of the Senators as less material than that of other members of the commonwealth? Menenius describes the belly's labours as entirely mental. It cares, digests and thinks. But should labours be regarded as any less material than fighting, farming or making? Ultimately Menenius's parable suggests that it is the

Senators as producers of parables whose labour is vital to the health of the body politic. Or to put it more accurately the material health of Rome as a commonwealth depends on the production of spaces for political thought, debate and discussion. The opening scene of *Coriolanus* can be seen as a pæan to the producers of parables: for Menenius the Senators but for Shakespeare's audience the people whose labour creates spaces for political debate and thought – writers and playwrights. It is these whom Menenius ultimately constructs as the defenders and maintainers of commonweal.

Menenius's use of a parable in order to create space for debate is, however, not depicted as in any way neutral or uninterested. The First Citizen warns him not to try and fob them off with a tale (Act 1, Sc 1, L 92). Despite this it does appear that at one level Menenius is seeking to distract the Citizens and buy time for his colleagues. The form of the parable, however, works to militate against the particular partial readings of it produced by Menenius and the First Citizen. This is because as a parable its meaning is inherently open, debatable and provisional. No one can own a parable or fix its meaning. Parables, like proverbs, embody a model of learning, interpretation and language that is inherently communal and ethical. Menenius's parable is not his, nor the First Citizen's – it does not, cannot, belong to anyone. Erasmus in the introduction to his *Adages* (1508) relates the collective nature of proverbs to the wisdom they contain. He goes on to argue that there is something inherently Christian about proverbial discourse, using the saying "Between friends all is common" to illustrate the point. He concludes the discussion of this proverb by commenting, "See what an ocean of philosophy, or rather theology, is opened up to us by this tiny proverb."[23] The phrase 'an ocean of philosophy' reflects the extent to which for Erasmus proverbs work as keys to reservoirs of collective knowledge and wisdom. This enabling function is a direct result for Erasmus of the non-authored, ancient provenance of proverbs. In Erasmus's thought it is also a product of the form of proverbs, which are at once wise and sparse, eloquent and simple. Proverbs open up an ocean of knowledge and also, most obviously in the *Adages*, stimulate the creation of another sea of wisdom. Their non-authored state means that they belong to everyone – to be read, enjoyed and passed on. In the *Adages* Erasmus creates an ideal textual community united in the mutual appreciation of proverbs, a community based upon proverbial ethics – the communal exchange, production and enjoyment of proverbs. The space of this community is one produced and protected by proverbial play. Menenius's parable works as an Erasmian proverb – it creates the space for the production of knowledge concerning the state of Rome through collective debate and exchange. The opening scene of *Coriolanus* equates parables with the theatre as symbolic spaces for the interpretative negotiation of political conflict. As has been suggested this in turn effectively places the producers of parables/plays at the centre of the commonwealth. But does anyone produce parables? Do they have authors? Is Menenius the author of 'his' parable?

In the opening scene of *Coriolanus* Shakespeare gives Erasmus's idealisation of proverbial discourse a specific political twist. Menenius's parable, which is not his, functions to reform Rome as a textual community.[24] It brings together Menenius and the Citizens in a moment of communal debate over the meaning of a parable. At another level the implication of the opening scene of *Coriolanus* is that the space created by the parable in Rome for non-violent communal debate of potentially deadly issues can be related to the space of Shakespeare's theatre. Proverbs, parables and plays can all operate as sites for political negotiation and the emergence of interpretative textual communities.[25]

There are, however, people for whom losing oneself in an ocean of knowledge, taking part in the mutual exchange and production of wisdom, being members of a textual community, is a horrific possibility – their names are Othello and Leontes, Brutus and Coriolanus.

Why is Coriolanus so opposed to political debate? When he first appears on stage he violently interrupts the debate that is in progress over the meaning of Menenius's parable. Coriolanus's response is dismissive and uncompromising. In particular, he implies that Menenius is at fault in wasting time arguing with the Citizens:

> Cor: He that will give good words to thee, will flatter
> Beneath abhorring. What would you have, you curs,
> That like nor peace nor war? The one affrights you,
> The other makes you proud. He that trusts to you,
> Where he should find you lions, finds you hares;
> Where foxes, geese: you are no surer, no,
> Than is the coal of fire upon the ice,
> Or hailstone in the sun.

Act 1, Sc 1, L 166–73

Coriolanus opens his speech by stating that to 'give good words' to the Citizens is a waste of time. The idea of 'good' words implies an opposite and that these 'bad' words are what should be given to the Citizens. Coriolanus's words also suggest an unequal relationship between Citizens and Senators with the latter *giving* the former words. The reason Coriolanus's speech silences the Citizens is not because it is eloquent, although it is, but rather because it is a gift of bad words designed to stop debate.

Coriolanus appears in these lines to be rejecting any possibility of a meaningful discussion with the Citizens. Certainly the effect of his speech is to stop the debate over the meaning of Menenius's parable. Interestingly there is no discussion over the meaning of Coriolanus's own use of proverbial phrases: "He that trusts you will find hares instead of lions" or "No surer than hailstone in the sun". This is largely because the intention informing Coriolanus's use of the language of proverbs is to close down debate. Coriolanus uses phrases and tags that sound proverbial not to create a space for political discussion but instead to sustain his polemical attack on the Citizens. That it works, however, should not obscure the extent to which Coriolanus's words are as rhetorically sophisticated as Menenius's. It is not the case that Coriolanus cannot speak to the people, does not know their language or lacks the skills necessary to engage in political debate. He uses proverbial discourse in a repetitive, accumulative way in this speech, piling up tags and phrases that all support his main theme – that the Citizens cannot be trusted. Coriolanus's speech echoes the one that Brutus made to the Plebeians at Caesar's funeral, not in terms of either content or form but rather in relation to its tone. Coriolanus, like Brutus, talks down to and at the Citizens.

Coriolanus, however, unlike Brutus does not care if the Citizens understand him. His exchanges with them invariably take the form of commands, threats and taunts. This is perhaps to be expected on the battlefield. In the streets and squares of Rome, however, it makes Coriolanus a liability to his fellow Senators. Even when, after much pleading, he agrees to ask the Citizens to consent to him becoming consul he does so with such ill grace that the Citizens soon turn against him. Coriolanus is finally exiled from Rome because he refuses to perform a role in public in order to win the approval of the Citizens. This refusal, while at one level being tragic, is based on Coriolanus's reductive view of the theatre. Shakespeare consistently emphasises that Coriolanus regards any form of acting or performance as inherently dishonourable. For example, during the exchange with his mother, Volumnia, before his last risible attempt to woo the people, Coriolanus equates acting with prostitution:

> Vol: I prithee now, sweet son, as thou hast said
> My praises made thee first a soldier, so,
> To have my praise for this, perform a part
> Thou hast not done before.
> Cor: Well, I must do't.
> Away, my disposition; and possess me
> Some harlot's spirit! My throat of war be turn'd,
> Which choired with my drum, into a pipe
> Small as an eunuch, or the virgin voice
> That babies lull asleep!

Act 3, Sc 2, L 106–14

Coriolanus conceives of any kind of acting as a form of feminising prostitution. He cannot imagine a situation in which performing a role would be positive. In particular, his sense of self is so absolute that the idea of playing is totally alien to him. This is, however, at one level rather contradictory. Coriolanus constantly stresses the extent to which his sense of self, who he is, is entirely non-performative – he is the man he is – but if this were the case then why is it so threatening to play a role? If one's sense of self is complete and gathered within oneself then it should be able to cope with a little performance.[26]

What Shakespeare illustrates in the person of Coriolanus, as he had years earlier in Brutus, is that the people most dismissive of the theatre, those whose identity leads them to reject any positive contribution for drama in the political sphere, are precisely the people who, unwittingly, are at the centre of the action – the leading actors in a political play, or more accurately a play of politics, that they are too blinkered to notice they are taking part in. Brutus dies in order to maintain a sense of self that is ultimately entirely performative. Shakespeare stresses this point by having Antony, the man of the theatre, pronounce Brutus's epitaph:

> Ant: This was the noblest Roman of them all:
> All the conspirators save only he
> Did that they did in envy of great Caesar.
> He only, in a general honest thought
> And common good to all, made one of them.

His life was gentle, and the elements
So mix'd in him that nature might stand up
And say to all the world, 'This was a man!'

Act 5, Sc 5, L 68–75

Antony claims that Brutus killed Caesar for the common good and that his actions can be judged by his status as a man. In the process he reveals the fundamental flaw in Brutus's political ideology. Brutus viewed himself as the defender of Roman republicanism, of liberty and virtue. He justified his action on the basis of his exceptionality. Antony's words celebrate Brutus and mark the moment when his history is turned into drama. Antony, the arch-actor, creates a myth that dramatises and obscures the reality of Brutus – the man who was constantly playing a role in a drama without even being aware of it. Coriolanus also meets his end in a moment of enforced theatre with his dead body displayed in the Volscian market place. In these Roman plays Shakespeare argues that politics and theatre are so closely linked that the most dangerous thing that anyone can do, for themselves and the commonwealth, is to desire a world in which the political and theatrical are entirely divorced. This is particularly the case when the people who should be the champions of the theatre as a space of liberty are the very people who attack and dismiss it.

Coriolanus, however, unlike Julius Caesar explicitly links the theatrical nature of politics with the resolution of conflict and violence. The ethics lacking in the earlier play are located in Coriolanus in the equation of the interpretative space created by Menenius's parable with Shakespeare's own theatre. In particular, the key difference between these two plays is that in Coriolanus the political sphere as a place for the negotiation over the meaning of empty signifiers, in particular Rome, is equated with a self-validating symbolic space of the parable and proverb. The theatre of politics and political theatre in Coriolanus allows and indeed demands that meaning is kept provisional and open.[27] Turning politics into drama creates a permanent brake on the collapse of the metonymic into the metaphoric. In these terms one could equate the difference between Julius Caesar and Coriolanus directly to their specific historical context. Coriolanus is an Elizabethan celebration of the fact that when the monarch is a woman her gender means that the relationship between ruler and body politic will also be metonymic – it can never be closed. Julius Caesar is a Jacobean warning of the dangers of a ruler whose place within the political order means that they can aspire to metaphoric totalisation – to make the metaphor of the body politic real.[28]

Shakespeare's Rome is a site of political struggle. It seems to suffer from constant crises of legitimation. But this is of course the point. Rome in plays like *Julius Caesar* and *Coriolanus* is a parable for the playing out of hegemonic struggle. It enables the staging and resolution of the conflicts that inevitably arise in a society in which the distribution of power and wealth is inequitable – one in which legitimacy has to be constantly produced. What these plays ultimately illustrate is that there never can be a final or total resolution of political conflict; there will always be a need for linguistic and textual spaces, empty signifiers, proverbs, parables and plays, within which political debate can take place.

Conclusion

In his study, *Cynicism and Postmodernity*, Timothy Bewes criticises postmodern theory for its obsession with authenticity as the only ground for political action and its consequent rejection of the possibility of purposeful rational politics. He writes:

> Postmodern politics is a mode of operation which fetishizes authenticity, in which metaphysical truths are hopelessly courted, rather than simply disregarded, and in which the political is reconceptualised as a realm of metaphysical harmony and personal integrity, rather than a sphere of tension generated by the projection of itself beyond existing limits, a necessarily *violent* procedure.[29]

Brutus is a postmodern politician. He is also, moreover, a postmodern literary critic. Brutus above all desires a world of authentic politics – one in which there is no need to put words like class, truth and real in quotation marks.[30] His obsession with a political authenticity that would deliver a true authentic Rome leads him to reject politics with its necessary compromises. Brutus destroys Rome's liberty because it fails to meet his own absolute and ultimately infantile standards. He acts as if he has already been defeated, as if Caesar has already won, when what Shakespeare shows us is that it is primarily Brutus's own loss of political confidence that makes Caesar's victory certain. Terry Eagleton, in his work *The Illusions of Postmodernism*, suggests that a similar failure of political courage is at the root of the Left's current malaise. He writes:

I have spoken of symptoms of political defeat; *but what if this defeat never really happened in the first place?* What if it were less a matter of the left rising up and being forced back, than of a steady disintegration, a gradual failure of nerve, a creeping paralysis?[31]

The lesson of Shakespeare's *Julius Caesar* is that the true protectors of liberty must not lose confidence in their ability to fight and win within the existing political order. Brutus is haunted by his own lack of confidence in popular politics, republican virtue and the theatre of politics. It is this that makes him turn to conspiracy in place of reason.

In *Coriolanus* Shakespeare depicts the virtue of the theatre as a place of political debate. In particular, this play reflects a positive turn in Shakespeare's politics. In *Julius Caesar* there seemed to be no way to resist Antony's exploitation of the theatre to produce political tyranny. In *Coriolanus*, however, the theatre's status as a privileged space for the negotiation of political conflict is located in the theatre itself as a space for thought, a place whose interpretative material practices, like those Erasmus equates with proverbs, are capable of forming the basis for a society of friends – a textual community united in the collective production of meaning through debate, exchange and pleasure.[32] This is an ideal that Brutus's obsession with authenticity would lead him to put into quotation marks, reject as hopelessly naive or dismiss as liberal humanist nonsense.

Notes

1 Andrew Hadfield has recently completed an important study of Shakespeare's republicanism. For an introduction to his conclusions see Andrew Hadfield, 'Shakespeare and Republicanism: History and Cultural Materialism', *Textual Practice*, 17 (2003), pp. 461–84.

2 Jürgen Habermas, *Communication and the Evolution of Society*, trans. Thomas McCarthy (Oxford: 1991), p.178.

3 Ibid., p.181.

4 Jürgen Habermas, *Legitimation Crisis*, trans. Thomas McCarthy (London: 1976), p.73.

5 Habermas comments that: "In traditional societies the type of [legitimation] crisis that arises proceeds from internal contradictions. The contradiction exists between validity claims of systems of norms and justifications that cannot explicitly permit exploitation, and a class structure in which privileged appropriation of socially produced wealth is the rule." Ibid., p.20.

6 This is not to repeat the argument of economic determinism. The fundamental issue that fractures all political orders is not their unequal distribution of wealth and power as an economic issue but as a political one. Althusser is right that the lonely hour of

the last instance never comes when the economy determines social change in a moment of revolutionary purity. All political orders are overdetermined because within all of them the last instance of injustice determines their conditions of existence. See Louis Althusser, 'Contradiction and Overdetermination', in *For Marx*, trans. Ben Brewster (London: 1990), pp.87–128.

7 Žižek points out that "… the dangerous ingredient of Nazism is not its 'utter politicization' of the entire social life, but, on the contrary, the suspension of the political via the reference to an extra-ideological kernel, much stronger than in a 'normal' democratic political order." Slavoj Žižek, 'Fantasy as a Political Category: A Lacanian Approach', *Journal for Psychoanalysis of Culture and Society*, 1 (1996), pp. 77–85, p.83.

8 For an excellent analysis of Coriolanus that draws on Habermas's idea of a legitimation crisis see Michael D. Bristol, 'Lenten Butchery: Legitimation Crisis in *Coriolanus*', in *Shakespeare Reproduced: The Text in History and Ideology*, ed. Jean E. Howard and Marion F. O'Connor (London: 1987), pp.207-24.

9 Marjorie Garber, *Shakespeare's Ghost Writers* (New York: 1987), p.71.

10 On Shakespeare's audience see Andrew Gurr, *Playgoing in Shakespeare's London* (Cambridge: 1987).

11 Brecht Bertolt, *Brecht on Theatre: The Development of an Aesthetic*, ed. and trans. John Willet (London: 1978), p.187.

12 Richard Wilson, '"Is This a Holiday": Shakespeare's Roman Carnival', in *Shakespeare: The Roman Plays*, ed. Graham Holderness, Bryan Loughrey and Andrew Murphy (London: 1996), pp.18–31, p.23.

13 Ernesto Laclau, *Emancipation(s)* (London: 1996), p.44.

14 Ernesto Laclau and Chantal Mouffe, *Hegemony and Socialist Strategy: Towards a Radical Democratic Politics* (London: 1985), p.127.

15 Ernesto Laclau, *The Politics of Rhetoric* (Colchester: 1998), p.13.

16 For the heterogeneous 'republican' nature of early modern English politics see Patrick Collinson, 'The Monarchical Republic of Queen Elizabeth I', in *Elizabethan Essays* (London: 1994), pp.31–58.

17 One can compare the way Brutus transforms the Plebeians from a politically engaged and active audience into a vile mob to a similar transformation that takes place in Elizabethan texts attacking the theatre. For a discussion of the image of Shakespeare's audience as it appears in the works of these writers see Jean Howard, *The Stage and Social Struggle in Early Modern England* (London: 1994).

18 Alexander Leggatt, *Shakespeare's Political Drama: The History Plays and the Roman Plays* (London: 1988), p.156.

19 *Coriolanus* has a number of important references to political events in the period 1607–8. For a discussion of Shakespeare's play as a piece of Jacobean political writing see Robin Headlam Wells, "Manhood and Chevalrie": *Coriolanus*, Prince Henry, and the Chivalric Revival', *Review of English Studies*, 51 (2000), pp. 395–422.

20 For the classic example of such responses see the various works produced by different Tudor regimes throughout the sixteenth century. Despite their large religious and political differences the governments of Henry VIII, Edward VI, Mary and Elizabeth all produced identical responses to the mass political movements that erupted throughout the sixteenth century. The development of popery and heresy as explanatory political tools in the reigns of Elizabeth and James simply confirmed existing magisterial assumptions concerning the status of popular disorder. See Tom Betteridge, *Literature and Politics in the English Reformation* (Manchester: 2004). For the development of

popery see Peter Lake, 'Anti-Popery: The Structure of a Prejudice', in *Conflict in Early Stuart England: Studies in Religion and Politics 1603–1842*, ed. Richard Cust and Ann Hughes (London: 1989), pp.72–106.

21 Stanley Cavell, *Disowning Knowledge: In Seven Plays of Shakespeare* (Cambridge: 2003), p.163.

22 Ibid., p.165.

23 Erasmus, *The Adages of Erasmus*, selected by William Barker (Toronto: 2001), p.14.

24 The idea of a textual community as both an interpretative and social entity is developed by Brian Stock in *Listening for the Text: On the Uses of the Past* (Philadelphia: 1990).

25 For the potentially dangerous political context within which *Coriolanus* was first produced see Annabel Patterson, *Shakespeare and the Popular Voice* (Cambridge: 1989).

26 The phrase 'gathered self' comes from Ben Jonson's poem *To Sir Thomas Roe* where it is used to celebrate Roe's stoic, anti-theatrical sense of self. Jonson writes:
    Be always to thy gathered self the same:
    And study conscience, more than thou wouldst fame.

27 This space is also inherently civic and communal. Cathy Shank has argued that: "Coriolanus is preoccupied with the workings of civic life and the role of language as a means of expressing and negotiating socio-political position. Key to its exploration of civic politics is its protagonist's refusal to partake in civic life or to moderate his excessive individualism for the common good ..." Cathy Shank, 'Civility and the City in *Coriolanus*', *Shakespeare Quarterly*, 54 (2003), pp. 406–23, p.423.

28 For example, while Elizabeth's gender meant that she was Governor of the Church of England, James was Head.

29 Timothy Bewes, *Cynicism and Postmodernity* (London: 1997), p.7/8.

30 Fredric Jameson comments that: "... the 'truth' of the concept of class (to speak like the Hegelians) lies ... in the operations to which it gives rise: class analysis, like materialist demystification, remains valid and indispensable even in the absence of the possibility of a coherent 'philosophy' or ontology of class itself." The truth of the concept Rome is valid because it allows as an empty signifier the emergence of public political debate. See Frederic Jameson, 'Actually Existing Marxism', in *Marxism beyond Marxism*, ed. Saree Makdisi, Cesare Casarino and Rebecca E. Karl (London: 1996), pp. 14–54, p.41.

31 Terry Eagleton, *The Illusions of Postmodernism* (Oxford: 1996), p.18.

32 For the ideal of Friendship as a basis for democratic politics see Jacques Derrida, *Politics of Friendship*, trans. George Collins (London: 1997).

CHAPTER FOUR

The redundancy of language in Othello

OTHELLO IS SHAKESPEARE'S ANGRY, violent repudiation of his drama. The play remorselessly exposes the hollow ethics of theatre as an act of consumption. *Othello* forces its audience to acknowledge the inferno of violence, hatred and irrationality that lurks in the margins of speech; it constantly juxtaposes poetry with violence, drama with hate and meaning with fantasy. In Iago Shakespeare creates not simply an alter ego for himself as playwright, but also a thing that incites, sustains and ultimately disappoints the audience's desire. Iago is the still centre at the heart of *Othello* – the point to which the play's meaning constantly returns and the void into which it disappears.

This chapter will examine the theatrical ethics of *Othello*. It will open by discussing Iago's deployment of racist and sexist imagery as a tool to incite the audience's desire and make them participate in 'his' play. The chapter will then move on to examine the extent to which Othello's sense of self makes him simultaneously an outsider, Other, and a representative, even clichéd, human subject. It will conclude by examining in detail the status of Iago and the function of Desdemona's, and Othello's mother's, handkerchief. It will argue that these things represent two opposing poles of interpretative possibility, the handkerchief in the way it endlessly multiplies meanings and Iago in his steadfast reduction of meaning to a single, albeit inscrutable, principle. It is in the tension between these two sites of hermeneutic failure that *Othello* reflects contemporary discussions over the status of language.

The opening of the play

Othello opens with Roderigo and Iago on stage apparently in the middle of a conversation.

> Rod: Tush, never tell me, I take it much unkindly
> That thou, Iago, who hast had my purse,
> As if the strings were thine, shouldst know of this.
> Iago: 'Sblood, but you will not hear me. If ever I did dream
> Of such a matter, abhor me.

Act 1, Sc 1, L 1–4

Shakespeare often opens a play in mid-conversation. At one level this is simply a good technique for engaging the audience's attention since it immediately forces them to participate in the play. There is no time to pause – one is plunged straight into the action. There is, however, more to this opening exchange than simply good salesmanship. The conversation between Iago and Roderigo that opens *Othello*, like that between Gloucester and Kent at the beginning of *King Lear*, ushers in a number of the key issues that will structure the following action. For example, Iago's insistence that he had never dreamt of 'such a matter' reflects the extent to which *Othello* is concerned with questions of truth and interpretation. One reading of this line is that Iago is simply telling the truth. If Roderigo's 'this' refers to the marriage between Othello and Desdemona then there is no reason to think that Iago did have prior knowledge of it. However, at another level it soon becomes clear that Iago's denial only pertains to the real world – or rather the 'real' commonsensical world of fools like Roderigo. It is precisely in his dreams and fantasies that Iago has known about the marriage between Othello and Desdemona. Iago, as a racist, knows that black men like Othello desire to marry white women like Desdemona. He knows, and indeed has seen, their marriage bed. It is a constant of the racist fantasy that for Iago is the truth of the surface world within which his exchange with Roderigo takes place.

It is, however, possible that Roderigo's 'this' is not a reference to Othello's marriage. In terms of the text there is simply not sufficient matter to determine what it refers to, and therefore to judge the status of Iago's denial. Within the first ten lines of the play Shakespeare creates a moment of interpretative hiatus which sets down a marker for the rest of the play.

One can, as I did in the preceding paragraph, make Roderigo's 'this' meaningful, fix it to the fact of Othello's marriage and in the process flesh out the matter of Iago's non-dreams – provide the detail of the dream that Iago denies having. But this would be to allow one's desire to make this conversation meaningful take precedence over the words themselves. *Othello* constantly offers its audience, and perhaps particularly those who are learned, whose status makes them peculiarly anxious to fill out the matter of the text and make it meaningful, the temptation to give in to their desire to produce meaning. It does so at a general thematic level but also in relation to its eponymous hero. Othello's downfall has many causes but central to it is his inability to tolerate any linguistic ambiguity or interpretative hiatus, either temporal or spatial. He cannot wait to see and hear the whole total truth of Desdemona for himself, and it is this totalising self-centred desire to know that prevents the emergence of the very truth he so desperately desires. Like Malvolio, although much more violently, Othello crushes the text in order to shape it to his desire.

What makes *Othello* a far more radical and demanding work than *Twelfth Night* is that in this play Shakespeare creates an image of the theatre in which the audience is made up of hundreds of Malvolios – all desperately seeking to crush the text to make it fit their desire.[1] Indeed he goes further than this since what makes Iago's ludicrous and largely inept plotting so successful is his ability to exploit the desire at the heart of the theatrical moment – the desire to participate in a collective act of interpretation as part of becoming a member of an audience. Stephen Greenblatt has pointed out that the production conditions of Shakespeare's drama – the lights were not dimmed, no attempt was made to isolate and awaken the sensibilities of each individual member of the audience, and the crowd did not disappear – meant that it depended on a 'felt community' to be successful.[2] Iago's evil is not simply a lie. It draws on a constitutive truth of Shakespeare's theatre, indeed any theatrical moment, which is that it is the desire of the audience to take part in a communal act of interpretation and in the process become part of a felt community – an audience – that makes the drama happen. It is the audience's desire that is materialised on stage in the bodies of the actors and the lines they speak. Of course, Iago is not concerned with community or truth – but he is expert, like Shakespeare, in exploiting an audience's desire to interpret and know. In particular, he consistently offers the audience the temptation to short-cut any hiatus over the production of meaning with his banal pack of racist and sexist fantasies. The horror at the heart of *Othello* is that it does not articulate any real basis from which one could resist the blandishments of people like Iago or Shakespeare. Iago's evil works because he knows that, as with Othello, the audience's desire to participate in a communal act of interpretation, to be part of a meaning-producing crowd, will in the end always take precedence over reason and thought. Antony will always beat Brutus, and indeed Antony is himself a chump for making such an effort to seduce the Roman crowd – all he really needed to do was produce a few crude racist jokes, some sexist smears, to ensure Brutus's political defeat.

The temptation of *Othello*'s opening exchange, to fill in the matter of Iago's dreams, is reinforced during the course of the scene. Shakespeare in this play consistently creates moments that are either banal or profound but which all function as provocations to interpret. For example, Iago tells Roderigo that:

> Iago: You shall mark
> Many a duteous and knee-crooking knave,
> That, doting on his own obsequious bondage,
> Wears out his time much like his master's ass,
> For nought but provender, and, when he's old, cashiered.
> Whip me such honest knaves! Others there are
> Who, trimmed in forms and visages of duty,
> Keep yet their hearts attending on themselves
> And, throwing but shows of service on their lords,
> Do well thrive by them, and, when they have lined their coats,
> Do themselves homage: these fellows have some soul
> And such a one do I profess myself. For, sir,
> It is as sure as you are Roderigo,
> Were I the Moor, I would not be Iago:
> In following him I follow but myself.

Act 1, Sc 1, L 43–57

In this speech Iago constructs a comparison between honest servants and those who simply perform the role. He argues that it is only the latter, those who wear a disguise, whose form has been trimmed to fit the part, that have 'some soul'. Clearly this is a provocative argument since it reverses the assumption that there is a connection between being truthful and having a soul – an essential animating non-corporal principle of being. Iago argues that it is only those servants who simply perform the role that remain true to their humanity, who refuse to be reduced to the state of their master's ass. For him having a soul means being able to perform, to disguise one's true intentions and in the process do homage to oneself. Iago's words can be read as the boasting of a disgruntled servant or the code of a malcontent. However, their theatrical context gives them a specific, and potentially disturbing, meaning. Iago is arguing that it is the performers who, although being servants, at least resist their place in the world – it is their fellows, duteous, non-performing, who, like an audience, passively accept their status as soulless fools. Iago is effectively telling his audience that he despises them as honest knaves who do not have the soul to perform, the courage to resist Iago's whip, but instead embrace it as their due.

In this context the famous line 'Were I the Moor, I would not be Iago' takes on a new, albeit banal, specifically theatrical meaning – 'Were I the actor playing Iago not playing Iago I would be playing the Moor'. This reading complements the rest of the speech where Iago goes on to tell Roderigo that he is simply acting a part in the service of his 'peculiar end'. Iago concludes by making another of his famously oblique claims, 'I am not what I am'. Again this can be read as simply a statement of the reality of the theatrical moment. Iago is not Iago – he is a man playing the role of Iago. In these terms Iago's 'peculiar end' is the actor's wage – his hidden but determining motivation. It is as though in this speech Shakespeare is offering the audience an interpretative choice – one can understand Iago's whole speech as a reference to the simple reality of the theatre or stay within the illusionary world of the theatrical moment. This is, however, not a real choice – or rather if it were Shakespeare would have failed as a writer – and Iago would have to put away his plots. If the audience hear Iago saying that he is an actor being paid to play a role then what price Shakespeare's drama or Iago's schemes? But they can't, don't or won't. Indeed Shakespeare, and Iago, know the audience will resist banal reality and instead opt for the interpretative pleasure of complexity, of trying to make sense of Iago's oblique words.

And pleasure is certainly what Iago goes on to give us as he and Roderigo proceed to tell Brabantio that his daughter, Desdemona, has married Othello:

Iago: Zounds, sir, you're robb'd, for shame put on your gown!
Your heart is burst, you have lost half your soul;
Even now, now, very now, an old black ram
Is tupping your white ewe! Arise, arise,
Awake the snorting citizens with the bell,
Or else the devil will make a grandsire of you,
Arise I say!

Act 1, Sc 1, L 85–92

There is a disjuncture in this speech between Iago's description of the marriage and the effects he states it *will* have upon Brabantio. It is, however, in some ways misleading to talk in the future tense here since Iago's words are not predictive – they are presented as statements of fact. Brabantio's heart *is* burst; he *has* lost half his soul. This is despite the fact that Iago cannot know these 'facts'. Indeed they are clearly less facts than simple assertions dressed up to sound factual. Given that Iago must know that Brabantio lacks knowledge of his daughter's wedding, and that therefore even if it were to break his heart it cannot yet have done so, why does he represent Brabantio's responses to it as if they have already taken place rather than as about to happen? Iago's words can be read as unproblematic on the basis that it is obvious that Brabantio will be shocked by Desdemona's elopement. To do so, however, is to come close to normalising the racism of the image Iago uses to actually 'tell' Brabantio his daughter has married Othello. This is because the extremity of Brabantio's reaction as imagined by Iago is structurally linked to the peculiarly aberrant, albeit privileged, nature of Desdemona's marriage within Iago's racist ideology. It is not simply that Desdemona has eloped but that in doing so she has placed herself within the centre of the drama of racism that bursts Brabantio's heart.

Iago's words to Brabantio, however, can also be understood less as an assertion of fact and more as a command. Iago is telling Brabantio that this is how he will react to the news of Desdemona's marriage. In the process Shakespeare again foregrounds the constructed theatrical nature of *Othello*. Iago/Shakespeare is telling Brabantio how he, or rather the actor playing the role, will respond to Desdemona's elopement since he already knows what is going to happen; he has read the script. Iago's insistence on the horror that Brabantio will feel when he finds out about the elopement, however, sits uneasily with the casual racism of his speech, 'an old black ram, Is tupping your white ewe'. This carnivalesque image, transgressing the boundaries between animal and human, is simultaneously banal and oblique. Its banality is a result of its deployment of racist and sexist tropes, for example the use of animalistic imagery to portray a sexual act between humans in order to suggest a lack of reason and love. By describing Desdemona's and Othello's marriage in these terms Iago is reducing it to an act of bestial sex. In the process he reproduces a moment of theatrical salesmanship similar to Shakespeare's at the play's opening. Iago describes the marriage between Desdemona and Othello in racist and sexual terms. And he does so through the use of an image that asks, indeed demands, that the audience suspend their reason in the process of making it meaningful. Iago's speech combines urgency with an image that can be made meaningful only if one accepts its racist sexist logic and do not question the ideological premises required to understand 'an old black ram, Is tupping your white ewe' as a representation of a black man and a white woman having sex. The temptation of racism is that it offers a solution to interpretative hiatus – it tempts one to interpret acts, words and events through a lens that always produces the same simplistic totalising answer. This is the basis of Iago's power. He constantly offers the audience, and particularly Othello, the possibility of short-circuiting interpretative hiatus, through racism and sexism. In particular, Iago uses carnivalesque imagery in order to satisfy the audience's, and later Othello's, voyeurism. The 'pleasure' engendered by the line 'an old black ram, Is tupping your white ewe' is that of making sense, understanding and consuming an inherently subversive 'comic' sexual image. In other words to make Iago's words meaningful one has, if only for a moment, to participate in his racist carnival.[3]

Racist discourse deploys a set of relatively trite formal tropes, which can then be endlessly varied in terms of content, being made more or less complex depending on the context. It succeeds as an ideology to the extent to which it can manipulate existing cultural desires. Slavoj Žižek comments that:

> ... in every ideological edifice, there is a kind of 'trans-ideological' kernel, since if an ideology is to become operative and effectively 'seize' individuals, it *has* to batten on and manipulate some kind of 'trans-idelogical' vision which cannot be reduced to a simple instrument of legitimising pretensions to power ... *it is only the reference to such a trans-ideological kernel which makes ideology 'workable'*.[4]

Ideology works to the extent to which it is able to latch on to existing and real cultural desires. In particular, ideology allows the non-satisfaction of these desires to be narrated and 'explained'. For example, the real desire for a society without antagonism and conflict is manipulated by ideology through a narrative of partial and flawed explanation. The example that Žižek uses to illustrate this argument is anti-Semitism. He argues that: "In the anti-Semitic ideological fantasy, social antagonism is explained away via the reference to the Jew as the secret agent who is stealing social *jouissance* from us (amassing profits, seducing women …).".[5] The important thing to note is that racism not only singles out a group as the explanation for social conflict; it also projects on to its chosen target its own disavowed desires.[6] This is one reason why racist ideologies invariably contain a strongly sexist element. Racism blames those it hates for stealing its desire and in the process creates a narrative of the collective theft of *jouissance* to explain social conflict. It is this ability to motivate minimally convincing explanatory narrations of the ills and traumas of society that empowers racist speech. Racism is not concerned with the real causes of society's troubles but it can nonetheless explain them – albeit in banal and superficial terms. It is the non-satisfaction of the real desire for a society free from antagonism that racism battens on to. Racist speech reflects the truth that any society in which wealth and power are unequally distributed will be marked by conflict. Racism, like other conservative ideologies, explains away this antagonism through lazy thinking, bogus science, distortions and lies – drawing on the reservoirs of violence, irrationality, infantilism and fear that George Steiner describes as "the undergrowth of language".[7]

Iago is a typical racist. He uses racially charged carnivalesque images of Desdemona and Othello having sex in order to shape the narrative within which Brabantio, and indeed the audience, understands their elopement. When Brabantio's initial response to the news of his daughter's marriage is incomprehension Iago upbraids him:

> Iago: Zounds, sir, you are one of those that will not serve God, if the devil bid you. Because we come to do you service, and you think we are ruffians, you'll have your daughter covered with a Barbary horse; you'll have your nephews neigh to you, you'll have coursers for cousins, and jennets for germans!
>
> Act 1, Sc 1, L 107–12

Iago's impatience with Brabantio is, however, misplaced since Iago has not yet told him, in plain English, that Desdemona has eloped. Iago creates a fantastical narrative of Othello's marriage prior to the articulation of the facts. He consistently presents Brabantio, and the audience, with sexualised racist images that can only be interpreted, even at a basic level, if one accepts that Othello as a Moor can be compared with a black ram or a Barbary horse.

Iago's racism also allows him to tap into Brabantio's existing anxieties concerning Desdemona and his position as her father. Once Brabantio understands what Iago is telling him he acknowledges that the events of the night are "not unlike my dream" (Act 1, Sc 1, L 141). Despite this prior knowledge, albeit in the form of a dream, Brabantio's basic reaction to Desdemona's elopement is to assume that Othello must have charmed her:

> Bra: Fathers, from hence, trust not your daughters' minds,
> By what you see them act. – Is there not charms,
> By which the property of youth and maidhood
> May be abused? Have you not read, Roderigo,
> Of some such thing?

Act 1, Sc 1, L 168–72

Brabantio generalises his experience as a lesson for all fathers before suddenly wondering if Desdemona had been enchanted by Othello. It is possible that Roderigo has indeed read of such charms – but it is as likely that he has seen them, and their results, being performed on stage, particularly in *A Midsummer Night's Dream*. Brabantio does not need to turn to books in order to explain what has happened. He simply needs to come to the theatre. Indeed this is particularly the case given that his main concern in this speech is his failure to properly read Desdemona's mind from her acts. It is Iago who offers Brabantio, and indeed the audience, a simple totalising solution to the disjuncture between appearance and reality, intention and act, signifier and signified. His racism, and indeed sexism, battens on to Brabantio's existing anxieties over his status as a father, his ability to understand and control Desdemona, to 'explain' her actions – and this is the same trick that Iago plays on Othello.

It is not, however, Brabantio who is the first or indeed most important target of Iago's racism. It is the audience. The first scene of *Othello* sets up the key dynamic of the drama – the tension between interpretative desire and failure. *Othello* is an essay on the cost of interpretation – a critique of people whose desire to know, to see, hear and consume the truth overrides their reason and wit. *Othello*'s first scene opens in the middle of a dialogue and concludes with a character bemoaning his failure to properly interpret the relation between his daughter's mind and her acts. During its course Shakespeare consistently foregrounds the play's status as a piece of theatre – the extent to which it is a written text being acted by paid actors speaking someone else's words. This self-referentiality is particularly marked around the figure of Iago. The audience is trapped between its constitutive desire to participate in a collective act of interpretation, to be an audience, and Shakespeare's constant reminders that what they are actually taking part in is a performance, a show – a gaudy piece of illusion put on simply to make money. It is the audience's desire to keep this reality at bay that Iago exploits. Despite his ineptitude, and the reductive banality of much of what he says, Iago knows that his audience are 'duteous and obsequious' knaves with 'free and open natures'. After all they have paid to be tricked and seduced. Their desperate desire to be part of a communal act of interpretation means that he can give them anything and they will lap it up. It is this which makes Iago's racist representation of Othello and Desdemona having sex, 'an old black ram tupping a white ewe', so effective. It does not matter if this image appals or excites one – what is important is that it incites an act of interpretation which depends upon a suspension of the audience's reason.

Iago exploits the inevitable metaphoric nature of language – that what is said is not what is – the gap between the signifier and signified. His racist imagery is seductive not because it marks this gap but on the contrary because it protects the fantasy at the heart of the audience's desire – that it is possible to engage in a communal act of interpretation that is compete and whole – that escapes, in Jacques Derrida's words, "the play of signifying references that constitute language".[8] Iago, who appears to have read Derrida, exploits language's inherent lack of wholeness. His racism protects the audience from having to acknowledge the failure of language and therefore interpretation. It does this by announcing its peculiar specific metaphorical status. Iago offers the audience the perfect image to indulge their voyeurism, an image of two people having sex which in its carnivalesque form demands an act of interpretation – we cannot but choose to understand the image of a black ram tupping a ewe as referring to two people having sex.[9] We have no choice if we want to remain part of the audience. It is this apparent lack of freedom which Iago exploits. He forces upon the audience the choice they have to make in order to protect the fantasy of a world of total transparent meaning – the desire for a truth beyond the play of representation, of a language that does escape the play of signifying references. Iago's gift to the audience is to protect this fantasy – that in a world without his racism, sexism and hatred the truth would be rendered up to us, complete, total, whole. Shakespeare, however, at the end of the play forces us to confront the extent to which it is this desire that is at the heart of the play's tragedy. There is always ideology – Iago simply does us the favour of making his explicit. And he hates us for being so grateful.

Othello *and telling the self*

Iago's racism allows the audience to protect the fantasy of pure language that escapes the play of the signifier and signified. Shakespeare's image of Venice repeats this motif but in the political sphere. The fantasy that is being sustained in relation to the portrayal of Venetian society in *Othello* is that of a society free of antagonism and conflict. Shakespeare creates in the figure of Othello a figure of the Other that functions to protect the natural organic wholeness of Venetian society and the humanist self. This can be illustrated by examining how the politics of Venice are portrayed in the play and the way the play depicts the emergence and collapse of Othello's sense of identity and selfhood.

Othello depicts Venice as a place where politics is conducted on the basis of reasoned public debate. This is perhaps most explicit in relation to the debate that takes place in Act 1 Scene 2 before the Duke and Senate over the twin problems of the imminent Turkish attack on Cyprus and Desdemona's elopement. Brabantio argues that Desdemona must have been seduced through the use of charms or drugs. When Othello denies this charge Brabantio's response is to repeat it and argue that nature itself rules against his daughter's actions:

> Bra: To fall in love with what she feared to look on?
> It is a judgement maimed and most imperfect,
> That will confess perfection so could err
> Against all rules of nature, and must be driven

> To find out practices of cunning hell,
> Why this should be. I therefore vouch again
> That with some mixtures powerful o'er the blood,
> Or with some dram conjured to this effect,
> He wrought upon her.
>
> Act 1, Sc 3, L 99–107

The Duke, however, will have none of this, telling Brabantio that:

> Duke: To vouch this is no proof,
> Without more certain and more overt test;
> Than these thin habits and poor likelihoods
> Of modern seeming do prefer against him.
>
> Act 1, Sc 3, L 108–10

The Duke's response to Brabantio's complaint is consistently pragmatic. He recommends patience and finally acceptance of what cannot be altered:

> Duke: The robbed that smiles steals something from the thief,
> He robs himself that spends a bootless grief.
>
> Act 1, Sc 3, L 209–10

Brabantio, however, is far from satisfied with this, telling the Duke that:

> Bra: These sentences to sugar or to gall,
> Being strong on both sides, are equivocal:
> But words are words: I never yet did hear
> That the bruised heart was pierced through the ear:
> I humbly beseech you, proceed to th' affairs of state.
>
> Act 1, Sc 3, L 217-21

At one level what seems to be achieved here is the resolution of conflict through public discussion. But it is noticeable that Brabantio rejects the Duke's platitudes, only agreeing to drop his case in order to allow more pressing public business to be discussed. In practice the issues raised by Desdemona's elopement and marriage to Othello are not conducive to reasoned debate. This is made clear by their eruption at the end of the debate:

> Duke: Let it be so.
> Good-night to every one. And, noble signior,
> If virtue no delighted beauty lack
> Your son-in-law is far more fair than black.
> First Sen: Adieu, brave Moor, use Desdemona well.
> Bra: Look to her, Moor, if thou hast eyes to see:
> She has deceiv'd her father, and may thee.

Act 1, Sc 3, L 288–94

These comments occur after the end of the public discussion over Othello's marriage and his appointment to command the Venetian force being sent to Cyprus to head off the Turkish invasion. They therefore take place in a moment of dramatic hiatus after the formal debate has taken place but before the action has moved on. This is not to suggest, however, that this exchange is unimportant since what is being enacted here is the policing of the boundary of the Venetian public sphere. These comments, with their coded racism and patriarchal fear, articulate what has been excluded from public debate and mark the limits of Venetian rationality.

It is this which makes Othello's position so tenuous. He is at once the defender of Venetian civilisation and an embodiment of its constitutive fears and hatreds. The tragedy of *Othello* is that not only does the play's eponymous hero fail to appreciate the reality of his place in Venice but it appears to be precisely his status as Other that makes him attractive to Desdemona. Othello tells the Duke, Brabantio and the assembled Senators that it was his life story that first attracted Desdemona to him. He describes her response to his stories as physically and emotionally intense:

> Oth: My story being done,
> She gave me for my pains a world of sighs,
> She swore in faith 'twas strange, 'twas passing strange;
> 'Twas pitiful, 'twas wondrous pitiful;

Act 1, Sc 3, L 159–62

Othello concludes his account of his and Desdemona's courtship by claiming that:

> Oth: She lov'd me for the dangers I had passed,
> And I loved her that she did pity them.

Act 1, Sc 3, L 168–9

It is, however, at one level a mistake to talk in terms of Othello's courtship of Desdemona since, in his version of what took place, theirs was an indirect displaced courtship. The stories that Othello told of his life, of slavery and redemption, of cannibals and anthropophagi, the tales that Desdemona greedily devoured, are the basis of Desdemona's love for Othello, and the substance of his sense of self.

Desdemona falls in love with Othello as he presents himself to her, and to himself, within a narrative of travel. In particular, Othello's version of his past constructs it as alien and foreign. His escape from this site of Otherness is enacted in the narrative that he tells Desdemona and embodied in the position that he holds within the Venetian state. In both cases, however, the extent to which Othello has really left behind the fantastical world of cannibals and anthropophagi is limited. As has been noted, Othello's Otherness lurks at the edge of his public position in Venice. At the same time it is clear that Othello himself is still in the grip of an Otherness that he at once seeks to narrate away and in the process enunciates as constitutive of his sense of self. Greenblatt comments that Othello's "… identity depends upon a constant performance … of his 'story', a loss of his own origins, an embrace and perpetual reiteration of the norms of another culture".[10] It is this performative element to Othello's subjectivity that Iago battens on to in order to corrupt and tempt him. Iago knows that Othello is aware that as far as Venetian society is concerned his identity is irreducibly Other/alien – and that this in turn generates in Othello a desire to assert through narrative his emergence from Otherness into selfhood. Iago encourages Othello to reverse this process as a way of dealing with the anxieties produced by his fear that Desdemona has betrayed him. He incites Othello to return to his point of origin, his racial Otherness, as a 'safe' site from which to explain Desdemona's betrayal.

At one level this reversal is predicated on Othello's acceptance of the racist logic of the travel discourse within which he narrates his life story. In these terms the tragedy of *Othello* can be explained away, can be made exceptional, by displacing Otherness, and its tragic effects, on to Othello. Such a move, however, fails to acknowledge the extent to which Othello's subjectivity is not exceptional but in its essential qualities entirely normal. The fact that Othello's sense of self is based on a narrated journey that circles around a core of Otherness is a reflection of its normality. Judith Butler comments that:

> Only by persisting in alterity does one persist in one's 'own' being. Vulnerable to terms that one never made, one persists always, to some degree, through categories, names, terms, and classifications that mark a primary and inaugurative alienation in sociality.[11]

Butler's argument here is that subjectivity is always based on the mediation between selfhood and discourse, between one's sense of self and the social collective matter, language, it is constructed from. Being a subject means using social tools to make, indeed to fill out, one's individual selfhood. The temptation that Shakespeare offers us in *Othello* is to see the eponymous hero's sense of self, its basis in a narration around Otherness, as exceptional or alien. This is despite the fact that Shakespeare also represents Othello as typical, not only in relation to his sense of self, but also in terms of the play's audience. Famously Iago describes Othello as having "a free and open nature", and predicts that he "will as tenderly be led by the nose ... As asses are" (Act I, Sc 3, L 397–400). Othello's desire to belong, to be part of Venetian society, is based upon an awareness of the precariousness of his social identity in Venice. Othello knows that at one level his sense of self is grounded on an irreducible Otherness. It is this which fuels his desire to belong, his desperate need for certainty, to see the truth, and which makes him so easy to seduce. In all this Othello can be seen as representing the audience. His desire to belong, like the audience's, takes precedence over his reason so that in the end he is prepared to sacrifice everything in order to sustain the explanatory racist and sexist narrative Iago has constructed for him.

The exchange between Iago and Othello that opens Act 4 of the play makes evident the extent of Iago's power over his victim. Throughout this dialogue Iago taunts Othello with questions, puns and hints all of which create interpretative spaces that he knows Othello will rush to fill. At one stage Othello asks the perfectly reasonable question, 'Has Cassio actually said Desdemona is his mistress?' Iago's response is typical of his confidence in his power over Othello:

> Oth: Hath he [Cassio] said anything?
> Iago: He hath, my lord, but be you well assured
> No more than he'll unswear.
> Oth: What hath he said?
> Iago: Faith, that he did – I know not what. He did –
> Oth: What? what?

Iago: Lie.
Oth: With her?
Iago: With her, on her, what you will.

Act 4, Sc 1, L 29–34

Iago's quotation of *Twelfth Night*'s sub-title, 'what you will', is no coincidence. There is nothing sophisticated about his manipulation of Othello in this exchange. Iago is no Antony. But he does know that Othello's will, his desire, will make up for his lack of subtlety or skill. In particular, Iago uses the word 'lie' to exploit Othello's desire to produce meaning, a need driven by his fear of a world of linguistic ambiguity and textual slippage. Lie in this exchange represents the instability of language and in particular the extent to which meaning is at one level arbitrary. Iago appears to have read not only Derrida but also Butler. He knows that subjectivity is based upon a dependence on language which in turn means that a person's sense of self can never be entirely personal or individual. Selfhood cannot escape language's sociability – the extent to which meaning is socially produced. Othello's response to this constitutive vulnerability is to seek to plaster over it in an ever more desperate and certain commitment to the fantastical narrative of Desdemona's betrayal that Iago has constructed for him.

It is not, however, only Othello's commitment to this fantasy that is on display in this scene. The interpretative cost of the audience's own investment in Iago's play is also Shakespeare's target here. Having promised to provide Othello with proof of Desdemona's adultery Iago proceeds to question Cassio about his relationship with a prostitute called Bianca. Iago's ploy is based on the assumption that the listening Othello will believe that Cassio is talking about Desdemona and not Bianca. In many ways this scene is a reversal of the box tree scene in *Twelfth Night* with Othello playing Malvolio and Iago Maria. In *Othello*, however, it is the person in hiding that crushes the text, or in this case the performance, to make it what they will. In the process Shakespeare turns the critical violence which in the box tree scene was directed at the critics of his theatre on his own audience. In particular, in this scene Shakespeare articulates a deep cynicism concerning the ability of an audience to actually see and understand what is in front of them – to resist the temptation to make of a play what they will. Certainly Othello is quite incapable of watching and listening to the exchange between Iago and Cassio in a rational way. Even

when Bianca herself appears on stage, and therefore potentially completely undermines Iago's plotting, Othello does not see what is in front of his
eyes. But of course in this he is simply behaving like all audiences do.
Othello sees what he wills as a way of warding off the chaos of a meaningless arbitrary world. Anything is better than that – even Iago's racist and
sexist fantasies.

Othello is finally prepared to sacrifice even his sense of self to keep
chaos at bay. By the time he comes to accuse Desdemona to her face of
being a whore it is clear that Othello's commitment to Iago's fantasy has
become complete:

> Des: I hope my noble lord esteems me honest.
> Oth: O, ay, as summer's flies are in the shambles,
> That quicken even with blowing. O thou weed
> Who art so lovely fair and smell'st so sweet
> That the sense aches at thee, would thou hadst ne'er been born!
> Des: Alas, what ignorant sin have I committed?
> Oth: Was this fair paper, this most goodly book,
> Made to write 'whore' upon? What committed!
> Committed? O thou public commoner!

> Act 4, Sc 2, L 66–74

Othello conceptualises Desdemona's alleged whoredom in this speech in
explicitly textual terms. He sees her as a page to be written on and moves
on from this to imagining her as a common text to be bought, sold and
consumed by other men. Othello's real fear, however, is marked in this
passage by his repetition of the word 'committed'. At one level this
appears to refer to his fear that Desdemona has committed adultery but
this explanation does not exhaust the meaning of this word. Indeed if it
did there would be no need for Othello to repeat it. Othello's repetition of
'committed' reflects the extent to which his violence is driven by an anxiety over meaning and a desperate desire to force signifier and signified
together – to close down and erase any difference, any pause or hiatus,
between word and meaning, to fix Desdemona's meaning in blood and
flesh on her face. His repetition of the word 'committed' marks this desire
and the inevitable failure that drives it since each time he repeats the
word its meaning subtly alters. At the centre of *Othello* is the fear of interpretative failure and it is this which gives the play its particular and peculiar density.

Iago and the boundaries of language

The problem with *Othello* as a play is, however, not only, or indeed principally, the eponymous hero's fall but the reason Iago makes it happen.[12] This is despite that fact that throughout *Othello* Iago reels out a number of plausible reasons for his actions. At the end of Act 1 he states that:

> Iago: I hate the Moor,
> And it is thought abroad that 'twixt my sheets
> He's done my office. I know not if 't be true,
> But I for mere suspicion in that kind,
> Will do as if for surety.

> Act 1, Sc 3, L 385–9

This seems a relatively unambiguous statement. However, it is important to note that Iago asserts his hatred of the Moor before giving any reasons for his hate. Earlier he appeared to tell Roderigo that he hated Othello because he felt slighted by Othello's promotion of Cassio to a position that Iago thought should have rightfully been his (Act 1, Sc 1, L 8–32). The truth is that Iago's hate precedes any rationalisation of it. The phrase in this speech 'Will do' refers directly to the fact that in terms of adultery suspicion is enough for Iago – he does not need facts. But these words also have another meaning which is that the possibility of Iago being cuckold to Othello will serve to justify his hate. The implication is that the crucial thing about the rumour of adultery is not its truthfulness but its validity as an excuse for Iago's hatred. In these terms 'Will do' can also be taken as referring to the audience's desire to understand why Iago causes Othello's downfall – to make sense and therefore in some ways contain the horror of the play. 'Will do' is Iago's contemptuous response to the need, his but far more pressingly the audience's, to provide his actions with a motivation, to make them meaningful. The rumour of adultery, like his early complaint about Cassio's appointment, will serve to justify his acts. Shakespeare, however, leaves no real doubt that Iago is making only the minimal effort to explain his behaviour to himself and us. This is why Iago is given so many different reasons for hating Othello – they are only there to create the minimal illusion of plausibility. Iago/Shakespeare, however, knows that the audience, like Othello, are so 'duteous and obsequious', have such 'open and free natures', that any old scrap of justification will do – they will lap it up like 'soulless knaves'.

The logic of Iago's 'Will do' is taken to its conclusion at the moment when he first tempts Othello to doubt Desdemona's faithfulness. Cassio has just been asking Desdemona to intercede for him with her husband when Othello enters with Iago. Deciding that it would be better to depart before meeting Othello Cassio takes his leave of Desdemona creating the opportunity for Iago to strike:

> Cas: Madam, I'll take my leave.
> Des: Why, stay and hear me speak.
> Cas: Madam, not now, I am very ill at ease,
> Unfit for mine own purposes.
> Des: Well, do your discretion.   [Exit Cassio]
> Iago: Ha, I like not that.
> Oth: What dost thou say?
> Iago: Nothing, my lord, or if – I know not what.

> Act 3, Sc 3, L 30–7

What does Iago's Ha mean? He seems not to know himself and yet Othello latches on to it. The *Oxford English Dictionary* gives the meaning of Ha as "An exclamation, of surprise, wonder, joy, suspicion, indignation etc according to the intonation". What defines Ha is its performance. Its meaning changes from moment to moment. Indeed it is debatable to what extent one can describe it as meaningful since its chief quality seems to be the extent to which it lacks a full or fixed meaning. It means nothing but also in Iago's hands everything since he uses it to incite Othello's fear of interpretative failure. Ultimately it is Othello's misunderstanding of Ha that leads him to his fate – or rather his desire to make this word of nothing, this sound, two letters, fit into the world of meaning. Later in this scene Iago again provokes Othello's fear of the protean quality of language:

> Iago: Did Michael Cassio, when you wooed my lady,
> Know of your love?
> Oth: He did, from first to last. Why dost thou ask?
> Iago: But for a satisfaction of my thought,
> No further harm.
> Oth: Why of thy thought, Iago?
> Iago: I did not think he had been acquainted with her.

Oth: O yes, and went between us oft.
Iago: Indeed?
Oth: Indeed? Ay, indeed. Discern'st thou aught in that?
Is he not honest?
Iago: Honest, my lord?
Oth: Honest? Ay, honest.
Iago: My lord, for aught I know.
Oth: What dost thou think?
Iago: Think, my lord?
Oth: Think, my lord? By heaven, thou echo'st me,
As if there were some monster in thy thought,
Too hideous to be shown.

Act 3, Sc 3, L 94–112

In this dialogue Iago again exploits Othello's anxieties over language. In particular, he constantly uses questions, repetitions and throw-away comments. It is as though Iago is not really committed to the conversation but simply following Othello's words. Indeed while it is true that at one level Iago does echo Othello the opposite is if anything even more striking – in this dialogue Othello directly echoes Iago at least twice as if he has lost the ability to generate his own words and has to parrot those of his tormentor.

Iago's Ha represents in Lacanian terms language's point of extimacy – the mark of Other at the centre of language.[13] Renata Salecl comments that: "Language inscribes itself as a whole by prohibiting something, by ruling something out of bounds."[14] Iago's Ha represents the prohibited thing ruled beyond the bounds of language, but which nevertheless constantly and illegally returns to disrupt the wholeness of language. It marks language's vulnerability to a point of Otherness that is at once alien to language and which gives it meaning – language's violent, irrational denied logic. Iago seduces Othello by drawing upon all that Ha represents – the undergrowth of language. Iago's plan works because it exploits Othello's awareness of his Otherness, the extent to which the narrative he tells of his life can never fully or finally write over the constitutive Otherness of his identity as Othello the Moor of Venice. Iago makes Othello experience language's own constitutive vulnerability and in the process awakes Othello's anxieties about the stability of his selfhood. Iago's Ha represents the fact that language is never complete, never full – that it always says less (or more) than the subject desires, that at its heart is lack.

The other side of language's failure is represented in the handkerchief that plays such an important part in Othello's fall. This mischievous object is raised by Othello, at Iago's prompting, to the signifier of Desdemona's honesty. If Iago's Ha reflects language's inevitable lack the handkerchief reflects language's promiscuous protean side – the extent to which meaning is always excessive. Othello's account of the handkerchief's past repeats motifs from the narrative he had earlier told of his life. In his narration of the handkerchief's journey, however, the movement is away from Venice backwards through the hands of his mother into the depths of time:

> Oth: That handkerchief
> Did an Egyptian to my mother give,
> She was a charmer and could almost read
> The thoughts of people.
> …
> … there's magic in the web of it [the handkerchief]
> A sibyl, that had numbered in the world
> The sun to course two hundred compasses,
> In her prophetic fury sewed the work;
> The worms were hallowed that did breed the silk
> And it was dyed in mummy, which the skilful
> Conserve of maidens' hearts.

Act 3, Sc 4, L 57–77

The source of the handkerchief's potency is pushed further and further back in Othello's account of its genesis as he attempts to fix its meaning. The narrative that Othello tells of his mother's handkerchief concludes by asserting that the materials from which it was made were themselves meaningful. It is as though the handkerchief is a text in which the gap between writing's exteriority and interiority has been bridged – in which the graphic word and its meaning are one. The handkerchief in Othello's eyes is an ur text – one whose materiality, the silk and ink, is at one with its meaning: a text that escapes the play of signification – in which signifier and signified are one. The fantasy that drives this representation of the handkerchief in the narrative that Othello tells is of a world, in his words implicitly feminine, of empowered prophetic speech that can escape the play of signification. The handkerchief is a text that in its stitches escapes the fall into textuality, which magically retains its pure oral state despite being a text.

Othello's representation of the handkerchief is, however, profoundly textual. The idea of a realm, feminine, popular or indeed prophetic, from which issue texts that combine meaning and matter, speech and text, is self-evidently a fantasy that can exist only in a textual world. Indeed in the early modern period it is a specifically humanist fantasy relating directly to humanist models of selfhood where subjectivity is marked by the creation of texts that speak the humanist's interior self. In particular, one finds in the work of Erasmus a constant tension between the valorisation of the individual interior self and an awareness of this self's dependence on the written text. Terence Crane comments that: "[For Erasmus] Discourse should be a direct counterpart of the inner self; those who try to make it something else – a false mask – indirectly reflect their own mendacity."[15] Crane goes on to point out that Erasmus's "whole value-system, based as it is on interiority … is compromised by the public exterior nature of writing".[16] As in *Twelfth Night*, in *Othello* Shakespeare reflects through the motif of the handkerchief upon a basic tension in humanistic, and specifically Erasmian, thought. In *Twelfth Night*, however, the use of Feste to reflect on the relationship between popular wisdom and writers like Erasmus is positive. In *Othello* Shakespeare is far more critical of humanism. In particular, while it is possible to see the eponymous hero's collapse of self as a product of his racial Otherness in fact Othello's sense of self is entirely normative in its vulnerability to language. What distinguishes Othello is that his race allows the audience to protect the fantasy of a humanist self as described by Crane – a self that escapes its dependence on textuality – by viewing Othello's self as peculiarly vulnerable because of his status as Other. But in terms of the individual's relationship to language Otherness is constitutive of selfhood – there can be no self without language which in turn means without the Other.[17] Shakespeare shows us in the figure of Othello the cost that some people have to pay in order to sustain the fantasy of the humanist self.

Othello constructs his mother's handkerchief as if its mythical roots allow it to escape its status as a text – and in the process simply emphasises its textual nature. The handkerchief is the symbolic partner of Iago's Ha. It marks the failure of language to be whole and transparent by embodying the fantasy of a world of inspired pure language and deconstructing it at the same time. The handkerchief springs from prophetic feminine roots, it weaves together signifier and signified, interiority and exteriority, *and* it is simply a text whose meaning spins off in every direction. In *Othello* Shakespeare enacts language's failure, the lack at its centre and its lack of a centre. And it is Iago who battens on to language's failure in order to seduce Othello. Iago reminds him both of the lack at the centre of his being, Ha, which he cannot narrate away and the extent to which his sense of self is built upon shifting words – a promiscuous web of language, the handkerchief.[18]

What makes Iago's seduction of Othello so radical, and indeed disturbing, is how banal it is.[19] Certainly Iago seems to have a profound understanding of how to seduce Othello, but Shakespeare makes sure that his ploys are exposed for everyone to see them for what they are, tricks and lies, banal acts of deception, innuendo and flattery. It is this banality that is the truth of *Othello* – dripping off the poetry and contaminating the drama. Iago operates as a kind of internal on-going prologue. Žižek has suggested that the prologue:

> … functions as the Freudian *Vorstellungsrepräsentanz* (representative of representing): an element which, on stage, within its diegetic reality of representation, holds the place of the mechanism of representing as such, thereby introducing the moment of distance, interpretation, ironic comment …[20]

Iago is *Othello*'s internal endless prologue. There is a constant sense during the play that he is only half involved in the action. Indeed, as has been suggested, Iago often seems to take a perverse pleasure in announcing to the audience the extent to which he is simply a cipher – an actor acting the part of a villain. If Iago is *Othello*'s prologue then it must be noted he shows no respect for dramatic conventions. He is a prologue who despises the rules of time and place, a prologue with soul.

Iago personifies Shakespeare's theatre. He is the tricks and lies that are the constitutive, but denied, logic of the theatre – the scaffold upon which Shakespeare hangs his poetry. *Othello* is built around a figure who encapsulates language's twin failures: Iago as Ha or handkerchief, meaning either nothing or everything, either a banal meaningless exclamation or a site of endless interpretation.[21]

Othello ends with Iago silent but about to be tortured. Having accepted his guilt Othello asks that Iago be made to explain his behaviour. Iago, however, rejects this request with a final oblique comment:

> Iago: Demand me nothing. What you know, you know.
> From this time forth I never will speak word.

Act 5, Sc 2, L 300–1

Iago's refusal to speak looks like a final act of rebellion against the people and society he despises – and in a sense it is, provided one acknowledges that the people it is really directed against are not those on stage but are rather the audience. This is because at one level the reason that Iago will never speak another word is that the play is ending. After all, despite the audience's desire to believe in Iago as a real person in fact he is simply a collection of someone else's words, a product of Shakespeare's trade produced to satisfy the audience's desire for drama. "What you know, you know." The people who really know are the audience. Far more so than even Othello they know what has taken place over the last two hours, what Iago has done. But what they know is nothing. Why does Iago destroy Othello? At the end of the play one is faced with two equally unacceptable answers to this question – the banal or flawed. One can simply give the answer that Iago hints at throughout the play which is that he is a villain. He destroys Othello because in terms of the conventions of Shakespeare's drama that is what villains do. Alternatively one can pick one of the justifications that Iago, and Shakespeare, drop throughout the play – class hatred, racism, sexism, alienation, etc. At the end of *Othello* one can choose either Ha or the handkerchief: an explanation that explains nothing – Iago is a villain; or one that 'will do' – that might satisfy the desire to explain Iago but which even as it is put forward will be undermined by one of the numerous other explanations that Iago/Shakespeare provides during the course of the drama.

At the end of *Othello* all that is left is the audience's desire to participate in the collective production of meaning.[22] It is this desire that Iago incites and exploits at the very beginning of the play with his racist sexist image of Desdemona and Othello having sex. It is this desire that is left hanging, unsatisfied by Iago's silence. This is why the audience, and in particular the learned among them, are prepared to turn the screw and tighten the rack in the Venetian torture chamber that Lobovico makes clear will be Iago's next stage. Iago's torture, however, will simply produce an endless, echoing Ha – violent, irrational and meaningless. It is this possibility, that in the end Iago's actions were without meaning, that their only real purpose was to provide drama, to make the play happen, that gives *Othello* its peculiar and disturbing feel. In the end the audience would rather torture Iago to keep alive the possibility of explanation than face the reality that they, like Othello, have allowed their open and free natures to be taken in by an incompetent, lying villain – and, unlike Othello, have paid for the privilege.

Conclusion

The issues raised by *Othello* seem strangely contemporary. In particular, there appears to be a strange and disturbing correspondence between Žižek's use of language and Iago's. The similarities between these two characters – the Lacanian plotter and Jacobean theorist – can be illustrated by examing briefly the opening section of Žižek's book, *The Plague of Fantasies*. This work opens with a section entitled 'The truth is out there' in which Žižek introduces one of the key themes of his study, that "The Unconscious is outside, not hidden in any unfathomable depths …".[23] Having made this claim, Žižek goes on to provide a number of examples from popular culture to support his argument. Among these are the differences between English, French and German toilets. Žižek then refers to what he suggests are "the three main hairstyles of the feminine sex organ's pubic hair – wildly grown, a French garden and punk/shaved".[24] The opening of *The Plague of Fantasies* is typical of Žižek's writing and reflects his preparedness to deploy examples to support his complex ideas that are at once humorous, shocking and potentially offensive. *The Plague of Fantasies*, as with all of Žižek's work, is at once complex and exciting but also repetitive and at times banal. As with *Othello* the choice it appears to offer the reader is either to allow the drama of theory to continue and in the process also allow the circulation of sexist/racist images or to renounce the pleasures of the text. Does Žižek, like Iago, rely upon the desire of his readers to make sense to sustain the gap in his work between its theoretical complexity and the relative simplicity of many of the examples he uses from popular culture? Does Žižek's work offer its readers the pleasure, made more intense by its forbidden nature, of consuming racist and sexist imagery? Indeed is the attractiveness of the sexist and racist images used by Žižek/Iago based on the fact that even in the face of the failure of language they work – they make sense in a world where language itself seems to consist of meaningless complexities or reductive banalities?

These questions can be related to the two main criticisms of Žižek's work – that it is constitutively based on racist and sexist imagery or that its rhetorical drive is in some way excessive. An example of the former is provided by Claudia Breger's critique of Žižek's work, 'The Leader's Two Bodies: Slavoj Žižek's Political Theology', in which Breger argues that:

> … Žižek outlines a world … not open to human agency and political change. Because the authoritarian shape of his vision is constitutively tied up with anti-Semitic and ant-feminist phantasms, it is especially problematic.[25]

For Breger Žižek's insistence on the essential truthfulness of Lacan's teaching means he is locked into a world dominated by a 'monstrous Lord' – one in which the space for thought has been entirely reduced and constrained. Robert Samuels on the other side argues that Žižek "is locked into a modernist Hegelian conception of universality that threatens to transform his entire corpus into a self-consuming rhetorical machine".[26] The choice in terms of these criticisms of Žižek's thought seems to boil down to a repetition of that in *Othello* between Ha and handkerchief – between critiquing Žižek's over-reliance on specific images or attacking his writing for its excessive mechanical productivity.

What lurks behind both these critiques is a desire for a critical idiom that says what it means, that is transparent and clear: a language that is not repetitive, machine-like, that does not constantly return to the same issues, dig over the same earth, one that in its form, the examples it deploys, shows its commitment to such liberal norms as anti-sexism and anti-racism. But critical thinking cannot be transparent or clear. It should not be comforting or safe. It has to be challenging. As Judith Butler points out, "The demand that language deliver what is already understandable appears to be a demand to be left alone with what one already knows."[27] Žižek's work is difficult and demanding. It is repetitive and it does have a mechanical quality to it. But this is because the issues he is raising are themselves at one level banal – culture does keep repeating itself, subjectivity is not endlessly performative and history is class struggle.[28] Despite the appearance of plurality, of human agency, of the possibility of political change, the truth is that modern society is banal and oppressive, writing is mechanical and there are fundamental traumas that humanity constantly returns to.[29] Žižek's agenda is profoundly political and ethical

– it is driven by a basic commitment to understanding the present in order to imagine a better future.[30]

Despite the pessimism of *Othello* Shakespeare, like Žižek, does not turn his back on the political or the ethical. Although Iago dominates *Othello* the play is Shakespeare's not his. In particular, although ultimately Desdemona cannot escape Iago's plots, she is depicted throughout the play as a site of resistance to Iago and all that he represents. Shakespeare goes out of his way to show her resisting and defeating Iago's sexism. Desdemona tells him that his sexist view of women is ignorant and impotent, that they are "old paradoxes, to make fools laugh i' th' alehouse" (Act 2, Sc 1, L 138–9). And despite her death it is Desdemona who wins in the end. It is her spirit that sustains Paulina's resistance to Leontes' tyranny in *The Winter's Tale*. Paulina, however, unlike Desdemona, knows her enemy – she has read Badiou.

Notes

1 Patricia Parker has suggested that the kind of voyeurism that sustains Malvolio's desire for Olivia is at the heart of *Othello*. She writes that "*Othello* itself … provokes a constant, even lurid, fascination with the offstage, or in this sense the ob-scene, starting from the vividly racialized rhetoric of Iago and Roderigo at its opening, focused on an unseen sexual coupling or imagined coupling, involving the 'monstrous' opening of a Venetian virgin by a 'lascivious Moor'." Patricia Parker, 'Fantasies of "Race" and "Gender": Africa, *Othello*, and bringing to light', in *Women, 'Race,' and Writing in the Early Modern Period*, ed. Margo Hendricks and Patricia Parker (London: 1994), pp.84-100, p.94.

2 Stephen Greenblatt, *Shakespearean Negotiations: The Circulation of Social Energy in Renaissance England* (Oxford: 1988), p.5.

3 For carnival in *Othello* see Michael D. Bristol, 'Charivari and the Comedy of Abjection in *Othello*', in *Materialist Shakespeare: A History*, ed. Ivo Kamps (London: 1995), pp.142–56.

4 Slavoj Žižek, *The Plague of Fantasies* (London: 1997), p.21.

5 Ibid., p.33.

6 Renata Salecl comments that "In racist hatred (let us remember that hatred is always the counterpart of love), the subject primarily objects to the other because of the way he or she enjoys …" Renata Salecl, *(Per)Versions of Love and Hate* (London: 1998), p.52.

7 George Steiner, *Language and Silence: Essays 1958–1966* (London: 1985), p.121.

8 Jacques Derrida, *Of Grammatology*, trans. Gayatri Chakravorty Spivak (Baltimore: 1974), p.7.

9 Katherine Eisaman Maus suggests that: "Iago functions as a sort of poet of monstrosity, lovingly dwelling on the gross issue, the monstrous birth, the unnatural thought, the palace into which foul things intrude." And he does all this for our entertainment. See Katherine Eisaman Maus, 'Proof and Consequences: Inwardness and its Exposure in the English Renaissance', in *Materialist Shakespeare: A History*, ed. Ivo Kamps

(London: 1995), pp.157–80, p.172.

10 Stephen Greenblatt, *Renaissance Self-Fashioning: From More to Shakespeare* (Chicago: 1980), p.245.

11 Judith Butler, *The Psychic Life of Power: Theories of Subjection* (California: 1997), p.28.

12 Andrew Hadfield argues that: "Whereas Venice is able to accommodate the black outsider and has institutions powerful enough to resist, if not nullify, indigenous prejudice, Iago, who is never assimilated, works from within to make sure that such harmony can never be achieved." Andrew Hadfield, *Literature, Travel and Colonial Writing in the English Renaissance* (Oxford: 1998), p.240.

13 For a discussion of the concept of extimacy see Jacques-Alain Miller, 'Extimité', in *Lacanian Theory of Discourse: Subject, Structure and Society*, ed. Mark Bracher, Marshall W. Alcorn, Jr and Françoise Massardier-Kenney (New York: 1994), pp.74–87, p.76.

14 Salecl, 1998, p.124.

15 Terence Crane, *The Cornucopian Text: Problems of Writing in the French Renaissance* (Oxford: 1979), p.44.

16 Ibid., p.47.

17 Or to put it another way there can be no subject without narrative. Butler comments that: "The grammar that governs the narration of subject formation is one that presumes that the grammatical place for the subject has already been established. In an important sense, then, the grammar that the narrative requires is a result of the narrative itself." Judith Butler, "'Conscience Doth Make Subjects of Us All', *Yale French Studies*, 88 (1995), pp.6–26, p.21.

18 On the handkerchief's excessive meaning see Elizabeth J. Bellamy, 'Othello's Lost Handkerchief: Where Psychoanalysis Finds Itself', in *Lacan, Politics, Aesthetics*, ed. Willy Apollon and Richard Feldstein (New York: 1998), pp.151–79.

19 Anne Righter points out that where Richard III's success can be regarded as a triumph of theatricality "Iago's abilities as an actor are far less important than his generalized will to destroy …". Anne Righter, *Shakespeare and the Idea of the Play* (London: 1962), p.165.

20 Slavoj Žižek, 'The Ambiguity of the Masochist Social Link', *Perversion and the Social Relation*, ed. Molly Anne Rothenberg, Dennis Foster and Slavoj Žižek (Durham, NC: 2003), pp.112–25, p.114.

21 Robert Watson has suggested that Iago shares many characteristics with the villainous Catholics that filled Elizabethan and Jacobean anti-Catholic propaganda. This is certainly the case in terms of the linguistic options that he incites – complete redundancy and meaningless expansion. Papist language is consistently constructed by English Protestant writers as filling up the space of religion with a mass of meaningless words – papistry produces endless text and it all means nothing worth knowing. For a discussion of the language of papistry see Tom Betteridge, *Literature and Politics in the English Reformation* (Manchester: 2004). For Iago's Catholic characteristics see Robert Watson, '*Othello* as Protestant Propaganda', in *Religion and Culture in Renaissance England*, ed. Claire McEachern and Debora Shuger (Cambridge: 1997), pp.234–57.

22 Robert Matz has recently argued that: "While Iago's accusations work to eliminate tensions that arise from contradictions within Venetian culture, as a partial outsider himself Iago also functions within the narrative logic of the play to keep the hands of 'proper' Venetians clean even as he does their work." One could argue that the proper Venetians whose hands are most dirty and therefore most in need of an Iago to clean them are the audience – they need above all to blame someone, preferably an outsider,

for their desire. See Robert Matz, 'Slander, Renaissance Discourses of Sodomy, and *Othello*', *English Literary History*, 66 (1999), pp.261–76, p.273.

23 Žižek, 1997, p.3.

24 Ibid., p.5.

25 Claudia Breger, 'The Leader's Two Bodies: Slavoj Žižek's Political Theology', *Diacritics*, 31 (2001), pp.73–90, p.75.

26 Robert Samuels, 'Žižek's Rhetorical Matrix: The Symptomatic Enjoyment of Postmodern Academic Writing', *Journal of Composition Theory*, 22 (2002), pp.327–54, p.331.

27 Judith Butler, 'Values of Difficulty', in *Just Being Difficult: Academic Writing in the Public Arena*, ed. Jonathan Culler and Kevin Lamb (Stanford, CA: 2003), pp.199–215, p.203.

28 In his response to Breger's criticism Žižek argues that: "… what lurks in the position of my critic is simply *the disavowal of psychoanalysis*. In the field from which she speaks, there is no place for the Freudian unconscious – it is as simple as that." Normative intellectual language at the moment cannot find a place for the radical a-historicism of psychoanalysis – the fact that as far as thinkers like Žižek are concerned the work of Freud and Lacan allowed the emergence of truths that transcend history. See Slavoj Žižek, 'The Rhetorics of Power', *Diacritics*, 31 (2001), pp.91–104, p.96.

29 Herbert Marcuse points out that "Socialism does not and cannot liberate Eros from Thanatos." Iago will always find enough hatred, fear and desire in language to weave his plots. Herbert Marcuse, *The Aesthetic Dimension: Toward a Critique of Marxist Aesthetics* (London: 1979), p.72.

30 It seems bizarre to criticise Žižek's lack of political engagement given studies like *Welcome to the Desert of the Real!* in which he argues that: "… we 'feel free' because we lack the very language to articulate our unfreedom. What this lack of red ink means is that, today, all the main terms we use to designate the present conflict – 'war on terrorism', 'democracy and freedom', 'human rights', and so on – are false terms, mystifying our perception of the situation instead of allowing us to think it. In this precise sense, our 'freedoms' themselves serve to mask and sustain our deeper unfreedom." In this context the intellectual needs to ensure that their work refuses the fantasy of freedom – of originality, creativity and human agency. Instead by being mechanical and repetitive, difficult and demanding, it can speak the current lack of freedom and therefore be part of the struggle to create a new meaningful language of freedom. See Slavoj Žižek, *Welcome to the Desert of the Real! Five Essays on September 11 and Related Dates* (London: 2002), p.2.

CHAPTER FIVE

Telling stories in Cymbeline *and* The Winter's Tale

Dying ain't so hard for men like you and me. It's living which is hard when all you have cared about has been butchered or raped.

Clint Eastwood, *The Outlaw Josey Wales*, 1976

*T*HE WINTER'S TALE is a lesson in ethics. It stages a confrontation between cynicism and politics, between philosophy and sophistry and between idealism and action. In this play Shakespeare returns to the relative optimism of *Richard III* in terms of his theatre and in the process develops an aesthetic that answers the despair of *Othello*. *The Winter's Tale* is an act of faith. Herbert Marcuse argued that:

> Art fights reification by making the petrified world speak, sing, perhaps dance. Forgetting past suffering and past joy alleviates life under a repressive reality principle. In contrast, remembrance spurs the drive for the conquest of suffering and the permanence of joy.[1]

Iachimo and Posthumus petrify their world turning it into a totalising inhuman metaphor when they 'bet' on Imogen's faithfulness. In treating her as an object they die to the world. Leontes creates a petrified fantasy world of shadows and empty words – a dead spectral realm conjured up to avoid encountering life.

In *The Winter's Tale* and *Cymbeline* Shakespeare revisits the issues that he addressed in *Othello* but applies to them the proverbial solution of *Coriolanus*. He develops in these late plays a sense of the theatre as an ethical space where truths are made. This chapter is in two parts. The first section discusses one of Shakespeare's neglected plays, *Cymbeline*, while the second examines the ethics of *The Winter's Tale*. In *Cymbeline* and *The Winter's Tale* Shakespeare plays with the audience's expectations. In both works the line between comedy and tragedy is extremely thin. Indeed these plays are constantly self-referential, disrupting any sense of continuity, either spatial or temporal, and often appearing to be designed to push theatrical plausibility to the limit. Why is this? Is it, as has been suggested, that at the end of his writing career Shakespeare simply got lazy or bored? Perhaps this is the case, but the turn to romance in *Cymbeline* and *The Winter's Tale* can also be seen as a deliberate attempt to address the theoretical and ethical issues raised by Iago's silence – it is to answer his Ha that Imogen suffers, Paulina makes her stand and Autolycus laughs.

Ethics in Shakespeare 1: Cymbeline

Living in the world means fighting to make meaningful words like justice, freedom and truth. When men like Leontes or Posthumus give in to their fears and fantasies they make the easy choice – they turn their backs on the world choosing instead the safety of death. The turn to romance reflected in *Cymbeline* and *The Winter's Tale* is driven by a desire to rescue language from the curse of Iago. In each of these plays tragedy rests on a knife-edge but is prevented by characters that refuse the comforts of cynicism and despair. It is this ethical refusal which relates Shakespeare's last plays directly to current critiques of postmodern thought.[2] At the heart of postmodernism is an infantile desire for a realm of the fully and totally authentic. The inevitable, indeed constitutive, failure of this desire is what motivates postmodern thinkers to announce the end of history and the futility of politics. In particular, postmodernism's hyper-valorisation of the authentic, and its congruent anger at its non-appearance, has driven postmodern theory to be particularly scornful of such concepts as justice, truth or ethics. Postmodernist thought insists that these ideals can only exist within language and that therefore they can never possess the degree of authenticity necessary for them to be meaningful. It is the combination of frustration, self-hatred, scorn and anger which makes postmodern writing so complex and at the same time empty. It constantly has to stage the impossibility of achieving the very thing it desires – an authenticity that it already knows it cannot have. The end result is the creation of an imaginary world in which action is impossible, in which critique consistently circles around the failure of language, and the idea of ethical action is regarded as either naive or dangerous. Timothy Bewes comments that: "The tortuous mincing of words which characterizes the classic texts of postmodern theory, finds its match in the installation of truth as a monstrous and impossible chimera at the heart of the political enterprise."[3] He goes on to argue that: "To place truth conceptually within quotation marks ... is as much a fetishization and an absurdity as the attempt to isolate if from the conditions of its articulation."[4] Postmodernism is obsessed with the failure of language, its lack of transparency and wholeness. Like Leontes, when its demand for complete and absolute authenticity fails, postmodern thought turns instead to the creation of fantasy worlds that in their tortuous obsession with the protean qualities of language simply confirm its own fantasies. Postmodernism represents a turn away from the world – surrendering to violence, irrationality, oppression and death. It is a world of shadows in which a blizzard of words prevents any engagement with the world – a protective postmodern linguistic cocoon.

Postmodern thought is profoundly sophistic and solipsistic. It tends to constantly turn inwards talking to and at itself. In the process postmodern discourse assumes the shape and sound of Leontes' or Othello's paranoid mutterings. This strange resemblance across five hundred years reflects the extent to which postmodernism is a recapitulation of long-standing themes within Western thought. For example, it is possible to see postmodernism's pessimistic approach to meaning, and in particular language, as a secular version of St Augustine's view of the irredeemably flawed and corrupt nature of human words. Margaret Ferguson comments that:

> According to Augustine's radical philosophy of Being, human language can never be truly 'literal' because all referents other than God are constituted by 'non-being' and are therefore, like the referent 'time', themselves figural with respect to the one absolutely literal truth.[5]

Ferguson argues that for Augustine language, like humanity, is drenched in sin. Its meanings can therefore never be full or complete because it shares in humanity's sinfulness – the curse of particularity and temporality. Authenticity, wholeness and totality can only exist in God and are simply beyond the fallen world of humans. Words are always flawed, partial and lacking – their integrity and meaning undermined by sin. Postmodernism shares in this sense of language's failure but gives it an additional twist by insisting that the fallen nature of language renders any attempt to produce the truth of the past, to critique the present or imagine a better future, futile.

It is this futility that Augustine and in a different context Shakespeare reject as a form of linguistic solipsism – a retreat from the world into a privatised corrupt language. In *Confessions* Augustine discusses how he learnt to talk and his education. He describes how the classical stories used as examples by his teachers corrupted his mind. It was not, however, the words themselves that were to blame for this corruption but the use his teachers made of them. "I bring no charge against the words which are like exquisite and precious vessels, but the wine of error is poured into them for us by drunken teachers."[6] Augustine's criticism of his teachers relates directly to his understanding of words as signs whose efficacy relates to how they are being used. The word is a 'precious vessel', an empty space, a mystery. Filling the word, adding something to its nothing, is for Augustine an inherently ethical act. He consistently critiques an emphasis on language as a formal structure or as rhetorical performance in comparison with its use to teach God's lessons. He writes:

> Look, Lord God, look with patience as you always do. See the exact care with which the sons of men observe the conventions of letters and syllables received from those who so talked before them. Yet they neglect the eternal contracts of lasting salvation received from you. This has gone to such lengths that if someone … pronounces the word 'human' contrary to the old school teaching … he is socially censured more than if, contrary to your precepts, he were to hate a human being, his fellow-man.[7]

The alternative to this formalist approach to language as articulated in Augustine's work is an emphasis on language's collective status and the extent to which this collectivity can itself enable humans to work away from their sinfulness. Augustine relates this possibility directly to the fact that God's grace has to operate through human instruments. In *On Christian Teaching* he argues that "the human condition would be wretched indeed if God appeared unwilling to minister his word to human beings through human agency".[8] Augustine's work constructs language as embodying in its very form the possibility of salvation. For example, in the *City of God* Augustine uses the rules of syntax as a

metaphor for the bonds that hold communities together, arguing that "…
the individual man is, like a single letter in a statement, an element, as it
were, out of which a community or realm is built up …".9 Augustine's
work suggests that the communal nature of language could provide the
basis for the creation of communities united in the pursuit of a truth that
would escape the here and now, that would be orientated to the future of
Christ's return, to the establishment of a reign of justice, truth and love.
Brian Stock comments that:

> [For Augustine] Love operates vertically, descending from the text to the
> reader, and horizontally, as readers relate to audiences. Christianity
> emerges as a textual community built around shared principles of inter-
> pretation.[10]

It is these textual communities that offer the possibility, if not the reality,
of escaping the prison house of language's failure – while the individual
cannot but be trapped by language, the community can at least imagine
escape.

Augustine's work seeks to push the reader to achieve a truth through
reading that paradoxically transcends the written text. In terms of the self
Augustine argues that self-knowledge, again paradoxically, is based on the
acceptance that one does not tell one's own life as narrative or story – that
we do not tell the tale we are. Stock comments that:

> At the end of [On Christian Doctrine], Augustine arrives at a position com-
> parable to that of Confessions 7–9. Through his analytical and autobio-
> graphical discussions, he concludes that it is illusory for men or women to
> believe that the narratives that they live are their own constructions, any
> more than they can be sure that a given interpretation of a text is com-
> pletely correct. As predestination operates inscrutably in Augustine's life,
> scripture creates for him a readerly universe that is never fully knowable.[11]

Augustine, particularly in his own Confessions, argues that embracing this
dependent state, the fact that one cannot have final control over the tale
that one is, that we are actors in a story told by someone else, is the basis
for ethics, truth and justice.

Shakespeare makes a similar argument in his last plays. He creates a
tension between those characters who desperately desire to tell themselves, to own or possess the narratives of who they are, and those which
accept the provisional nature of language as a provocation for ethical
action – as the very ground that makes ethics possible. In particular, in

Cymbeline Shakespeare critiques the death to the world embodied in the moment of commodification. Karl Marx famously approved of Shakespeare's depiction of money as, in Marx's words, the "alienated ability of mankind".[12] Marx argued that Shakespeare was particularly concerned with two properties of money: 1) it is the visible divinity – the transformation of all human and natural properties into their contraries, the universal confounding and distorting of things: impossibilities are soldered together by it; 2) it is the common whore, the common procurer of people and nations.[13] In *Cymbeline*, however, it is language, particularly poetry, rather than money that Shakespeare depicts as the alienated ability of mankind. It is language, and in particular that of the villain of the play, Iachimo, that solders contraries together. It is Iachimo's linguistic skills, his abilities as a writer, which enable him to turn the play's hero, Imogen, into a commodity – a common whore to be consumed voyeuristically by the audience. It is his words that destroy, or more accurately write over, her chastity. In *Cymbeline* ethical action is compared with the desire to consume, with Iachimo's commodification of Imogen, and is related directly to the emergence of a textual interpretative community that explicitly embraces the collective nature of language, selfhood and truth.

Cymbeline opens with two Gentlemen on stage discussing recent events at court:

> First Gent: You do not meet a man but frowns: our bloods
> No more obey the heavens than our courtiers
> Still seem as does the king's
> Sec. Gent: But what's the matter?
> First Gent: His daughter, and the heir of's kingdom (whom
> He purpos'd to his wife's son – a widow
> That late he married) hath referr'd herself
> Unto a poor but worthy gentleman. She's wedded,
> Her husband banish'd; she imprison'd, all
> Is outward sorrow, though I think the king
> Be touch'd at very heart.

Act 1, Sc 1, L 1–10

These opening lines seem almost provocatively evocative of earlier plays by Shakespeare. The lack of names reminds one of the Chorus's speech at the beginning of *Romeo and Juliet*. The themes of inheritance and banishment echo the concerns of *King Lear*. Above all *Cymbeline's* opening reminds one of the exchange between Iago and Roderigo at the beginning of *Othello*. This is because the First Gentleman's account seems designed to simultaneously satisfy and whet the audience's desire to know what is happening on stage. At one level the First Gentleman tells the audience all they need to know. *Cymbeline* is going to be a play centred upon a forbidden royal marriage. But who are the lucky couple? What are their names? Even more perplexing is the First Gentleman's claim that the court's sadness is 'outward sorrow'. Although at one level this is simply a reference to the fact that the courtiers are pretending to be sorrowful it also repeats the meta-theatrical motif from *Othello*. As with Iago's instructions to Brabantio at the beginning of *Othello* this line can be read as a deliberate, and indeed provocative, reference to the fictionality and theatricality of *Cymbeline* as a play. 'Outward show' is what actors do. And by suggesting that the courtiers are all performing their sorrow the First Gentleman makes Cymbeline's court a stage.

This sense of unreality is increased by the rush of events that the audience is presented with in the First Gentleman's comments. The overwhelming impression that is created by these opening lines is of partiality and belatedness. The First Gentleman's speech makes it impossible to ignore the extent to which *Cymbeline* is part of a larger narrative that has already started and will carry on long after the play has finished. The opening of *Cymbeline* reflects Shakespeare's exploitation of the generic conventions of romance in order to foreground the fictionality and communality of his drama. The First Gentleman's comments serve to locate the play within a narrative of tales, histories and myths. They are the drama's point of origin and the moment when, in an entirely arbitrary, provisional and self-reflective fashion Shakespeare decided to cut his narrative out from the tapestry of romance.[14]

As the first scene progresses Shakespeare appears to be playing with his audience. Having started the scene without any names the First Gentleman goes on to give an extremely detailed account of Posthumus's parentage and childhood. This speech is immediately preceded by the First Gentleman's rather strange claim that, in praising Posthumus, "I do extend him … within himself, Crush him together, rather than unfold His measure duly" (Act 1, Sc 1, L 25–7). The account of Posthumus's lineage that follows this rather elliptical statement, however, clearly does extend 'him' beyond himself and into a romance narrative of orphanage and royal adoption. The idea of extending someone into themself is oxymoronic since it combines two contradictory movements – extension and enclosure. The language reminds one of Ben Jonson's stoic celebration of Sir Thomas Roe's 'gathered self', but as with Jonson's poem there is a tension between gathering and publication – can a gathered self remain in its state of stoic completeness once it has been textualised or narrated?[15] Posthumus as he is presented by the First Gentleman in the first scene of *Cymbeline* sounds like a stoic hero who has wandered into a romance.

The First Gentleman's imagery of enclosure and expenditure also echoes that of Shakespeare's much earlier text, *The Rape of Lucrece*, where the husband of the eponymous hero of the poem, Collatine, celebrates Lucrece's chaste purity in language that constructs her as a commodity in order to impress his fellow Roman officers and more tragically his general, Tarquin:

> ... he the night before, in Tarquin's tent
> Unlock'd the treasure of his happy state:
> What priceless wealth the heavens had him lent,
> In the possession of his beauteous mate ...

> L 15–18

The narrative of *The Rape of Lucrece* goes on to ask why Collatine is:

> ... the publisher
> Of that rich jewel he should keep unknown
> From thievish ears, because it is his own?

> L 33–5

Collatine's publication of his wife's chastity makes something that should be hidden and enclosed public. More importantly it commodifies Lucrece's worth by turning it into words, something to be circulated, handled and exchanged. The language Collatine uses to praise Lucrece is commercial and monetary, in direct contrast to that used by the poem's narrator who equates Lucrece's beauty, chastity and worth to her sovereignty. When the First Gentleman extends Posthumus's worthiness into a romance narrative he also becomes the publisher of that which at one level should remain hidden. The crucial difference, however, is that, while Collatine's publication of Lucrece's worth deploys the language of commerce, the First Gentleman speaks within the discourse of romance. Collatine makes Lucrece into an object to be owned and possessed while the First Gentleman turns Posthumus into a character within a tale, within a romance, within a play.

Ironically it is Posthumus who later in the play repeats Collatine's lethal authorship of his wife as a commodity when he bets on his wife's, Imogen's, chastity with Iachimo, a dissolute Italian nobleman:

> Post: My mistress exceeds in goodness the hugeness of your unworthy thinking. I dare you to this match: here's my ring.
> Phi: I will have it no lay.
> Iach: By the gods, it is one. If I bring you no sufficient testimony that I have enjoy'd the dearest bodily part of your mistress, my ten thousand ducats are yours, so is your diamond too ...

> Act 1, Sc 5, L 141–8

This exchange between Posthumus and Iachimo repeats the tension between expansion and contraction. Posthumus's rejection of Iachimo's huge thinking is answered in the latter's implicit reduction of Imogen to her 'dearest bodily part' – in other words her sex. Iachimo is betting that he can 'have' the nothing, the part, which marks Imogen as a woman. Posthumus's strange phrase 'hugeness of your unworthy thinking' relates at a specific level to Iachimo's sexist view of woman and in particular his assumption that they are all wanton. In a more general sense, however, this phrase can be related to a misogynistic fear of women. Iachimo's 'huge unworthy thinking', or rather Posthumus's fantasy of it, reflects the horror of the male gaze when confronted with the nothing to see of femininity.[16] Iachimo's huge thinking is a reference to the misogynistic fantasy of filling up and obscuring femininity as the signifier of lack; Mercutio's Queen Mab speech is another example of this huge thinking and reflects its inevitable failure – male thinking can never be so large as to write over the trauma, the horror, when confronted with its own lack. Iachimo's huge thinking can also be related directly to Petrarchan poetry which was predicated on the endless production of texts that simultaneously sought to fill up and hide this feminine place of horror, and incited its voyeuristic consumption.[17] Posthumus's participation in the bet, like Collatine's publication of Lucrece, makes him a party in the commodification of his wife. It reflects the extent to which he shares, if only as a disavowed desire, in Iachimo's huge thinking. Like Collatine he cannot resist using his wife as an object to be exchanged between other men – the thing that, like a Petrarchan sonnet, allows men to share and exchange their huge thinking.[18]

It is, however, important to note that this exchange between Posthumus and Iachimo is interrupted by Philario's attempt to stop the bet being placed. Philario is a friend of Iachimo and throughout the scene attempts to act as a moderating influence. The importance of his interjection here is that it creates the possibility for either of Iachimo or Posthumus, perhaps particularly the latter, to pull back from the brink. That this does not happen reflects Shakespeare's desire to make explicit the choice being made by Iachimo and Posthumus – that both of them of their own free wills are choosing to treat Imogen as a commodity and place huge thinking, empty words, before her status as a fellow human being. Posthumus's acceptance of the bet means he accepts the commodification of Imogen and that therefore Iachimo is bound to win since he does not need to possess the reality of Imogen's body but only its symbolic value as a commodity.

Iachimo leaves Posthumus in Italy and travels to Britain where he meets Imogen. At this point, however, his plans suffer a temporary setback. Iachimo tries to seduce Imogen by telling her that Posthumus has been unfaithful:

> Iach: O dearest soul: your cause doth strike my heart
> With pity that doth make me sick! A lady
> So fair, and fasten'd to an empery
> Would make the great'st king double, to be partner'd
> With tomboys, hir'd with that self exhibition
> Which your own coffers yield! with diseas'd ventures,
> That play with all infirmities for gold
> Which rottenness can lend Nature! Such boil'd stuff
> As well might poison poison!

Act 1, Sc 7, L 118–26

It is easy to dismiss Iachimo's speech as simply a lie. As far as one knows Posthumus has not been visiting tomboys or harlots. But is this speech itself not a reflection of the fact that Posthumus has taken part in at least one diseased venture – the bet? Indeed when he accepted the commodification of Imogen did he not make her a tomboy, an object to be passed around and consumed by men for their pleasure? Iachimo's speech is an attempt to poison Imogen's mind; indeed at one level it is poison – venomous wine poured into her ear. And the source of this venom is the man she loves.

Iachimo's words, however, also reflect the misogynist horror at the heart of his huge thinking with their metaphoric collapse of money, disease, sex and language. In particular, even when he is trying to compliment Imogen he appears to find it impossible to keep at bay his desire to consume her 'best part'. The phrase 'self exhibition' refers specifically to the money that Imogen gave Posthumus. It also, however, implies a collapse of selfhood into money and suggests that Imogen's generosity is itself in some way part of the same economy as Iachimo's and Posthumus's diseased venture. The reference to 'boil'd stuff' refers to the treatment for venereal disease, but is also the corollary of the reduction of Imogen to her best part. It implies a reduction of the human to a porridge or mess of matter – in other words what is left after the best part has been subtracted.

Iachimo's attempt to seduce Imogen, however, ultimately fails because she refuses her part in his and Posthumus's misogynist drama:

> Iach: I dedicate myself to your sweet pleasure,
> More noble than that runagate to your bed,
> And will continue fast to your affection,
> Still close as sure.
> Imo: What ho, Pisanio!
> Iach: Let me my service tender on your lips.
> Imo: Away, I do condemn my ears, that have
> So long attended thee. If thou wert honorable,
> Thou wouldst have told this tale for virtue, not
> For such an end thou seek'st, as base, as strange.

> Act 1, Sc 7, L 136–44

Imogen's rejection of Iachimo's suit reflects her chastity. It also acts as a model for the audience. Imogen listens to all Iachimo's words and then makes the moral decision to reject them – she refuses his seduction. This rejection, however, does not prevent Imogen from being 'taken' by Iachimo who, having asked her pardon, tricks her into keeping a chest of his safe in her bedchamber. After she has gone to sleep Iachimo emerges from his trunk and rhapsodises over the sleeping Imogen. This is a deeply disturbing scene which conjures up images of violation and rape:

> Iach: The crickets sing, and man's o'er-labour'd sense
> Repairs itself by rest. Our Tarquin thus
> Did softly press the rushes, ere he waken'd
> The chastity he wounded. Cytherea,
> How bravely thou becom'st thy bed! fresh lily!
> And whiter than the sheets! That I might touch!
> But kiss, one kiss! Rubies unparagon'd,
> How dearly they do't: 'tis her breathing that
> Perfumes the chamber thus: the flame o' th' taper
> Bows toward her, and would under-peep her lids,
> To see th'enclosed lights, now canopied
> Under these windows, white and azure lac'd
> With blue of heaven's own tinct. But my design:
> To note the chamber ...

Act 2, Sc 2, L 11–24

Iachimo imagines himself as Tarquin posed before the sleeping Lucrece. The reference to 'our Tarquin' is, however, ambiguous. It could simply be a reference to Iachimo's and Tarquin's shared nationality, Italian, except that Iachimo is a Roman whereas Tarquin was an Etruscan. More importantly the reference to Tarquin lends this scene a political colouring since it was Tarquin's rape of Lucrece that provoked the Romans to rise against the Etruscan tyranny and set up a republic. What are the politics of Iachimo's performance as Tarquin? Can one compare what is taking place on stage at this moment in *Cymbeline* with *The Rape of Lucrece*'s construction of Lucrece as the embodiment of Roman republicanism and Tarquin as representative of foreign monarchical tyranny?

Before answering these political questions, it is important to note that Iachimo's use of the word 'our' gives this moment a specifically theatrical edge since at one level 'our Tarquin' is his *and* the audience's. In other words as Iachimo hovers over Imogen he is being Tarquin at this moment in the drama – for himself and the audience. The image of the taper straining to peep under Imogen's lids, to penetrate her closed eyes, is a metaphor for rape. This creates a relationship between Tarquin's rape of

Lucrece and Iachimo's incitement of the audience's desire to participate in his consumption of Imogen's best part. Iachimo consumes Imogen as the audience's Tarquin. His words force her to give up the secrets of her body to the audience while she sleeps:

> Iach: On her left breast
> A mole cinque-spotted: like the crimson drops
> I' th' bottom of a cowslip. Here's a voucher,
> Stronger than ever law could make; this secret
> Will force him to think I have pick'd the lock, and ta'en
> The treasure of her honour. No more: to what end?

> Act 2, Sc 2, L 37–42

Catherine Belsey has recently commented in detail on the politics of *The Rape of Lucrece* arguing that a central issue in this text is consent. She comments that: "The installation of the Republic which is the consequence of [Lucrece's suicide] affirms a model of state politics based on consent."[19] The difference between Imogen's story and Lucrece's is, however, that whereas the latter is literally raped and then kills herself Imogen is the victim of a fantasy. The issue remains one of force and consent but in *Cymbeline* what is forced upon the woman is not literal violence but the symbolic violence of commodification.

Iachimo does not rape Imogen but his words do publish her as a commodity to be consumed by himself and the audience. Indeed there is clearly a level at which the audience's presence is necessary to motivate and sustain the commodification of Imogen. The audience need Iachimo's words in order to 'see' him 'winning' the bet. But this explanation does not fully explain why Shakespeare gives him such a long and detailed speech, in particular as the longer Iachimo spends on stage at this moment the more plausibility seeps from Shakespeare's drama. But to put the issue in these terms is to misunderstand the theatrical politics of this moment. Iachimo is the audience's Tarquin, but he is also their Collatine. He needs them in order to publish Imogen's sovereignty – to write her as a commodity to be consumed. In this scene he behaves like Iago manipulating the audience, turning them into duteous fools, Brutus's vile bondsmen. In the process the audience become the slaves to Iachimo's Etruscan tyranny – as their Tarquin he consumes Imogen's sovereignty on their behalf. Iachimo makes the audience party to his plots and hates by battening on to their voyeuristic desire to consume Imogen. Unlike Iago, however, Iachimo seduces himself. It is as though he comes to believe as he hovers over Imogen that he is indeed taking possession of her when in fact all he, and the audience, has consumed is a simulacrum of her sovereignty – an outer shell of Iachimo's own construction whose hugeness can never fill out its empty centre.

Cymbeline, however, unlike *Othello* does not end in tragedy. This is not because Posthumus is any more sensible than Othello. Shakespeare explicitly creates a comparison between Imogen's refusal to credit Iachimo's lies and Posthumus's acceptance of them. What really distinguishes *Cymbeline* from *Othello* is that while the latter ends with silence the former concludes with a riot of interpretation. In the penultimate scene Posthumus is in jail. He falls asleep and has a vision in which he is visited by his dead father, mother and younger brothers. These Ghosts upbraid Posthumus for his failings but their complaint is interrupted when Jupiter appears from the heavens and assures them that Posthumus will be happily reunited with Imogen. Jupiter departs but not before placing a tablet on Posthumus's breast, "wherein Our pleasure his full fortune doth confine" (Act 5, Sc 4, L 109–10). When Posthumus awakes he discovers Jupiter's tablet but finds that he cannot make sense of what is written on it – which is hardly surprising given that it is so elliptical:

> Post: When as a lion's whelp shall, to himself unknown, without seeking find, and be embrac'd by a piece of tender air: and when from a stately cedar shall be lopp'd branches, which, being dead many years, shall after revive, be jointed to the old stock, and freshly grow, then shall Posthumus end his miseries, Britain be fortunate, and flourish in peace and plenty.

Act 5, Sc 4, L 138–45

It is only at the very end of the play that a Soothsayer explains the riddle to Posthumus and the rest of the characters assembled on stage. This creates the strange sense that the ending of *Cymbeline* repeats itself – or rather that it concludes with a series of regressions. Jupiter foretells the end, but is not understood; the action is brought to a conclusion and only then does the Soothsayer appear on stage to unite meaning and action. He brings order to the world of the play – or more accurately makes the order that has emerged meaningful. *Cymbeline* ends, as it began, by announcing its fictionality. In particular, it foregrounds its status as a story cut from a tapestry of stories, a romance that forms part of a far wider textual community of tales, myths and histories.

There are two types of expansion and constriction in *Cymbeline*. Iachimo's and Posthumus's bet is sustained by a misogynistic logic that commodifies women. It is as a commodity that Iachimo, the audience's Tarquin, consumes/rapes Imogen – and it is as a commodity that she is forced to consent to the audience's voyeurism. The other form of expansion and constriction in *Cymbeline* is, however, generic. The play's romance form is based upon the simultaneous cutting out of the matter of the story, its tales, myths and historical 'facts', and their expansion into a narrative. This process of narratological production is moreover integral to the play. *Cymbeline* consistently announces itself as a work of fiction. If this sounds profoundly postmodern it is, but with a fundamental twist. Postmodernism fetishises the production of meaning, and the extent to which this process is always in some ways flawed – excessive or stalled. This failure is postmodernism's endlessly protean object of study and the particular fact that prevents its production of truths. In these terms the bet between Iachimo and Posthumus is also postmodern in its balance between Iachimo's huge thinking and Imogen's best part. As has been suggested the linguistic nature of this bet means that Posthumus will always lose but the important thing to also note is that so will Iachimo. The bet allows Posthumus and Iachimo to weave together their ideological edifice – it serves as a point of justification for their huge thinking – and keeps at bay the worrying possibilities of huge thinking/boiled stuff and the particular part. The crucial point to note here is that the bet's endless productivity serves to protect Posthumus and Iachimo from the danger of the encounter – it functions to keep permanently open and deferred the moment when the subject has to make a choice, to be ethical. It is this which drives the commodification of Imogen since by turning her into a commodity Posthumus and Iachimo create a situation in which they never need to face the reality of her as a woman – they turn her into the fantasy that sustains their misogynistic reality and in the process make her pay the price for their infantile refusal of ethics.

Cymbeline, however, unlike postmodern thought does not respond to this logic with a weary acceptance of its inevitability. Instead it offers its own generic status, its romantic form, as an alternative to Iachimo's huge thinking. It is this ethical move at the level of form and genre that gives the Soothsayer at the end of the play his authority. It is not that he pro-duces the truth or reality from the play's various plots – this has already happened. The Soothsayer is a figure for the Lacanian critic – his domain is one of meaning not facts.[20] All he adds to the play, which is, however, in some ways everything, is a distance between its being and meaning. It is this space that enables the production of truth and a space for ethics. And it is precisely this gap or possibility that the bet allows Iachimo and Posthumus to obscure and erase. *Cymbeline* constructs itself as a space for thought – or rather the play presents us with two possible responses to the inevitable non-appearance of the Real. One can either create a thing, the bet, in order to avoid ever confronting the trauma of the Real or one can live with it; one can either remain huddled with Posthumus and Iachimo in their permanently stalled postmodern phantasmagoria or embrace the world with Imogen and Žižek.

Ethics in Shakespeare 2: The Winter's Tale

The work of the French philosopher, Alain Badiou, is centrally concerned with questions of truth and ethics. In *Manifesto for Philosophy* Badiou's focus is on the tension between philosophy and sophistry which he sees as a constant within the history of Western thought. In this work Badiou argues that during the twentieth century, and perhaps particularly with reference to postmodernism, sophistry has been in ascendancy but that there is now an urgent need for a return to philosophy. Badiou argues that: "Philosophy shall only exist insofar as it proposes, to match the needs of our times, a new step in history of the category of truth. It is truth which is the new idea in Europe today."[21] He goes on to suggest, however, that in order for philosophy to be possible it must be desired and that this in turn requires a break with historicism – with the idea that the possibilities of thought are constrained by history. Were this break to take place, Badiou argues, philosophy would re-appear:

> … as what it is, a bright opening of eternity, without God or soul, from the very fact that its effort puts us in agreement with the following: that there are truths. Such is the orientation of what I do not hesitate to consider, for thought, as a *duty*.[22]

Badiou's work is predicated on the human duty to pursue or think truths. His insistence on this relates directly to his work on ethics.

In his discussion of ethics, *Ethics: An Essay on the Understanding of Evil*, Badiou starts by examining the meaning of the term ethics and proposes that it needs to understood in terms of 'the destiny of truths'.[23] What Badiou means by this rather elliptical phrase only becomes apparent after he has dismissed the idea of an ethics based on differences. He argues, "No light is shed on any concrete situation by the notion of the 'recognition of the other'."[24] Badiou goes on to suggest that: "Only a truth is ... *indifferent to differences*. This is something we have always known, even if sophists of every age have always attempted to obscure its certainty: a truth is *the same for all*."[25] This leads Badiou to argue that: "The only genuine ethics is of truth*s* in the plural – or more precisely, the only ethics is of processes of truth, of the labour that brings *some* truths into the world."[26] It is for Badiou philosophy's duty to create a space for thought that allows these truths to emerge. Badiou's conception of the ethics of truths stresses the extent to which the ethical has to involve more than one – that it has to be an ethics *of*, an ethics of process, not a given or an injunction. In other words the ethical is inherently provisional and collective. It is also for Badiou inherently material. He argues that: "Ethics is the principle that judges the practice of a Subject, be it individual or collective."[27] For Badiou the ethical should be understood in almost utilitarian terms. For him ethics can only really exist as a principle of judgement at the level of practice. This leads Badiou to argue that any attempt to totalise a truth, to make it the truth and therefore a basis for an ethics as law or morality, is evil. He writes, "Every absolutization of the power of a truth organizes an Evil."[28] For Badiou the desire to totalise a truth is evil and produces evil since it ignores the extent to which truths exist within language, within the community. And it is when the ethical is based upon a totalised truth that it becomes an evil justification for the closure of thought.

In *Cymbeline* and even more so *The Winter's Tale* the space for thought is threatened by three evils, flattery, desire and consumption. In *The Winter's Tale* it is the failure of Leontes as ruler that causes tragedy. He insists on totalising his view of the world, and rejects the rather pathetic attempts of his counsellors to resist his tyrannical corruption of the political realm. It is Paulina who insists on forcing open the prison doors of Leontes' sophistic fantasy – she embodies the antidote to the flattery of his counsellors who by simply reflecting back on him his fantasies encourage him to close off the real world, to die into a misogynistic cocoon. The conclusion of *The Winter's Tale* is a defence of the theatre as a space in which truths can be produced. It is, however, in the figure of Autolycus that Shakespeare reflects most radically on the ethics of his art.

The Winter's Tale opens with what appears to be an Augustinian morality tale. When Hermione presses Polixenes to tell her about his and Leontes' boyhood he replies with a strange metaphoric account which is centred upon the concept of original sin:

> Pol: We were as twinn'd lambs that did frisk i' th' sun,
> And bleat the one at th'other: what we chang'd
> Was innocence for innocence: we knew not
> The doctrine of ill-doing, nor dream'd
> That any did. Had we pursu'd that life,
> And our weak spirits ne' er been higher rear'd
> With stronger blood, we should have answer'd heaven
> Boldly 'not guilty', the imposition clear'd
> Hereditary ours.
> Her: By this we gather
> You have tripp'd since.
> Pol: O my most sacred lady,
> Temptations have since then been born to's: for
> In those unfledg'd days was my wife a girl;
> Your precious self had then not cross'd the eyes
> Of my young play-fellow.

Act 1, Sc 2, L 66–80

Polixenes produces an image of his childhood with Leontes as an Edenic state of innocence without the burden of original sin, 'the curse hereditary ours'. He goes on to suggest that it was only after meeting their future wives that Leontes and he knew sin. What makes Polixenes' speech disturbing is the way it mingles images of innocence with references to sex. For example, the line 'our weak spirits ne'er been higher rear'd With stronger blood' implies that in their state of innocence Leontes and Polixenes did not know desire. The actual imagery, moreover, suggests that this lack of desire had a specific form which was that they did not have erections. This reading appears to be rather reductive. It should be noted, however, that for Augustine involuntary erections were *the* sign of original sin – the thing that above all displayed man's inability through his free will to save himself. This context gives Polixenes' claim that 'Temptations have since been born to us' a specific sexual meaning as if it was only when they met their future wives that he and Leontes fell from grace. There is also a strange gender slippage in this line with the suggestion that at one level Polixenes and Leontes have given birth to their own temptations. Polixenes' short account of his childhood with Leontes reproduces in miniature the story of Adam and Eve, particularly in its suggestion that in their childhood the two future kings escaped the fate of humanity. Polixenes obviously intends his words to conjure up an Edenic image of a pre-sexual paradise – and they do achieve this, but only if one ignores the extent to which the cost of this image is a denial of his and Leontes' humanity, an arrogant assumption that the two young princes once escaped the fate of their fellow humans, and the extent to which Polixenes' image is constitutively dependent on his wife and Hermione bearing the burden of sin.

It is Polixenes' speech, and the thoughts it contains, which is the pro-logue to Leontes' sudden and apparently inexplicable fall into jealousy. Leontes initially bases his suspicions that Hermione and Polixenes have had an affair on their courtly behaviour. Shakespeare, however, goes out of his way to depict how quickly Leontes' jealousy generates its own matter. In particular, it very soon becomes apparent that for Leontes his jealousy performs the same function as the bet does for Posthumus and Iachimo. It provides the motivation for him to retreat from the world – to die into a language of sterile productivity. Very early on in his jealousy Leontes tries to theorise what has happened to him:

> Leon: Affection! thy intention stabs the centre:
> Thou dost make possible things not so held,
> Communicat'st with dreams; – how can this be? –
> With what's unreal thou coactive art,
> And fellow'st nothing: then 'tis very credent
> Thou may'st co-join with something; and thou dost
> (And that beyond commission) and I find it,
> (And that to the infection of my brains
> And hard'ning of my brows).

> Act 1, Sc 2, L 138–45

This speech is notoriously difficult to understand and at one level is designed to sound incoherent. Part of the problem is, however, that Leontes is a more sophisticated thinker than he is sometimes given credit for. Affection's fellowship with nothing is premised on Leontes' understanding that even 'nothing' has a place within the symbolic order – it is something. Indeed the problem with the argument that nothing may join with something is not that it is nonsense but that it is a tautology – every nothing is a negation of something and therefore no nothing is nothing – it is something's nothing. Lurking behind Leontes' words is an awareness that reality is a nothing made meaningful by a fantasy something that in turn blocks the emergence of the Real nothing.

Leontes' meditation on affection can be related directly to the Lacanian Real. Žižek comments that:

> The Real is ... simultaneously both the hard, impenetrable kernel resisting symbolization *and* a pure chimerical entity which has in itself no ontological consistency. ... the Real is the rock upon which every attempt at symbolization stumbles, the hard core which remains the same in all possible worlds (symbolic universes); but at the same time its status is thoroughly precarious; it is something that persists only as failed, missed, in a shadow, and dissolves itself as soon as we try to grasp it in its positive nature.[29]

The Real is at once the only real something that exists outside the symbolic universe and a nothing always beyond one's grasp. The crucial thing about Leontes' meditation on affection is not what the words mean but their form; the complexity of the language sustains Leontes' fantasy that he can fix the place of the Real – prevent it oscillating between hard kernel and fleeting shadow. In particular, what Shakespeare shows us in Leontes is a man retreating from the world into a utopian solipsistic fantasy – a linguistic world of his own making.

It is therefore a mistake to see Leontes' jealousy as irrational or mad. The problem with Leontes is that he is too rational, too sane. He sees the world for what it is and the horror leads him to create a fantasy that protects him from this knowledge. Indeed Leontes' fantasy, while it is particularly productive, is formally rather old-fashioned. It is as though what Leontes is doing in the first three acts of *The Winter's Tale* is creating a parodic version of Othello's jealousy – *acting* as a jealous husband. This is made explicit when Leontes first confronts Hermione with his suspicions:

Leon: You, my lords,
Look on her, mark her well: be but about
To say 'she is a goodly lady', and
The justice of your hearts will thereto add
''Tis pity she's not honest, honorable':
Praise her but for this her without-door form
(Which on my faith deserves high speech) and straight
The shrug, the hum or ha, these petty brands
That calumny doth use …

Act 2, Sc 1, L 64–72

The reference to ha echoes *Othello* but here Leontes is acting as his own Iago. Indeed this speech is a dramatisation of his self-intoxication. What Leontes fears is being a cuckold and ironically his way of addressing this fear is to perform it in public before the whole court as a cuckolded husband in an imaginary play. Leontes' 'petty brands' are words whose meanings are banal and fixed. At the same time what these branded words produce, and indeed are, is a dangerous supplement, an addition that spells Hermione's doom. Ha and hum are at once banal and productive; they brand Hermione as a whore and incite the constant production of discourse – Leontes looks like Othello but he seems to have read Benedick's jest book.

Leontes' fantasy works to protect him from having to embrace the reality of language's lack of totality. It does this by creating an explanation for language's protean quality – Hermione's adultery. By placing Hermione within the discourse of cuckoldry Leontes creates a structure that allows the simultaneous production of 'petty brands' and endless words circulating out of control, whispers, nudges, hints, the 'hums' and 'has' of cuckoldry. Leontes' jealousy is profoundly productive but what it produces is a mass of empty words. Leontes speaks the language of Petrarchan poetry; his fantasy is replete with the language of commodity. It is, however, in the field of politics that Leontes' fantasy is most destructive. Like Coriolanus, Leontes desires a monological political world in which only his voice is heard – one can therefore see him as a figure for Henry VIII who clearly shared this infantile desire.[30] Leontes' fantasy fills up the space of his court with words, petty brands, which stifle and erode the space for thought. In particular, they create an apolitical political space – a court in which debate and discussion have been replaced by the paranoid tortured hum of Leontes' conspiracy theories.

Leontes' accusation of adultery works in the same way as the bet between Posthumus and Iachimo by creating a fantasy in which the cost of language, in particular its lack, is conceptualised within a discourse of commodification and displaced from the male subject on to the female object. In other words Hermione and Imogen are made into objects, dehumanised, in order to protect the fantasy of a humanity that escapes the burden of language, the curse 'hereditary ours'. Leontes and Posthumus effectively deny their humanity, they die to the world, when they create tyrannical fantasies as a way of obscuring their human dependence on language, a dependency that involves a separation from the world, an acceptance of the non-appearance of an unmediated authentic world. To be human is to be inauthentic and mediated. It is this inauthentic humanity that the bet and the discourse of cuckoldry allow Posthumus and Leontes to displace on to Hermione and Imogen while they pursue the dangerous fantasy of the truly authentic.

Paulina's response to Leontes' tyranny is political and ethical. She constructs her right to speak within the discourse of counsel by presenting herself to Leontes, and his lords, as a physician:

> Paul: Good my liege, I come, –
> And, I beseech you hear me, who professes
> Myself your loyal servant, your physician,
> Your most obedient counsellor, yet that dares
> Less appear so, in comforting your evils,
> Than such as most seem yours …

Act 2, Sc 3, L 52–7

It is a reflection of how far Leontes has fallen that his response to Paulina's intervention is to brand her a 'mankind witch' with a 'boundless tongue' who deserves to die.

> Leon: I'll ha' thee burnt.
> Paul: I care not
> It is an heretic that makes the fire,
> Not she which burns in't. I'll not call you tyrant;
> But this most cruel usage of your queen –
> Not able to produce more accusation
> Than your own weak-hing'd fancy – something savours

Of tyranny, and will ignoble make you,
Yea, scandalous to the world.

Act 2, Sc 3, L 113–20

Paulina's reference to heresy creates a further historical echo of the reign of Henry VIII and has the effect of relating Leontes' tyranny with Henry's.[31] More importantly what this speech does is incite the audience to make the ethical political judgement that Paulina explicitly rejects. The world within which the scandal of Leontes reverberates is the theatre. Paulina may stop short of naming Leontes as tyrant but this speech is clearly inviting the audience to do so. In particular, throughout this scene Paulina claims the right to speak as the spokesperson of a truth. She does not claim any authority for herself or attempt to make any general accusations – she does not call Leontes a tyrant. But what Paulina absolutely insists upon is her right to speak the truth of Hermione's faithfulness and in the process enacts the opening up of the court as a space for thought. In the first part of *The Winter's Tale* it is Paulina's voice that re-politicises a fantasy masculine world – she is the one who puts the truth, its status and worth, back into circulation.

Paulina's moral stand can be related directly to Badiou's critique of postmodern thought. Žižek comments that:

> The fundamental lesson of postmodernist politics is that *there is no Event*, that 'nothing really happens', that the Truth-Event is a passing illusory short circuit, a false identification to be dispelled sooner or later by the reassertion of difference or, at best, the fleeting promise of the Redemption-to-come, towards which we have to maintain a proper distance in order to avoid catastrophic 'totalitarian' consequences; against this structural skepticism, Badiou is fully justified in insisting that – to use the term with its full theological weight – *miracles do happen* ...[32]

Leontes' scepticism drives him to create a fantasy event, a non-event. Its fantastical status is reflected in its sterile effects and the way it closes down the space of the political. Leontes' non-event, his fantasy of Hermione's adultery, fills the court with whispers and shadows – it creates a world of much ado about nothing, a world in which nothing, empty words and huge thinking, comes of nothing, Leontes' misogynist fear of women. Politics becomes the impotent and ultimately pointless pursuit of the truth. It takes on a judicial and indeed metaphysical form as Leontes sinks further and further into his fantasy, and this sinking is the point. Leontes creates the fantasy of Hermione's adultery in order to justify his scepticism, to explain the failure of his infantile desire to return to the state of Edenic bliss that he shared with Polixenes and to escape the inauthentic mediated world of human life, love and politics.

The lesson that Paulina teaches Leontes at the end of *The Winter's Tale* is that to be an ethical human means accepting the duty to act, to embrace the event, without complete or full knowledge, that being human involves taking a risk; acting without full transparency, authenticity or knowledge. It means turning one's back on the postmodern insitence that any political action is meaningless because all politics involves compromises, failures and illusions. Žižek comments that:

> ... there is no political 'taking sides' without minimal reference to some ethical normativity which transcends the sphere of the purely Political ... the 'Yes!' of the Hegelian 'reconciliation' is, in the last analysis, precisely a 'Yes!' to complementarity: a 'Yes!' of fully accepting that one cannot simultaneously 'know it' and 'do it'; a 'Yes!' of bidding farewell to the Enlightenment illusion of a self-transparent activity ...[33]

At the end of *The Winter's Tale* Paulina stages an act of faith. This is not, however, a religious moment despite Paulina's demand that the participants in her ceremony awake their faith. Indeed to understand it in religious terms is to avoid the radical implications of this moment.[34] When Hermione first awakes, Leontes comments that "If this be magic, let it be an art Lawful as eating" (Act 5, Sc 3, L 110–11). Later in the scene Paulina replies to Polixenes' request for an explanation of what has happened by telling him, "That she is living, Were it but told you, should be hooted at Like an old tale ..." (Act 5, Sc 3, L 115–17). The play ends with Leontes inviting everyone on stage to join him in retelling the tale:

> Leon: Good Paulina,
> Lead us hence, where we may leisurely
> Each one demand, and answer to his part
> Perform'd in this wide gap of time, since first
> We were dissever'd: hastily lead away.

> Act 5, Sc 3, L 151–5

The Winter's Tale ends at its beginning. The actors leave the stage for another stage to start telling the story again. Indeed has not the audience just sat through a retelling of the story with each of the characters answering their part on demand? The implication of Leontes' final words is that the play is about to start again, that the tale is endless.

The Winter's Tale concludes by invoking a number of key scenes from Shakespeare's earlier work – Richard III's seduction of Anne, Antony's performance at Caesar's funeral and Lear's love test. Paulina, like Richard, uses the totalising power of metaphor to create a moment of theatrical seduction. However, while Anne is seduced into Richard's evil world in which meaning is entirely performative Paulina seduces her audience, on stage and off, into romance. She uses metaphor to produce a truth. And, unlike Richard, Paulina foregrounds the constructed willed nature of this truth – the ethical supplement that she adds to this moment is her demand of faith. It is in this demand that Paulina answers Brutus's scepticism towards the theatre since it is precisely his lack of faith in the theatre as a site for the political that leads to tyranny. At Caesar's funeral Antony uses the possibilities of the theatrical moment to create a community united around a desire to avenge the death of Caesar. The effects of this are, however, tragedy and tyranny. At the end of *The Winter's Tale* Paulina creates a just community – but it is one of equals, a community of tale tellers who when they leave the stage do so in order to enact their acceptance that they too are told. It is this which makes Leontes' leading role at the end of the play so significant. At the end of *The Winter's Tale* Leontes accepts that he is not the narrator of his own life – he accepts, indeed embraces, that he is a part in someone else's story. What is produced at the end of *The Winter's Tale*? Nothing. Just more words, more story – an old wives' tale.[35] But unlike Lear's horror at Cordelia's nothing – a horror driven by his desire to interpret, to see himself in her – Leontes' response to Paulina's nothing – the faith required to make the miracle of Hermione's rebirth happen – is to embrace and perpetuate it.[36] Leontes, in Augustinian terms, accepts at the end of *The Winter's Tale* that the narrative he lives is not his own – that he is part of a tale, a larger romance narrative, part of Augustine's syntactical community.

The final scene of *The Winter's Tale* celebrates the theatre as a proverbial space. Indeed the second half of the play displays to the audience, by deploying romance conventions, the emergence of a textual community produced by tale telling. In particular, Shakespeare, as he did in *Coriolanus*, creates an image of the theatre in the second part of *The Winter's Tale* as a space for thought in contrast to the closed, tyrannical world of

Leontes' court. The nothing that men like Othello, Mercutio, and Leontes in the first part of *The Winter's Tale* find so threatening becomes in the second part of *The Winter's Tale* the basis for the emergence of the theatre as a site for the production and exchange of proverbial wisdom. *The Winter's Tale* is much ado about nothing, an old wives' tale; it is what you will, but with a crucial twist, an added ethical supplement, Autolycus.

In *Aesthetic Theory* Theodor Adorno suggests that:

> Even artworks that incorruptibly refuse celebration and consolation do not wipe out radiance, and the greater their success, the more they gain it. Today this luster devolves precisely upon works that are inconsolable. Their distance from any purpose sympathizes, as from the abyss of ages, with the superfluous vagrant who will not completely acquiesce to fixed property and settled civilization.[37]

Autolycus is Shakespeare's superfluous vagrant. His presence in the second part of *The Winter's Tale* is what sustains its ethics as a proverbial space. This is because Autolycus, like Puck and even Iago, embodies Shakespeare's labour as a writer. His claim to be 'a snapper-up of unconsidered trifles' relates him directly to the role of Shakespeare as an author – what is *Cymbeline* if not a collection of unconsidered trifles: bits and patches of stories, tales and histories? Howard Felperin has argued that:

> Autolycus' ballads re-enact in a comic or surrealistic form not only Leontes' opening fantasies of illicit pregnancy and condign punishment, but his – and our – eagerness for verification, for grounding what must forever remain linguistic and poetic possibility in historical fact or empirical truth.[38]

Felperin argues that Autolycus operates as a comic Iago battening on to the desire of Leontes, and the audience, for a truth that escapes the play of signification. However, this is only part of the story since by turning Leontes' fantasies into the matter of his songs Autolycus renders them harmless and makes them the reason for comedy. This is not to suggest that Autolycus operates for anything other than purely mercenary reasons but that for him, unlike Iago, these are open and obvious. Even his play-acting is transparent. Autolycus is an actor, a writer and a playwright. His business as a picker-up of unconsidered trifles is to sell the scraps he 'finds' back to his audience.

Autolycus, however, is far more than a parasite. In the penultimate scene it is Autolycus who provides the on-stage audience for the three

Gentlemen to recount the reconciliation between Leontes, Perdita, Polixenes and Florizel. The First Gentleman describes in detail the effect on Leontes and Camillo of the Shepherd's confession that he had found Perdita. His partial account is, however, immediately up-staged by the entry of a Second Gentleman whose response to a request for news foregrounds the extent to which what he has seen is beyond reason:

> Sec. Gent: Nothing but bonfires: the Oracle is fulfilled; the king's daughter is found: such a deal of wonder is broken out within this hour, that ballad makers cannot be able to express it.
>
> Act 5, Sc 2, L 22–5

A Third Gentleman then enters to finish the story. It is left to the First Gentleman to comment that "The dignity of this act was worth the audience of kings and princes; for by such was it acted" (Act 5, Sc 2, L 79–80). This line can be seen as a sly dig at the critics of Shakespeare's theatre who constantly complained about the fact that on stage actors played kings – here it is the other way around. More importantly the First Gentleman's line is a reminder that the actual audience is not watching the reconciliation of the kings. They have to hear what has happened through the reported speech of unnamed Gentlemen. Indeed the situation for the audience is even worse than this since the Gentlemen consistently construct what they have seen as beyond language – so wonderful that it defies the descriptive poetic powers of even ballad makers. What is happening at this moment is Shakespeare is making the audience, in advance of Paulina's injunction, engage in an act of faith – this scene only makes sense if one believes what one is hearing. Autolycus operates here as a reason for story telling – he is the excluded party, the audience, that provokes the Gentlemen to tell their winter's tale, their romance of loss, discovery and reconciliation.

Autolycus is superfluous to the plot of *The Winter's Tale* – or rather the story could easily get along without him. If he does make things happen this is purely by chance. This is in some ways strange since, as has been suggested, Autolycus can be seen as a representation of Shakespeare as a playwright. Surely if anyone is in charge of the play it is the person who writes it – who makes it happen. It is this which created the disturbing similarities between Iago and Shakespeare. In Autolycus, however, it is as though Shakespeare is embracing the logic of proverbial wisdom with its denial of ownership or originality. Autolycus's trifles are not his – he only borrows them, exchanges them and moves on. Autolycus, like Erasmus with his proverbs, is a producer of a sea of knowledge. He patches together bits and pieces of learning and puts them into circulation. In the process he creates a textual community, imagined specifically against the tyranny of Leontes' court, united through its endless consumption of ballads – endless because the will to consume in the pastoral scenes of *The Winter's Tale* is consistently equated with the will to spend and share. It is as though the collective nature of the ballads, Autolycus's own lack of ownership, makes the songs he sells escape the logic of ownership and control – they are unconsidered trifles, superfluous vagrants, Erasmus's proverbs or Shakespeare's plays.

The Winter's Tale enacts the unveiling of love as the creation for a space for thought – in other words the progress of love in this play can be equated with the work's ethics. Alain Badiou has suggested that:

> Love initially involves the One of solipsism, which is the confrontation or hand-to-hand combat between the cogito and the grey darkness of being in an endless, compulsive repetition of words. Next comes the Two, which arises within the event of an encounter and the incalculable poem of its designation by a name. Lastly, there is the infinity of the sensible world that the Two penetrates and deploys, and where it progressively unravels a truth of the Two itself. This numericity (one, two, infinity) is specific to the process of love.[39]

Leontes starts *The Winter's Tale* caught in the grey world of words. Under Paulina's tutelage he learns to embrace the cost of the encounter – he learns to love for the first time. It is, however, Autolycus, and what he represents, that marks the unravelling of love through the world of the play, and indeed out into the audience, in the generic and formal intricacies, demands and possibilities of the world of the proverb, ballad and romance – and above all in the space of the play.[40]

Conclusion

Žižek has criticised the way in which contemporary culture generates parodic or empty versions of things, concepts and events. He writes:

> On today's market, we find a whole series of products deprived of their malignant property: coffee without caffeine, cream without fat, beer without alcohol ... And the list goes on; what about virtual sex as sex without

sex, the Colin Powell doctrine of warfare with no casualties (on our side, of course) as warfare without warfare, the contemporary redefinition of politics as the art of expert administration as politics without politics, up to today's tolerant liberal multiculturalism as an experience of the Other deprived of its Otherness ...[41]

Literary criticism without aesthetics, without an explicit engagement with the question of the truths of great writing, is empty or pointless. It is virtual criticism with its malign quality, its ability to question the ethics of writing, removed. Timothy Bewes has recently suggested that:

> The urgent need ... is for political critique at every stage to *mediate* contemporary, 'immediate' reality. Contrary to almost all received opinion, we are living not in a more mediated society than ever before, but a less mediated one. Reality is increasingly what appears to be, just as political agendas are increasingly what they are professed to be – yet this is evidence not of the overcoming of reification but of its proliferation, of a model of truth based not on revelation and mediation but on consistency and immediacy.[42]

Leontes desires a world of authenticity and immediacy. He regards the need for mediation, in the first part of *The Winter's Tale*, as inherently corrupting; it is the fact that his knowledge of Hermione's faithfulness, indeed at a more profound level of the world itself, has to be mediated through language that he cannot accept – that he experiences as a fall into dependency and horror, sin and language, somethings and nothings. This fall leads Leontes to die to the world and to retreat into a safe postmodern linguistic cocoon. His escape from his grey state can be taken as a model for the future of literary criticism – of the need to renounce the empty pleasures of virtual criticism and embrace the risk, the danger, of a criticism that engages in the ethical human duty of producing truths.

Notes

1   Herbert Marcuse, *The Aesthetic Dimension: Toward a Critique of Marxist Aesthetics* (London: 1979), p.73.
2   Postmodernism is a complex and contentious term. In this chapter when I refer to postmodernism I am using it to describe a mode of thought, a way of thinking. Postmodernists, if there are such people, would probably not accept the characterisation of their 'beliefs' that informs this chapter. On postmodernism see Frederic Jameson, *The Cultural Turn: Selected Writings on the Postmodern, 1983–1998* (London: 1998).
3   Timothy Bewes, *Cynicism and Postmodernity* (London: 1997), p.170.

4 Ibid., p.170.

5 Margaret W. Ferguson, 'Saint Augustine's Region of Unlikeness: The Crossing of Exile and Language', *Georgia Review*, 29 (1975), pp.844–64, p.856.

6 St Augustine, *Confessions*, trans. Henry Chadwick (Oxford: 1992), p.19.

7 Ibid., p.21.

8 St Augustine, *On Christian Teaching*, trans. R.P.H. Green (Oxford: 1997), p.5.

9 St Augustine, *City of God*, trans. Henry Bettenson (London: 1972), p.138.

10 Brian Stock, *Augustine the Reader: Meditation, Self-Knowledge, and the Ethics of Interpretation* (Cambridge, MA: 1996), p.196.

11 Ibid., p.206.

12 Karl Marx, *Economic and Philosophic Manuscripts of 1846* (Moscow: 1959), p.123.

13 Ibid., p.123.

14 *Cymbeline* is drawn from many different texts. Although Shakespeare's main source appears to be Holinshed – Cymbeline 'was' an ancient English king – the play itself seems also deliberately iconoclastic in its use of this source.

15 Jonson writes:

That thou at once, then, nobly mays't defend

With thine own course the judgement of thy friend,

Be always to thy gathered self the same …

Ben Jonson, *Selected Poetry*, ed. George Parfitt (London: 1992), p.39.

16 Luce Irigaray comments that for the misogynist the female "sexual organ represents *the horror of nothing to see*". Luce Irigaray, *This Sex Which Is Not One*, trans. Catherine Porter (Ithaca, NY: 1985), p.26.

17 On Petrarchan poetry see Gary Waller, *English Poetry of the Sixteenth Century* (Harlow: 1993).

18 Irigaray comments that: "The exchanges upon which patriarchal societies are based take place exclusively among men. Women, signs, commodities, and currency always pass from one man to another; if it were otherwise, we are told, the social order would fall back upon incestuous and exclusively endogamous ties that would paralyze all commerce. Thus the labour force and its products, including those of mother earth, are the object of transactions among men and men alone. This means the *very possibility of a sociocultural order requires homosexuality as its organising principle*." Irigaray, 1985, p.192.

19 Catherine Belsey, 'Tarquin Dispossessed: Expropriation and Consent in *The Rape of Lucrece*', *Shakespeare Quarterly*, 52 (2001), pp.315-35, p.335.

20 This is a paraphrase of Žižek's suggestion that "the detective's domain, as well as that of the psychoanalyst, is … thoroughly one of *meaning*, not of 'facts'." The Soothsayer, like the detective and the analyst, works at the level of analysis; he makes meaning after the event. Slavoj Žižek, 'The Detective and the Analyst', *Literature and Psychology*, 36 (1990), pp.27-46, p.37.

21 Alain Badiou, *Manifesto for Philosophy*, trans. Norman Madarasz (New York: 1999), p.101.

22 Ibid., p.137.

23 Alain Badiou, *Ethics: An Essay on the Understanding of Evil*, trans. Peter Hallward (London: 2001), p.3.

24 Ibid., p.27.

25 Ibid., p.27.

26 Ibid., p.28.

27 Ibid., p.2.

28 Ibid., p.85.

29 Slavoj Žižek, *The Sublime Object of Ideology* (London: 1989), p.169.

30 Henry's desire to produce a monological public sphere in which only his voice was heard was given its exemplary expression in the frontispiece to the Great Bible. See David Scott Kastan, '"The Noyse of the New Bible": Reform and Reaction in Henrician England', in *Religion and Culture in Renaissance England*, ed. Claire McEachern and Debora Shuger (Cambridge: 1997), pp.46–68.

31 For Henry VIII as a tyrant and the Elizabethan understanding of his use of the heresy law as a specific form of tyranny see Tom Betteridge, *Literature and Politics in the English Reformation* (Manchester: 2004), Ch. 4.

32 Slavoj Žižek, *The Ticklish Subject: The Absent Centre of Political Ontology* (London: 1999), p.135.

33 Slavoj Žižek, *The Indivisible Remainder: An Essay on Schelling and Related Matters* (London: 1996), p.213.

34 S.H. Lim comments that: "By not permitting faith and theological dogma the final say on what the ultimate significance of the highly provocative enlivening of Hermione's statute may be, *The Winter's Tale* interrogates the very ground on which claims to definitive knowledge and transcendent truth are built." This is undoubtly the case, although what *The Winter's Tale* is ultimately concerned with is the idea of proverbial wisdom as the source for the production of truths. See S.H. Lim, 'Knowledge and Belief in *The Winter's Tale*', *Studies in English Literature*, 41 (2001), pp.317–34, p.331.

35 Amelia Zurcher has recently commented on the way in which *The Winter's Tale* "purifies the notion of the tactic" in a political context but avoids making any larger strategic claims – an avoidance that Zurcher relates directly to the play's romance genre. I would argue, however, that the emphasis on tactics in this play relates it to the world of the proverb and that this is in itself a strategic political move. See Amelia Zurcher, 'Untimely Monuments: Stoicism, History, and the Problem of Utility in *The Winter's Tale* and *Pericles*', *English Literary History*, 70 (2003), pp.903–27.

36 Anne Righter comments in relation to Leontes' concluding words that "The play goes on eternally; it has become a synonym for life itself." Anne Righter, *Shakespeare and the Idea of the Play* (London: 1962), p.180.

37 Theodor Adorno, *Aesthetic Theory*, trans. Robert Hullot-Kentor (London: 1997), p.82.

38 Howard Felperin, '"Tongue-Tied our Queen": The Deconstruction of Presence in *The Winter's Tale*', in *Shakespeare and the Question of Theory*, ed. Patricia Parker and Geoffrey Hartman (New York: 1985), pp.1–18, p.15.

39 Alain Badiou, 'Beckett's Generic Writing', *Journal of Beckett Studies*, 4 (1994), pp.13–21, p.18/19.

40 Ronald W. Cooley has commented on what happens to Autolycus at the play's end. He points out that "it is difficult to determine just where to locate Autolycus, or the actor playing Autolycus, *physically*, at the end of the play". He goes on to suggest that: "The play's silence on his ultimate fate, and the nonsense and inconclusiveness of the penultimate scene, liberate Autolycus, rather than containing him. They suggest that the artistic and political apparatus of the play and the state have, in the end, no place to put such a person." Autolycus's lack of place at the end of the play may, however, represent not his liberation from the play but the liberation of the play's message, its ethics, from the closed world of the stage into the audience. See Ronald W. Cooley, 'Speech versus Spectacle: Autolycus, Class and Containment in *The Winter's Tale*', *Renaissance*

and Reformation, 3 (1997), pp.5–23, p.18.

41 Slavoj Žižek, *The Puppet and the Dwarf: The Perverse Core of Christianity* (Cambridge, MA: 2003), p.96.

42 Timothy Bewes, *Reification or The Anxiety of Late Capitalism* (London: 2002), p.174/5.

Conclusion: Mystery and ethics in Shakespeare's drama

S HAKESPEARE'S LAST PLAY was probably *King Henry VIII* (*All is True*). However, it is almost certainly inaccurate to refer to Shakespeare as the author of this work since it is now commonly accepted that it was the product of two playwrights – William Shakespeare and John Fletcher.[1] *Henry VIII* as it appears in the new Arden edition is a tapestry of sources, influences and texts that Shakespeare and Fletcher wove together to produce their play. The composite nature of *Henry VIII* makes the play's sub-title, 'All is True', seem particularly provocative. How can the totality of such a diverse work be true? Whose truth? Whose all? 'All is True' is also a problematic phrase to associate with a history of the Henrician Reformation – or at least Henry VIII's divorce and the birth of the future Queen Elizabeth. *Henry VIII* is a history play obsessed with truth.[2] At its heart is a restaging of Henry's divorce of Katherine of Aragon. This scene is designed to valorise the production of historical truth through the enactment of past events. In particular, what Shakespeare and Fletcher stage in this moment is the ability of staged history to generate truths that have been silenced by the prevailing historical tradition. When Katherine tells Henry that "I desire you do me right and justice" (Act 2, Sc 4, L 11), the scope of her demands extends beyond her husband into the theatre and across history. Katherine's justice, like Isabella's in *Measure for Measure*, never actually appears on stage and the audience is left wondering where it has gone. In *Henry VIII*, however, it does return in the play's insistent portrayal of Katherine's innocence and Henry's culpability.[3]

The play ends with Archbishop Cranmer's famous prophetic speech over the infant Elizabeth:

> Cranmer: Truth shall nurse her;
> Holy and heavenly thoughts still counsel her.
> She shall be loved and feared. Her own shall bless her;
> Her foes shake like a field of beaten corn,
> And hang their heads with sorrow. Good grows with her.

Act 5, Sc 4, L 28–32

In Cranmer's prophecy Elizabeth is a paragon of princely virtues but his words sit uneasily with the preceding scene where a Porter and a Man debate the problems caused by the crowd seeking to get into the palace to celebrate the royal birth. The Man tells how he was doing well keeping the people at bay until overwhelmed by a 'file of boys' to which the Porter replies:

> Porter: These are the youths that thunder at a playhouse and fight for bitten apples, that no audience but the 'Tribulation' of Tower Hill or the 'Limbs' of Limehouse, their dear brothers, are able to endure. I have some of 'em in *Limbo Patrum* – and there they are like to dance these three days – besides the running banquet of two beadles that is to come.

Act 5, Sc 3, L 57–63

In this speech the Porter characterises the boys who defeated the Man as members of the same gangs, the Tribulation of Tower Hill and Limbs of Limehouse, which terrorise the playhouses. He goes on to say that he has some of their comrades in prison and that in three days' time they will be publicly flogged by the beadles. The tension between the formality of Cranmer's words and the informal nature of the preceding scene could be accounted for by the joint authorship of *Henry VIII* – except that it seems likely Fletcher wrote both scenes. The question of authorship is, however, less important than the way *Henry VIII* forces its audience to confront the historical cost of divorce – of separating the world of the populace from that of the court. Cranmer's historical prophecy effectively looks forward to the time in which the Porter and the Man, given the Jacobean content of their dialogue, actually exist.

In its self-reflective staging of the tension that exists within history between past and present, its enactment of de Certeau's historical 'as if', *Henry VIII* returns to the historiographic debates of the first tetralogy, and particularly *Richard III*. The audience of *Henry VIII* are forced to incessantly change registers from high politics, to the saint's life of Katherine's final hours, to the teeming world of a Jacobean crowd and finally Cranmer's prophetic collapse of history itself. The 'All' of *Henry VIII* can be read as Shakespeare's entire dramatic output as represented in the play's kaleidoscope of voices, forms and genres. The word 'true' in the play's sub-title, like its generic claim to be history, is a provocation to the audience. Everything in this play has its truth, is true, but the truth itself is something that has yet to be produced. Rather than offer the audience the simple choice between falsehood and truth *Henry VIII* makes them decide between truths. In the process it creates an image of the theatre as a site for the interrogation and production of truths.[4]

There is something particularly appropriate about the authorial debates surrounding *Henry VIII*. It would be possible to plot in Shakespeare's work from the moment of Lear's howl and Iago's Ha a steady erosion of the authorial function. This is not to suggest for a moment that Shakespeare did not write plays like *Cymbeline* or *The Winter's Tale*. But the turn to romance can clearly be seen as requiring a new self-reflective model of authorship – one that is self-consciously aware that it is only one voice cutting out from the tapestry of romance the story it wishes to tell. In *Henry VIII* this process is taken even further since in this play Shakespeare's authorial role is almost spectral – a ghostly presence haunting the play, but also policing its boundaries.

Henry VIII sits at the edge of Shakespeare's canon. The debates over its authorship reflect a need within literary criticism to define a body of work as written by Shakespeare – to police which texts can be labelled Shakespeare's. This desire is, however, at one level quite inexplicable, particularly from a historicist perspective. Why should it matter who wrote *Henry VIII*? From a historicist stand-point the authorship of a text is a relatively minor question of fact. If the most important thing about *King Lear* is its reflection of the historically traumatic death of feudalism and the emergence of capitalism then who wrote the play cannot be of much note. Such questions are simply a detail compared with the clash of grand historical and social forces reflected in the drama. Literary criticism, however, if it is going to be more than a form of history-lite needs to define its object of study, of which the works of Shakespeare are perhaps the prime example, on the basis of its own discursive norms – in terms of author-ship, literariness and aesthetics. The only defendable reason from a liter-ary critical perspective for studying the plays and poems Shakespeare wrote in the period *c.* 1580–1620 is that his writing, as a sustained unified body of work, engages with questions of truth in relation to love, politics and language. It is Shakespeare's truthfulness that makes him a great writer.

When Thomas Mann was sent a letter stripping him of his honorary doctorate by the University of Bonn as a punishment for his opposition to the Nazis he replied in a famous letter that contained a justification of the role of the artist:

> The mystery of the Word is great; the responsibility for it and its purity is of a symbolic and spiritual kind; it has not only an artistic but also a gener-al ethical significance; it is responsibility itself, human responsibility quite simply … the duty of keeping pure its image in the sight of humanity.[5]

Mann's political writings of the 1930s consistently return to the duty of the writer to be politically engaged. Mann saw Nazism and Stalinism as totalising ideologies that offered their adherents the infantile possibility of escaping the world. He argued that beyond all the publicly espoused aims and goals of these movements – socialism, the defence of the father-land, etc. – was a desire to escape the burdens of the self. Mann argued that:

> The real objective [of young Nazis and Communists] is the ecstasy of free-dom from the self, from thought, and especially morality and reason; and of course from fear also, the fear of life which drives them to huddle together, warm, loudly singing.[6]

Mann's critique of the political tyrannies of his day was that they sought to totalise meaning by reducing the space for politics, ethics and thought. The other side of this totalisation was the ecstasy of escape from the self that they offered their adherents.[7] Mann's response to these twin evils was to emphasise the mystery of the word and the human duty to engage in the ethical practical activity that this mystery made possible. For Mann the mysterious quality of words was not a reason to retreat from politics into obscurantism, fanaticism or sophistry. It was the antidote to tyranny. The mystery of the word creates the space for thought. To close it down, to totalise it, was for Mann to betray one's humanity. To retreat from the self into the happy embrace of irrational totalising ideologies, huddling together within one's linguistic cocoon, was for him a betrayal of one's duty as a human to engage in the pursuit of truths.

Mann's defence of the political seems to uncannily echo contemporary debates over postmodernism. In particular, one can relate his emphasis on the mystery of the word to a number of important critiques of postmodern thought. In his recent study, *Reification or The Anxiety of Late Capitalism*, Timothy Bewes makes a compelling argument for the importance of imagining a space outside or beyond language. Bewes argues that the existence of this possibility is "… a characteristic of dialectical, as of tragic and religious thought, and it signals a refusal to be determined by linguistic necessity, a refusal of the world in the 'reified' form in which it currently appears …".[8] For Bewes this third term or category that 'escapes' the logic of the signifier and signified is necessary for any kind of political critique or indeed action. Without it one ends up in Leontes' closed linguistic world – a place in which there is nothing outside language. Bewes writes that:

> Both tragic and dialectical thought refuse the world *while remaining in it* … While in tragedy the result of this irresolvable contradiction is pathos, in dialectical thinking the possibility of change is implicit in the realization … that in this world, subject and object are in a state of alienation.[9]

For Bewes the defining characteristic of postmodernism is a denial of alienation. This takes the form, he argues, of a reduction of the field of analysis to a formalist and sophistic emphasis on language as a closed totalising system. Bewes writes that: "We are living in an unprecedentedly reflective world in which the desire for an unreified, untainted existence has become a mainstream of cultural and political value."[10] The cost of this desire is, however, illustrated by Leontes and Lear, Othello and Brutus. Leontes wants an untainted world and his consciousness of his own taint leads him to create a tyranny. Brutus desires political purity and instead produces the very tyranny he feared. Iago's seduction of Othello is predicated on his ability to simultaneously incite and contain Othello's fear of the protean tainting qualities of language. Lear wants to hear what cannot be said. He wants to make language say more than it can. But his absolute terror of the idea that language might lack, that it might not be able to say all, that Cordelia's nothing refers to something beyond language, beyond Lear's grasp, leads him to tragedy and madness. The desire for an untainted world is, as Bewes comments, a mainstay of modern Western culture – but it is also a desire that, as one sees very clearly from Shakespeare's work, invariably has violent and tragic results.[11]

The desire for a world free from mediation, for an authentic, untainted existence, is postmodern reification. Being human, however, means being mediated, being alienated, being tainted. Polixenes' myth of a pre-Edenic state reflects a desire for a natural authentic world before the fall into desire but Shakespeare insists on the textual mediated nature of this fantasy – that even as Polixenes imagines a world free from the 'curse hereditary' his words are marked by alienation, desire and sensuous humanity. Bewes and Mann assert the need for a category or realm that cannot be reduced to the functional – a space for thought that resists the totalisation of meaning on the basis of the here and now. Kent, Albany and Edgar attempt to make Cordelia's death meaningful, to textualise it and place it within a narrative, but its meaning escapes their words. It is a mystery but one that demands from the audience an ethical engagement – an attempt to understand its truth. Bewes and Mann, albeit in very different ways, are dialectal thinkers. Their work seeks to imagine a space in which the alienation of subject to object can, indeed must, be thought.

Shakespeare's work shares in this dialectical agenda. New Historicism, however, like much postmodern cultural criticism, lacks this quality. Even the best New Historicist work is invariably based on an undertheorised assertion that literature is not capable of producing truths that transcend a work's historical context. In these terms New Historicism is a profoundly postmodern form of criticism. In *Shakespearean Negotiations* Stephen Greenblatt gave a sophisticated and moving explanation of his new critical methodology. In strangely nostalgic terms he told his readers that:

> I had dreamed of speaking with the dead, and even now I do not abandon this dream. But the mistake was to imagine that I would hear a single voice, the voice of the other. If I wanted to hear one, I had to hear the many voices of the dead. And if I wanted to hear the voice of the other, I had to hear my own voice. The speech of the dead, like my own speech, is not private property.[12]

What makes this passage moving is its emphasis on failure, an acceptance that there never can be an authentic dialogue with the dead. Underlying this passage is a yearning for a world in which speech is private, personal, real, in which one can hear the singular voice of the dead, Shakespeare's voice, without mediation. It is this desire, and the acceptance that it can never be satisfied, that reflects the postmodern nature of Greenblatt's work – that despite all its wit, skill and insight at its heart is a sense of failure, a loss of confidence, a sense that all the history, all the grand narratives and fascinating anecdotes, cannot make the dream real.

The turn to historicism within literary criticism, of which New Historicist work is simply the most obvious example, embodies an uncritical acceptance among literary critics of key basic premises of postmodernism – that the encounter never really happens, that there can be no third term, no escape from language, and that therefore concepts like truth, ethics and aesthetics are meaningless. Above all literary critics have lost sight of the mystery of the world as a space for thought. The turn to historicist and contextual studies can be seen as an exemplary postmodern move since what it represents is a desire to obscure the basic dialectical quality of reality – to avoid the trauma/mystery at its heart by producing matter, narratives, contexts and histories.[13]

Slavoj Žižek's work consistently and, as some critics have pointed out, repetitively comes back to the Real as the ahistorical thing/nothing at the heart of symbolisation. In *The Puppet and the Dwarf* he writes:

> ... the Real is ... that invisible obstacle, that distorting screen, which always 'falsifies' our access to external reality, that 'bone in the throat' which gives a pathological twist to every symbolisation, that is to say, on account of which every symbolization misses its object.[14]

Postmodernism is a lament for the inevitable loss of real or complete symbolisation. It is predicated, like New Historicism, on a nostalgia for a world of authenticity and transparency, a world where one could talk to the dead, a world that escapes the 'bone in the throat' of the Real. This nostalgic longing serves to justify postmodernism's refusal of the political and ethical. Postmodernism effectively argues that, 'If there was a world without the failure of symbolisation, a world where one could talk to the dead, then politics and ethics would be meaningful. But as this world can never exist there is no requirement to engage with ethical questions. Indeed to raise the question of ethics is simply a reflection of one's naivety and lack of sophistication.' For Žižek this argument is simply wrong. If the failure of symbolisation is a fact of language then concepts like ethics, politics and truth have only ever existed in a failed partial state. The mystery of the word, in Mann's words, is not an excuse for giving up on the political sphere, but rather that which makes ethical action possible. Žižek argues that "we should abandon all ethical arrogance, and humbly acknowledge how lucky we are to be able to act ethically".[15] For literary critics Žižek's work offers the possibility of a return to ethical criticism – to a literary criticism whose ethics are based on its engagement with the truths produced in the writing of people like Shakespeare.

Michel de Certeau has suggested that:

> The literary text is like a game. With its sets of rules and surprises, a game is a somewhat theoretic space where the formalities of social strategies can be explained on a terrain protected from the pressure of action and the opaque complexity of daily struggle. In the same way, the literary text, which is also a game, delineates an equally theoretic space, protected as is a laboratory, where the artful practices of social interaction are formulated, separated, combined, and tested.[16]

There is nothing innocent or playful about Shakespeare's engagement with language. The truths that are enacted in Puck's dust, Iago's silence and Paulina's faith relate directly to the 'opaque complexity of daily struggle'. Shakespeare's plays are theoretic spaces which consistently foreground the forces that threaten their existence. Ironically these are not usually simple tyranny or prohibition. Far more often they take the form of the cultural forces that made Shakespeare's plays possible – the audience's voyeuristic desire to consume ('what you will'/'as you like it'), the commodification of people and products (Imogen and *Much Ado About Nothing*) and the totalisation of meaning (dying to the world into a linguistic cocoon).[17] Shakespeare locates the resistance to these reductive forces not in grand gestures or ethical assertions but in the emergence of theoretic spaces for thought, proverbs, parables and stories: spaces or perhaps more accurately stages for meditation, history, political struggle, friendship, faith and the communal production of truths.

Notes

1   In his judicious Introduction to the new Arden edition of *Henry VIII* Gordon McMullan draws an important conclusion from the authorial and textual debates surrounding the play. He writes that: "… [*Henry VIII*] requires us to reconsider the very basis of our understanding of the way in which texts – particularly early modern dramatic

texts – come into being." Gordon McMullan, 'Introduction', *Henry VIII*, William Shakespeare, ed. Gordon McMullan (London: 2000), pp.1–199, p.199.

2   McMullan points out that the word truth appears in the play twenty-five times. Ibid., p.2/3.

3   It is worth noting that the scene where Katherine faces Henry in front of Cardinal Wolsey's divorce commission uncannily echoes the moment in *The Winter's Tale* when Hermione faces her accuser.

4   Anston Bosman comments that: "Amid the surreption and conspiracy that characterises Shakespeare's version of the Henrician Court, we are repeatedly encouraged to place our trust in the Gentlemen's commentary on offstage developments." Bosman's argument can be related to the historiographic agenda of *Henry VIII* since the Gentlemen's trustworthiness is an aspect of their status as the audience's on-stage guides. They can therefore be seen as honest historical Pucks supporting the play's plot and guiding the audience in the process. See Anston Bosman, 'Seeing Tears: Truth and Sense in *All is True*', *Shakespeare Quarterly*, 50 (1999), pp.459–76, p.462.

5   Thomas Mann, *Order of the Day: Political Essays and Speeches of Two Decades*, trans. H.T. Lowe-Porter (New York: 1942), p.109.

6   Ibid., p.72.

7   Mann's critique of the seductive 'choice' the tyrannies of the 1930s offered their adherents can be related directly to Étienne Balibar's recent argument concerning the relationship between identities and violence. Balibar argues that there are two equally extreme possibilities in terms of identity – being absolutely one and no one. He goes on to suggest that "… certain situations of violence with which we are faced occur not simply when individuals or groups are carried towards one of these extremes, but when these respective impossibilities meet, when individuals or groups seek a way out in a violent oscillation from one pole to the other". Balibar's suggestion can clearly be applied to Mann's work but it is also applicable to a figure like Othello who is caught in a violent debilitating struggle over the nature of his identity. It is in this context, as in Mann's, that racism as a 'solution' to the mystery of the word is so seductive. See Étienne Balibar, *Politics and the Other Scene*, trans. Christine Jones, James Swenson and Chris Turner (London: 2002), p.29.

8   Timothy Bewes, *Reification or The Anxiety of Late Capitalism* (London: 2002), p.47.

9   Ibid., p.54.

10 Ibid., p.106.

11 Bewes's solution to this desire for authenticity is to argue for a political critique that at every stage mediates contemporary, 'immediate' reality. Ibid., p.174.

12 Stephen Greenblatt, *Shakespearean Negotiations: The Circulation of Social Energy in Renaissance England* (Oxford: 1988), p.20.

13 Charles Altieri comments that "so long as we freely spin out undecidable textual possibilities we can claim to explain nothing but our ability to generate textual meanings". Of course it is precisely this endless textual productivity that is attractive for postmodern and New Historicist critics since, like the handkerchief in *Othello*, it works to defer the end of interpretation. Charles Altieri, *Cannons and Consequences* (Evanston, IL: 1990), p.13.

14 Slavoj Žižek, *The Puppet and the Dwarf: The Perverse Core of Christianity* (Cambridge, MA: 2003), p.67.

15 Ibid., p.159.

16 Michel de Certeau, *Heterologies: Discourse of the Other* (Minneapolis: 1986), p.23.

17 Theodor Adorno comments that "The greatness of works of art lies solely in their power to let those things be heard which ideology conceals." This is particularly so in the case of Shakespeare whose work consistently and self-reflectively stages the workings of ideology – the closure, distortion and reduction of language in the service of totalising desires. See Theodor Adorno, 'Lyric Poetry and Society', *Telos*, 20 (1974), pp.56–71, p.58.

Bibliography

Adorno, Theodor, 'Lyric Poetry and Society', *Telos*, 20 (1974), pp.56–71

Adorno, Theodor, *Aesthetic Theory*, trans. Robert Hullot-Kentor (London: 1997)

Aers, David, 'A Whisper in the Ear of Early Modernists: Or, Reflections on Literary Critics Writing the "History of the Subject"', in *Culture and History 1350-1600: Essays on English Communities, Identities and Writing*, ed. David Aers (Hemel Hempstead: 1992), pp.177–202

Althusser, Louis, *Essays on Ideology*, trans. Ben Brewster (London: 1971)

Althusser, Louis, *Lenin and Philosophy and Other Essays*, trans. Ben Brewster (London: 1971)

Althusser, Louis, 'Contradiction and Overdetermination', in *For Marx*, trans. Ben Brewster (London: 1990), pp.87–128

Althusser, Louis, 'From Capital to Marx's Philosophy', in *Reading Capital*, Louis Althusser and Étienne Balibar (London: 1997), pp.11–70

Altieri, Charles, *Cannons and Consequences* (Evanston, IL: 1990)

Asher, Lyell, 'Lateness in *King Lear*', *Yale Journal of Criticism*, 13 (2000), pp.209–28

Augustine, St, *City of God*, trans. Henry Bettenson (London: 1972)

Augustine, St, *Confessions*, trans. Henry Chadwick (Oxford: 1992)

Augustine, St, *On Christian Teaching*, trans. R.P.H. Green (Oxford: 1997)

Bacon, Robert, 'The History of the Reign of K.Henry the Eighth, K.Edward, Q.Mary, and Part of the Reign of Q.Elizabeth', in *The History of the Reign of King Henry VII*, ed. Brian Vickers (Cambridge: 1998), pp.209–14

Badiou, Alain, 'Beckett's Generic Writing', *Journal of Beckett Studies*, 4 (1994), pp.13–21

Badiou, Alain, *Manifesto for Philosophy*, trans. Norman Madarasz (New York: 1999)

Badiou, Alain, *Ethics: An Essay on the Understanding of Evil*, trans. Peter Hallward (London: 2001)

Balibar, Étienne, *The Philosophy of Marx*, trans. Chris Turner (London: 1995)

Balibar, Étienne, *Politics and the Other Scene*, trans. Christine Jones, James Swenson and Chris Turner (London: 2002)

Barthes, Roland, 'The Discourse of History', trans. Stephen Bann, *Comparative Criticism*, 3 (1981), pp.3–20

Bellamy, Elizabeth J., 'Othello's Lost Handkerchief: Where Psychoanalysis Finds Itself', in *Lacan, Politics, Aesthetics*, ed. Willy Apollon and Richard Feldstein (New York: 1998), pp.151–79

Belsey, Catherine, 'Tarquin Dispossessed: Expropriation and Consent in *The Rape of Lucrece*', *Shakespeare Quarterly*, 52 (2001), pp.315–35

Benjamin, Walter, 'Theses on the Philosophy of History', in *Illuminations*, ed. Hannah Arendt, trans. Harry Zohn (London: 1973), pp.245–55

Bergeron, David M., 'Deadly Letters in *King Lear*', *Philological Quarterly*, 72 (1993), pp.157–76

Betteridge, Tom, *Tudor Histories of the English Reformations 1530–1583* (Aldershot: 1999)

Betteridge, Tom, 'The Place of Sodomy in the Historical Writings of John Bale and John Foxe', in *Sodomy in Early Modern Europe*, ed. Tom Betteridge (Manchester: 2002), pp.11–26

Betteridge, Tom, *Literature and Politics in the English Reformation* (Manchester: 2004)

Bewes, Timothy, *Cynicism and Postmodernity* (London: 1997)

Bewes, Timothy, *Reification or The Anxiety of Late Capitalism* (London: 2002)

Blundeville, Thomas, *The True Order and Methode of Wryting and Reading Hystories* (London: 1574)

Booker, M. Keith, '"Nothing That Is So Is So": Dialogic Discourse and the Voice of the Woman in *The Clerk's Tale* and *Twelfth Night*', *Exemplaria*, 3 (1991), pp.519–37

Bosman, Anston, 'Seeing Tears: Truth and Sense in *All is True*', *Shakespeare Quarterly*, 50 (1999), pp.459–76

Brayton, Dan, 'Angling in the Lake of Darkness: Possession, Dispossession, and the Politics of Discovery in *King Lear*', *English Literary History*, 70 (2003), pp.399–426

Brecht, Bertolt, *Brecht on Theatre: The Development of an Aesthetic*, ed. and trans. John Willet (London: 1978)

Breger, Claudia, 'The Leader's Two Bodies: Slavoj Žižek's Political Theology', *Diacritics*, 31 (2001), pp.73–90

Bristol, Michael D., 'Lenten Butchery: Legitimation Crisis in *Coriolanus*', in *Shakespeare Reproduced: The Text in History and Ideology*, ed. Jean E. Howard and Marion F. O'Connor (London: 1987), pp.207–24

Bristol, Michael D., 'Charivari and the Comedy of Abjection in *Othello*', in *Materialist Shakespeare: A History*, ed. Ivo Kamps (London: 1995), pp.142–56

Butler, Judith, '"Conscience Doth Make Subjects of Us All"', *Yale French Studies*, 88 (1995), pp.6–26

Butler, Judith, *The Psychic Life of Power: Theories of Subjection* (California: 1997)

Butler, Judith, *Antigone's Claim: Kinship between Life and Death* (New York: 2000)

Butler, Judith, 'Values of Difficulty', in *Just Being Difficult: Academic Writing in the Public Arena*, ed. Jonathan Culler and Kevin Lamb (Stanford, CA: 2003), pp.199–215

Cahill, Edward, 'The Problem of Malvolio', *College Literature*, 23 (1996), pp.62–82

Cavell, Stanley, *Disowning Knowledge: In Seven Plays of Shakespeare* (Cambridge: 2003)

Certeau, Michel de, *Heterologies: Discourse of the Other* (Minneapolis: 1986)

Certeau, Michel de, *The Writing of History*, trans. Tom Conley (New York: 1988)

Colebrook, Claire, *New Literary Histories: New Historicism and Contemporary Criticism* (Manchester: 1997)

Collinson, Patrick, 'The Monarchical Republic of Queen Elizabeth I', in *Elizabethan Essays* (London: 1994), pp.31–58

Cook, Carol, '"The Sign and Semblance of Her Honour": Reading Gender Difference in *Much Ado About Nothing*', in *Shakespeare and Gender: A History*, ed. Deborah Barker and Ivo Kamps (London: 1995), pp.75–103

Cooley, Ronald W., 'Speech versus Spectacle: Autolycus, Class and Containment in *The Winter's Tale*', *Renaissance and Reformation*, 3 (1997), pp.5–23

Copjec, Joan, *Read my Desire: Lacan against the Historicists* (Cambridge, MA: 1995)

Crane, Terence, *The Cornucopian Text: Problems of Writing in the French Renaissance* (Oxford: 1979)

Delaney, Paul, '*King Lear* and the Decline of Feudalism', *PMLA*, 92 (1977), pp.429–40

Derrida, Jacques, *Of Grammatology*, trans. Gayatri Chakravorty Spivak (Baltimore: 1974)

Derrida, Jacques, 'Remarks on Deconstruction and Pragmatism', in *Deconstruction and Pragmatism*, ed. Chantal Mouffe (London: 1996), pp.77–88

Derrida, Jacques, *Politics of Friendship*, trans. George Collins (London: 1997)

Dobin, Howard, *Merlin's Disciples: Prophecy, Poetry, and Power in Renaissance England* (Stanford, CA: 1990)

Dolar, Mladen, 'Beyond Interpellation', *Qui Parle*, 6 (1993), pp.75–96

Dollimore, Jonathan, *Radical Tragedy: Religion: Ideology and Power in the Drama of Shakespeare and his Contemporaries* (New York: 1989)

Dubrow, Heather, 'The Newer Historicism', *Clio*, 25 (1996), pp.421–38

Eagleton, Terry, 'History, Narrative and Marxism', in *Reading Narrative: Form, Ethics, Ideology*, ed. James Phelan (Columbus, OH: 1989), pp.272–82

Eagleton, Terry, *The Illusions of Postmodernism* (Oxford: 1996)

Easthope, Anthony, *Poetry as Discourse* (London: 1983)

Erasmus, *The Adages of Erasmus*, selected by William Barker (Toronto: 2001)

Felperin, Howard, '"Tongue-Tied our Queen": The Deconstruction of Presence in *The Winter's Tale*', in *Shakespeare and the Question of Theory*, ed. Patricia Parker and Geoffrey Hartman (New York: 1985), pp.1–18

Ferguson, Arthur B., *Clio Unbound: Perception of the Social and Cultural Past in Renaissance England* (Durham, NC: 1979)

Ferguson, Margaret W., 'Saint Augustine's Region of Unlikeness: The Crossing of Exile and Language', *Georgia Review*, 29 (1975), pp.844–64

Fox, Adam, *Oral and Literate Culture in England 1500–1700* (Oxford: 2000)

Gallagher, Catherine and Greenblatt, Stephen, *Practicing New Historicism* (Chicago: 2001)

Garber, Marjorie, *Shakespeare's Ghost Writers* (New York: 1987)

Grady, Hugh, 'On the Need for a Differentiated Theory of (Early) Modern Subjects', in *Philosophical Shakespeares*, ed. John J. Joughin (London: 2000), pp.34–50

Greenblatt, Stephen, *Renaissance Self-Fashioning: From More to Shakespeare* (Chicago: 1980)

Greenblatt, Stephen, *Shakespearean Negotiations: The Circulation of Social Energy in Renaissance England* (Oxford: 1988)

Gurr, Andrew, *Playgoing in Shakespeare's London* (Cambridge: 1987)

Guy, John, 'Tudor Monarchy and its Critiques', in *Tudor Monarchy*, ed. John Guy (London: 1997), pp.78–109

Habermas, Jürgen, *Legitimation Crisis*, trans. Thomas McCarthy (London: 1976)

Habermas, Jürgen, *Communication and the Evolution of Society*, trans. Thomas McCarthy (Oxford: 1991)

Hadfield, Andrew, *Literature, Travel and Colonial Writing in the English Renaissance* (Oxford: 1998)

Hadfield, Andrew, 'Shakespeare and Republicanism: History and Cultural Materialism', *Textual Practice*, 17 (2003), pp.461–84

Halpern, Richard, *The Poetics of Primitive Accumulation: English Renaissance Culture and the Genealogy of Capital* (Ithaca, NY: 1991)

Hardt, Michael and Negri, Antonio, *Empire* (Cambridge, MA: 2000)

Harsnett, Samuel, 'A Declaration of Egregious Popish Impostures', in *Shakespeare, Harsnett, and the Devils of Denham*, ed. F.W. Brownlow (London: 1993)

Hobday, Charles, 'Clouted Shoon and Leather Aprons: Shakespeare and the Equalitarian Tradition', *Renaissance and Modern Studies*, 23 (1979)

Hohendahl, Peter Uwe, 'A Return to History? The New Historicism and its Agenda', *New German Critique*, 55 (1992), pp.87–104

Holderness, Graham, *Cultural Shakespeare: Essays in the Shakespeare Myth* (Hatfield: 2001)

Holderness, Graham and Carter, Naomi, 'The King's Two Bodies: Text and Genre in *King Lear*', *English*, 45 (1996), pp.1–31

Howard, Jean, *The Stage and Social Struggle in Early Modern England* (London: 1994)

Howard, Jean and Rackin, Phyllis *Engendering a Nation* (London: 1997)

A Hundred Merry Tales, 1526 (London: 1887)

Hunt, Maurice, 'Ordering Disorder in *Richard III*', *South Central Review*, 6 (1989), pp.11–29

Hutson, Lorna, 'On Not Being Deceived: Rhetoric and the Body in *Twelfth Night*', *Texas Studies in Literature and Language*, 38 (1996), pp.140–74

Irigaray, Luce, *This Sex Which Is Not One*, trans. Catherine Porter (Ithaca, NY: 1985)

Jameson, Frederic, 'Actually Existing Marxism', in *Marxism beyond Marxism*, ed. Saree Makdisi, Cesare Casarino and Rebecca E. Karl (London: 1996), pp.14–54

Jameson, Frederic, *The Cultural Turn: Selected Writings on the Postmodern, 1983–1998* (London: 1998)

Jonson, Ben, *Selected Poetry*, ed. George Parfitt (London: 1992)

Kastan, David Scott, *Shakespeare and the Shapes of Time* (London: 1982)

Kastan, David Scott, 'Is There a Class in this (Shakespearean) Text?', *Renaissance Drama*, 24 (1993), pp.101–21

Kastan, David Scott, '"The Noyse of the New Bible": Reform and Reaction in Henrician England', in *Religion and Culture in Renaissance England*, ed. Claire McEachern and Debora Shuger (Cambridge: 1997), pp.46–68

Kastan, David Scott, *Shakespeare after Theory* (New York: 1999)

Kinney, Daniel, 'Kings' Tragicomedies: Generic Misrule in More History of Richard III',

Moreana, 86 (1985), pp.128–50

Knowles, Richard, 'Cordelia's Return', *Shakespeare Quarterly*, 50 (1999), pp.33–50

Laclau, Ernesto, *Emancipation(s)* (London: 1996)

Laclau, Ernesto, *The Politics of Rhetoric* (Colchester: 1998)

Laclau, Ernesto and Mouffe, Chantal, *Hegemony and Socialist Strategy: Towards a Radical Democratic Politics* (London: 1985)

Lake, Peter, 'Anti-Popery: The Structure of a Prejudice', in *Conflict in Early Stuart England: Studies in Religion and Politics 1603–1642*, ed. Richard Cust and Ann Hughes (London: 1989), pp.72–106

Larocco, Steve, 'Contentious Intimations: John Donne, *Richard III*, and the Transgressive Structures of Seduction', *Exemplaria*, 7 (1995), pp.237–67

Leggatt, Alexander, *Shakespeare's Political Drama: The History Plays and the Roman Plays* (London: 1988)

Levy, F.J, *Tudor Historical Thought* (San Marino, CA: 1967)

Lim, S.H., 'Knowledge and Belief in *The Winter's Tale*', *Studies in English Literature*, 41 (2001), pp.317–34

Malcolmson, Cristina, '"What You Will": Social Mobility and Gender in *Twelfth Night*', in *The Matter of Difference: Materialist Feminist Criticism of Shakespeare*, ed. Valerie Wayne (Hemel Hempstead: 1991), pp.29–57

Mann, Thomas, *Order of the Day: Political Essays and Speeches of Two Decades*, trans. H.T. Lowe-Porter (New York: 1942)

Marcuse, Herbert, *The Aesthetic Dimension: Toward a Critique of Marxist Aesthetics* (London: 1979)

Markels, Julian, '*King Lear*, Revolution, and the New Historicism', *Modern Language Studies*, 21 (1991), pp.11–26

Marx, Karl, *Economic and Philosophic Manuscripts of 1844* (Moscow: 1959)

Matz, Robert, 'Slander, Renaissance Discourses of Sodomy, and *Othello*', *English Literary History*, 66 (1999), pp.261–76

Maus, Katherine Eisaman, 'Proof and Consequences: Inwardness and its Exposure in the English Renaissance', in *Materialist Shakespeare: A History*, ed. Ivo Kamps (London: 1995), pp.157–80

Mazzio, Carla, 'The Melancholy of Print: *Love's Labour's Lost*', in *Historicism, Psychoanalysis, and Early Modern Culture*, ed. Carla Mazzio and Douglas Trevor (New York: 2000), pp.186–227

McMullan, Gordon, 'Introduction', *Henry VIII*, William Shakespeare, ed. Gordon McMullan (London: 2000), pp.1–199

Menon, Madhavi, '*Richard II* and the Taint of Metonymy', *English Literary History*, 70 (2003), pp.653–76

Miller, Jacques-Alain, 'Extimité', in *Lacanian Theory of Discourse: Subject, Structure and Society*, ed. Mark Bracher, Marshall W. Alcorn, Jr and Françoise Massardier-Kenney (New York: 1994), pp.74–87

Morrill, John, *The Nature of the English Revolution* (London: 1993)

Murray, Timothy, *Drama Trauma: Spectres of Race and Sexuality in Performance, Video, and Art* (London: 1997)

Nical, Brian, 'As If: Traversing the Fantasy in Žižek', *Paragraph*, 24 (2001), pp.140–55

Norbrook, David, *Poetry and Politics in the English Renaissance* (Oxford: 2002)

Parker, Patricia, 'Fantasies of "Race" and "Gender": Africa, *Othello*, and bringing to light', in *Women, 'Race,' and Writing in the Early Modern Period*, ed. Margo Hendricks and Patricia Parker (London: 1994), pp.84–100

Patterson, Annabel, *Shakespeare and the Popular Voice* (Cambridge: 1989)

Patterson, Lee, 'Critical Historicism and Medieval Studies', in *Literary Practice and Social Change in Britain 1380–1530*, ed. Lee Patterson (Berkeley, CA: 1990), pp.1–14

Patterson, Lee, 'On the Margin: Postmodernism, Ironic History, and Medieval Studies', *Speculum*, 65 (1990), pp.87–108

Plissart, Marie-Françoise and Derrida, Jacques, 'Right of Inspection', *Art and Text*, 32 (1989), pp.20–97

Poster, Mark, 'The Question of Agency: Michel de Certeau and the History of Consumerism', *Diacritics*, 22 (1992), pp.94–107

Rackin, Phyllis, *Stages of History* (London: 1990)

Reynolds, Susan, *Fiefs and Vassals: The Medieval Evidence Reinterpreted* (Oxford: 1994)

Ricoeur, Paul, *The Reality of the Historical Past* (Milwaukee: 1984)

Righter, Anne, *Shakespeare and the Idea of the Play* (London: 1962)

Salecl, Renata, 'I Can't Love You Unless I Give You Up', in *Gaze and Voice as Love Objects*, ed. Renata Salecl and Slavoj Žižek (Durham, NC: 1996), pp.179–207

Salecl, Renata, *(Per)Versions of Love and Hate* (London: 1998)

Salecl, Renata and Žižek, Slavoj, 'Introduction', in *Gaze and Voice as Love Objects*, ed. Renata Salecl and Slavoj Žižek (Durham, NC: 1996), pp.1–4

Samuels, Robert, ' Žižek's Rhetorical Matrix: The Symptomatic Enjoyment of Postmodern Academic Writing', *Journal of Composition Theory*, 22 (2002), pp.327–54

Selden, John, '*Jani Anglorum Facies Altera*', 1610, in *Tracts Written by John Selden*, trans. Redman Westcot (London: 1683)

Shank, Cathy, 'Civility and the City in *Coriolanus*', *Shakespeare Quarterly*, 54 (2003), pp.406–23

Simpson, James, *Reform and Cultural Revolution 1350–1547* (Oxford: 2002)

Spelman, Sir Henry, 'The Original Growth, Propagation and Condition of Feuds and Tenures of Knight-Service', in *The English Works of Sir Henry Spelman* (London: 1723)

Spotswood, Jerald W., 'Maintaining Hierarchy in *The Tragedie of King Lear*', *Studies in English Literature*, 38 (1998), pp.265–80

Steiner, George, *Language and Silence: Essays 1958–1966* (London: 1985)

Stock, Brian, *Listening for the Text: On the Uses of the Past* (Philadelphia: 1990)

Stock, Brian, *Augustine the Reader: Meditation, Self-Knowledge, and the Ethics of Interpretation* (Cambridge, MA: 1996)

Sullivan, Garrett and Woodbridge, Linda, 'Popular Culture in Print', in *English Literature 1500–1600*, ed. Arthur F. Kinney (Cambridge: 2000), pp.265–86

Terdiman, Richard, 'The Response of the Other', *Diacritics*, 22 (1992), pp.2–10

Traub, Valerie, 'Desire and the Differences It Makes', in *The Matter of Difference: Materialist Feminist Criticism of Shakespeare*, ed. Valerie Wayne, (Hemel Hempstead: 1991), pp.81–114

Van Pelt, Tamise, 'Entitled to be King: The Subversion of the Subject in *King Lear*', *Literature and Psychology*, 42 (1996), pp.100–12

Veeser, H., *The New Historicism* (New York: 1989)

Waller, Gary, *English Poetry of the Sixteenth Century* (Harlow: 1993)

Watson, Robert, '*Othello* as Protestant Propaganda', in *Religion and Culture in Renaissance England*, ed. Claire McEachern and Debora Shuger (Cambridge: 1997), pp.234–57

Wells, Robin Headlam, '"Manhood and Chevalrie": *Coriolanus*, Prince Henry, and the Chivalric Revival', *Review of English Studies*, 51 (2000), pp.395–422

Wilson, Richard, '"Is This a Holiday": Shakespeare's Roman Carnival', in *Shakespeare: The Roman Plays*, ed. Graham Holderness, Bryan Loughrey and Andrew Murphy (London: 1996), pp.18–31

Wolf, Amy, 'Shakespeare and Harsnett: "Pregnant to Good Pity"?', *Studies in English Literature*, 38 (1998), pp.251–64

Yachnin, Paul, 'Reversal of Fortune: Shakespeare, Middleton and the Puritans', *English Literary History*, 70 (2003), pp.757–86

Zavarzadeh, Mas'ud, 'Pun(k)deconstruction and the Postmodern Political Imaginary', *Cultural Critique*, 22 (1992), pp.5–46

Žižek, Slavoj, 'The Object as a Limit of Discourse: Approaches to the Lacanian Real', *Prose Studies*, 11 (1988), pp.94–120

Žižek, Slavoj, *The Sublime Object of Ideology* (London: 1989)

Žižek, Slavoj, 'The Detective and the Analyst', *Literature and Psychology*, 36 (1990), pp.27–46

Žižek, Slavoj, *For They Know Not What They Do: Enjoyment as a Political Factor* (London: 1991)

Žižek, Slavoj, *Enjoy Your Symptom! Jacques Lacan in Hollywood and Out* (New York: 1992)

Žižek, Slavoj, *The Metastases of Enjoyment: Six Essays on Woman and Causality* (London: 1994)

Žižek, Slavoj, *The Indivisible Remainder: An Essay on Schelling and Related Matters* (London: 1996)

Žižek, Slavoj, 'Re-visioning "Lacanian" Social Criticism: The Law and its Obscene Double', *Journal for Psychoanalysis of Culture and Society*, 1 (1996), pp.15–25

Žižek, Slavoj, 'Fantasy as a Political Category: A Lacanian Approach', *Journal for Psychoanalysis of Culture and Society*, 1 (1996), pp.77–85

Žižek, Slavoj, *The Plague of Fantasies* (London: 1997)

Žižek, Slavoj, 'Introduction: Cogito as a Shibboleth', in *Cogito and the Unconscious*, ed. Slavoj Žižek (Durham, NC: 1998), pp.1–8

Žižek, Slavoj, *The Ticklish Subject: The Absent Centre of Political Ontology* (London: 1999)

Žižek, Slavoj, 'Class Struggle or Postmodernism? Yes, Please', in *Contingency, Hegemony, Universality: Contemporary Dialogues on the Left*, ed. Judith Butler, Ernesto Laclau and Slavoj Žižek (London: 2000), pp.90–135

Žižek, Slavoj, 'The Rhetorics of Power', *Diacritics*, 31 (2001), pp.91–104

Žižek, Slavoj, *Welcome to the Desert of the Real! Five Essays on September 11 and Related Dates* (London: 2002)

Žižek, Slavoj, 'Cultural Studies versus the "Third Culture"', *South Atlantic Quarterly*, 101 (2002), pp.19–32

Žižek, Slavoj, 'The Ambiguity of the Masochist Social Link', *Perversion and the Social Relation*, ed. Molly Anne Rothenberg, Dennis Foster and Slavoj Žižek (Durham, NC: 2003), pp.112–25

Žižek, Slavoj, *The Puppet and the Dwarf: The Perverse Core of Christianity* (Cambridge, MA: 2003)

Zunder, William, 'Shakespeare and the End of Feudalism: *King Lear* as *Fin-de-Siècle* Text', *Shakespeare Studies*, 78 (1997), pp.513–21

Zurcher, Amelia, 'Untimely Monuments: Stoicism, History, and the Problem of Utility in *The Winter's Tale* and *Pericles*', *English Literary History*, 70 (2003), pp.903–27

Index